THE·KING

Anoedd bid bet y Arthur
The world's enigma, Arthur's grave

Welsh, 9th or 10th century

GRAEME·FIFE

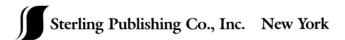 Sterling Publishing Co., Inc.   New York

DEDICATION

To friends,
for succour of this reluctant nomad

Library of Congress Cataloging-in-Publication Data

Fife, Graeme.
    Arthur the King / Graeme Fife.
        p.   cm.
    Reprint. Originally published: London : BBC Books, 1990.
    Includes bibliographical references (p.   ) and index.
    ISBN 0-8069-8344-2
      1. Arthur, King. 2. Arthurian romances—History and criticism.
   3. Britons—Kings and rulers—Biography. 4. Great Britain—History—
To 1066. I. Title.
[DA152.5.A7F54   1991]
942.01′4—dc20
[B]   90-24599
                                              CIP

10   9   8   7   6   5   4   3   2   1

Published in 1991 by Sterling Publishing Company, Inc.
387 Park Avenue South, New York, N.Y. 10016
Originally published in Great Britain
by BBC Books © 1990 by Graeme Fife
Distributed in Canada by Sterling Publishing
℅ Canadian Manda Group, P.O. Box 920, Station U
Toronto, Ontario, Canada M8Z 5P9
Manufactured in the United States of America
All rights reserved

Sterling ISBN 0-8069-8344-2

CONTENTS

ACKNOWLEDGEMENTS

My heartfelt thanks to David Evans and all his staff at the unsung BBC Reference Library for their unfailing patience and indispensable help; not only in procuring and granting extended loan of books, even out-of-the-way titles; but also for chasing obscure references.

Suzanne Webber, Senior Commissioning Editor at BBC Books, gave me vital encouragement and guidance at every stage. Sarah Hoggett has been a splendid editor, thoughtful, sensitive, painstaking.

My thanks to John Powell for asking me to write the radio series, which is dedicated to the memory of David Buck, and for assembling such a magnificent cast.

Thanks, too, to Jennifer, Suzanna, Kate and Grahame at BBC Books for their help and enthusiasm; to Hilary Dickinson for last-minute work; to Michael Walsh, Librarian at Heythrop College, for valuable insights on theological matters and allowing me free run of his shelves; to Tony Richardson at the Tower of London Armouries for scholarly expertise; to Jane for support in the early days; to Jim for help beyond the call of duty; to Helen for practical help and forbearance all along; and above all to Lindy for putting up with the whole business.

INTRODUCTION

..li autour plenierement   Let us prize
Qui firent livres et escriz   Writers who made books and records
Des nobles faiz et des bons diz Of noble deeds and fine words
Que li baron et li seignour   That we have of barons and lords
Firent de tens ancianour.   In olden days.

Wace, **Romance of Rollo**, Prologue

Now. The mist falling away, see him, a moment, dipped in ardent flame, Arthur the King, at daybreak. Flaring sun out of the dawn's forge glints off polished silver of helmet, of fine mail, of the long blade of Excalibur, leaning out from his hand like the dragon's tongue licking the dark earth. Arthur, once King and to be King. Arthur come again. And think of high Tintagel, where the sea's white teeth gnaw relentlessly at the ankles of the cliff. And think of Merlin, now cramped an enternity in Nimuë's rock cell, him who once conversed with winds and fire and wolves and eagles as cosily as the brackish foam chatters with the beach sand along the tideline. And of Guenever, White Phantom, her of the grey eyes and double-vaulted heart, her marriage gift the Round Table. And Arthur's knights who sit there; hear their names, every one, in the young stream's chuckling over pebbles, the ageless spring welling out from under the hill:

Gawain, Perceval, Lancelot du Lac, Erec, Yvain, Cligès, Bedivere, Dinadan, Pellinore, Tristram. And their lovers – Fair Isolde, Elaine, the Lady of Astolat. Before the mist comes down once more, before the mist comes down like smoked glass to veil them over. Gone.

From shadowy origins, Arthur has come to epitomise the heroic, more specifically the chivalric ideal: besiege and carry the Giant's castle, vanquish the villain Black Knight, slay the dragon and rescue the damsel . . .thence home to Queen and good fellowship, feasting and lute music. All in a day's work. Not quite the chirpy Cockney sparrow; nor yet the bluff, though tender-hearted northener, but elements of them too. A thoroughly British hero, a prince among men when manly virtue is in decline as successive generations always reckon it to be.

But who was the real Arthur? The hunt for him

5

is never straightforward. At every count he stalls our pursuit, one step ahead, like that most cunning of mediaeval quarries the hart. One of this majestic beast's favourite tricks was what the huntsmen called the ruse, or doubling back. The hart would retrace its steps, leap sideways into a stream, follow that a way, then spring out onto the far bank and off into the thicket leaving the hounds a long distance off, baying at a dead end. So Arthur refuses to be cornered. He is Celtic warlord clad in mediaeval robes or armour, lionised in French romance; he is patron of gallant, noble and Christian virtues honoured throughout Europe, yet cuckolded by his closest friend. He is first cousin to warriors of the Celtic twilight who did battle with ogres, dragons and supernatural powers and yet inspirer, too, of the Quest for the Holy Grail. Arthur has many aspects.

In his preface to Malory's *Morte d'Arthur*, which he printed in 1485, Caxton singles out nine worthies of the universal world, that is the landmass centred on the Mediterranean: Hector of Troy, Alexander the Great, Julius Caesar; Joshua David and Judas Maccabaeus; King Arthur, Charlemagne and Godfrey de Bouillon. It's an interesting company. It embraces conquerors of empire – Alexander (Asia), Caesar and Charlemagne (Europe); religiously inspired generals – Joshua and Judas; a prince of the most ancient pedigree – Hector; kings of Jerusalem – David and Godfrey. All are known figures of living history. The odd man out is Arthur though he might be a role model for each and every one of them. Perhaps the best and most enduring of all the nine worthies, he differs from the rest in that history rather blushes at the mention of his name. Legend, on the other hand, brags much of him: that he conquered most of Europe and the cold north, defeated the Roman emperor and captured Rome; that he lead his Christian armies against the paynim (pagans), paving the way for Charlemagne and

Godfrey; that he was the foremost king of royal blood, divinely blessed, in the world and, like Judas Maccabaeus, the Hammer of the Syrians, possessed a life-preserving sword. Finally, if he did not become King of Jerusalem himself, he sent his knights there to prepare the ground for Godfrey de Bouillon and the First Crusade:

> For the French book makes mention – and is authorised – that Sir Bors, Sir Hector, Sir Blamor and Sir Bleoberis went into the Holy Land, thereas Jesus Christ was quick and dead. And as soon as they had established their lands . . .these four knights did many battles upon the miscreants, or Turks. And there they died upon a Good Friday for God's sake.
> Malory Book XXI chapter 13

The fascination of Arthur the King is perennial. From his very first appearance in the twelfth-century romances, all subsequent ages have cast him in their own mould. In the mid-fifteenth century, when the Wars of the Roses strangulated England, Malory harked back to Arthur's golden time when the island basked in a glorious peace. The Elizabethan poet Edmund Spenser cast his praise of England's *Faerie Queene*, her with 'the stomach of a king and a King of England too', in Arthur's world of gallant derring-do. A hundred years on, in 1691, Purcell and Dryden marked their own nostalgia for the old monarchy lost, with an operatic piece *King Arthur or the British Worthy*. When the French revolutionaries ousted their mediaeval-style monarchy in 1789, a marching song of the new Republican army mocked the *ancien régime* in a send-up of Arthur's knights:

> *Chevaliers de la Table Ronde,*
> *Goûtons voir si le vin est bon.*

Drunk, élitist and idle, like the Bourbon oppressors. Elsewhere, in royalist Europe, these knights of the Round Table epitomised the chivalric order which more egalitarian epochs interpreted as gallantry, gentlemanly conduct, grace under pressure. And for Victorian England, in the high noon of Empire, what better image of grandeur and glory could there be than great Arthur the King and his Queen Guenever in Camelot? The pre-Raphaelite painters, the Poet Laureate Tennyson, establishment composers like Sullivan and Parry answered the call and hailed the new golden age of peace and industry in fulsome Arthurian terms.

Across the Channel, in emergent Germany, Wagner made his own propagandist use of Arthurian legend, and writers in this last century of the second millennium have returned again and again to the deep seam of inspiration with Arthur's story laid in the hidden quarry under the hill. As Morgan le Fay says to the dying Arthur in the radio series which this book accompanies:

> . . . leave the unquenched sun behind you. They will take it to be you, that sun, Arthur, all of them lay claim to *their* bright once glory in my belonging.

Arthur, though, is confined by no grave. The monks of Glastonbury claimed to have discovered both his and Guenever's burial place in the twelfth century, because immortality and resurrection had to be reserved uniquely to Christ. Tradition clings, however. Malory writes:

> Yet some men say in many parts of England that King Arthur is not dead, but had by the will of our Lord Jesus into another place; and men say that he shall come again, and he shall win the Holy Cross.

> Book XXI chapter 7

But under which hill, precisely, does Arthur slumber in his long sleep, knights by him, waiting for the horn to sound the alarm so that they can ride out once more to save the kingdom? The mysterious conical Tor at Glastonbury, set down in the Somerset flats like a shield boss? Below the ancient fort at Cadbury Hill by Yeovil a few miles distant? Or Alderley Edge in Cheshire, or the triple yoke of hills at Eildon in the Scottish borders or Craig y Dinas in central Glamorgan? Perhaps not in these islands at all, but rather in the snow-tipped mountains of Savoy between Switzerland and France or the desert ranges of Arabia. Or does he, after all, share the vaults below Mount Etna in Sicily with the lame smith god Vulcan who roars his own name in the erupting fire and lava of the volcano?

If the legend swaggers and blows, history can only whisper 'maybe' and 'perhaps' and 'possibly'. Who was this Arthur, who had been king and would be king again? And why did his story suddenly emerge in twelfth-century Europe to become all the rage, and then disappear, almost completely, in the thirteenth? (Except in England where local interest did not flag.)

I hope in this book to offer some answers to these and other questions. Not conclusive answers, necessarily, but answers which make sense in historical context and give some clue as to why Arthur, defying the odds, resolutely *refuses* to die.

If all ages claim Arthur, it goes without saying that all ages have their view of him. My view is only the latest, and a determinedly personal one, too. Yet it differs significantly from most, for I see Arthur as he was originally intended: a mediaeval king. Other accounts dwell preponderantly on his misty, mysterious Celtic aspect. But I believe that Arthur, a literary figure, remember, does not reach back from the twelfth century into the Dark Ages and beyond. He stands, first and foremost, for the new concept of god-given kingship at the very start of what we now identify as the mediaeval renaissance in Europe. Then he reaches ahead through every century in the course of modern history.

The era of the romances marks a watershed between the Dark Ages – collapse of the Roman Empire, barbarian invasion, dissolution of tribal society – and the modern world. This world's new foundations – Feudalism, Church religion and absolute monarchy – are still more or less recognisable today. But how is it that Arthur, a very unhistorical figure, should so convincingly exemplify high authority, as feudal lord, defender of Christian faith, unchallenged king? Because he did not exist as such? Because Camelot is a fiction? Because better a hero with no feet at all than feet made of clay? Possibly; but the answer is not as easy as that. For,

imagine a pentangle of cities, grouped round the Mediterranean, interlinked by powerful forces of attraction and repulsion: Troy and Constantinople, old and new capitals of Greek Asia; Jerusalem (or Sion), capital of Christ's kingdom on earth, and Rome, capital of His Church on earth; Baghdad, capital of Mahomet's Islam. And inside this pentangle, century after century, explode the fires of war, culminating in the bloodiest conflagration of all: the Crusades.

It is the object of this book to suggest that, somewhere about this tense pentangle, in which *still* hangs the fate of Europe, floats, but precisely where we do not know, Arthur's Camelot.

Note: all the translations are my own unless otherwise attributed.   G.F.

CHAPTER ONE

ORIGINS: GREATER BRITAIN

Transformed by Merlin's potions into the likeness of the absent King Gorlois, Uther Pendragon, king of the Britons, arrives before the gates of Tintagel fortress at twilight. The guard admits whom he takes to be his royal master. That night King Uther spends with Gorlois' Queen Ygerna, whom he loves to distraction. That night she conceives Arthur, most famous of men.

Book VIII

Thus, in the words of Geoffrey of Monmouth, a canon of the English church teaching at Oseney by Oxford in the 1120s, Arthur the King is born.

Geoffrey wrote his *Historia Regum Britanniae* (*History of the Kings of Britain*) as a continuation of Virgil's *Aeneid*. In his epic poem, composed, for propaganda purposes, to the order of Augustus, Rome's first Emperor, Virgil describes how the Trojan Prince Aeneas escapes from the burning city of Troy, carrying with him the sacred relics and divine images of his people, out of the clutches of the attacking Greeks. After hair-raising adventures, a descent to Hell, a tragic love affair and heroic enterprise, he reaches Italy and founds a new Troy, called Alba Longa, on the future site of Rome.

Geoffrey of Monmouth takes up the story. Aeneas' son and grandson succeed him. But his great-grandson, Brutus, has the misfortune (or temerity?) to shoot his father dead with a stray arrow on a royal hunting expedition. Hounded out of Italy he flees to Greece, on to Gaul, where he conquers the non-Celtic territory known as Aquitaine, and then crosses the Channel to his eventual home, the island known in those days as Albion. The mediaevals loved a name that resonated through associations, the more complex the better, and the ring of Alba Longa in Albion was too harmonious an echo for a seasoned wordspinner like Geoffrey of Monmouth to resist. The name of the island changed in Brutus' honour to Britain and becomes, by this token, a cadet refounding of old Troy. Moreover, Brutus' older sons Locrinus and Kamber add the names Logres (England) and Cambria, modern Cwmru and Cumbria. The Benjamin of the family, Albanactus, merely confirms the more than sentimental link between old home and new. Albany later became south-east England (Cornwall being south-west). And in 1398 a Dukedom of Albany, Scotland north of the Clyde and Firth, was bestowed on an ancestor of mine, Robert

Stewart Earl of Fife. However.

Geoffrey traces the history of Britain up to A.D. 689, through an account of her kings (most of dubious historicity) from Brutus to Cadwallader who, rounding off the story, dies, an exile, in Virgil's Rome. Geoffrey wrote his chronicle, much as the Roman poet had done, for royal masters; in his case the Norman conquerors of England. The *Historia*, though, probably wasn't a direct commission and, sadly, Geoffrey's Anglo-French superiors took less shine to him than Augustus to Virgil, but he did his best for them.

Of course, by the time Geoffrey wrote the *Historia*, Britain, as such, no longer existed. The Normans conquered an island renamed England five hundred years before by the invading Saxons. But the old Romano-Celtic word for the island worked, even for Geoffrey's Norman readers, as a poignant talisman of former greatness. Nostalgia, therefore, but with an added, vital ingredient – pedigree – ensured the popularity of this new history. Like the Roman Emperors they artfully emulated, mediaeval kings craved a solid gold genealogy. What other example of grandiose pomp and splendour had they to ape than that of the empurpled Caesars? And Augustus had looked back to *his* ancestor, Aeneas, Prince of Troy. So, Geoffrey provided the Norman overlords of England with a direct blood-link to the selfsame royal house. Thereby he gave them scriptural authority, written approval for their sovereignty over the recently acquired domain known in former times as Greater Britain. But of all the kings in his book, it was the freedom fighter Arthur who stirred the Norman blood, caught their imagination. This was the king they all dreamed of being compared to. Arthur commanded lands and palaces and castles. He secured the oath and loyalty of lesser kings and princes almost by sheer force of his majesty. Arthur was, pre-eminently, a winner. Arthur burst off the page into dazzling reality. In

Arthur, his shield emblazoned with the Virgin Mary and child, appears as king of the thirty kingdoms of the earth, including France, Denmark, Rome, Egypt, Babylon.

essence, Arthur, they decided, was the most Norman of them all. More significantly, though, Arthur's appeal extended much further. The literary portrait of this great king held up a mirror of splendour and magnificence in which twelfth- and thirteenth-century kings, of England, France and other realms across all Europe, saw themselves reflected, twice, three times life size. Whatever his original intention in writing the *Historia*, Geoffrey had introduced to European culture and literature a king who stood head and shoulders above the rest. For, where the other kings of Britain paraded in the *Historia* made apparently small, if any, impression on its readers, the hitherto obscure Arthur established himself almost instantly as *the* king. Why?

There are two probable answers. First, Arthur's story had been part of an oral tradition of bardic romance amongst the surviving Celts of Greater Britain (Wales and Cornwall), for centuries. Geoffrey certainly didn't invent Arthur. On the other hand, there can be no doubt that *his* account it was that gave startling birth to the Arthurian legend as *we* know it. What clues, then, can be gleaned from the life and work of Geoffrey himself? Why, and in what historical context, did he write the *Historia*? To what sources did he refer?

GEOFFREY OF MONMOUTH

Geoffrey was born, of mixed Welsh and Breton blood, in Monmouth about the end of the eleventh century. He became a teaching canon at St George's college on Oseney island near Oxford and composed his history, in Latin, sometime before 1136. He signs himself *Galfridus Monemutensis* and, on an Oxford charter of 1125, *Galfridus Arturus*. Clearly his preoccupation with Britain's great champion had begun early.

Oxford had declined as a bustling market town even before the Norman invasion. Now, while not yet a university, it had become an important centre of learning. Scholars flocked there from all over England and Wales; France, too. They exchanged books, ideas and, most important for us, stories by word of mouth. Geoffrey declares in his prologue and the section on Arthur, that he had received from Walter the Archdeacon, Provost of St George's, an original treatise (now lost) 'in the British (i.e. Welsh) tongue', from which he culled his information for the *Historia*. More likely his material came from tales and myths, folklore and legend, both Celtic and classical in origin, swapped by the learned visitors who thronged Oxford; anyone, in fact, who had an ear for local history, a nose for interesting data from the great stockpile of culture, old religion and curiosities gathered in from every angle of what had been Arthur's realms. Above all, he must have relished the stories passed on by fireside narrators, many of them professional storytellers, from generation to generation.

We do know of two written sources used by Geoffrey, both extant: Gildas' *De Excidio Britanniae*, ('On the Ruination of Britain'), circa A.D. 540, and the eighth-century *Chronicles* of Nennius.

Gildas was born somewhere north of the old Roman frontiers of Britain, in the Pictish kingdom of the Clyde. However, he came south and received a full Roman-style education, probably in a monastery, in the Somerset wetlands near Severn Sea. Ordained priest, Gildas (later to be canonised as Gildas the Wise) composed, probably in middle age, his *De Excidio*, a polemic on 'the miseries, the errors and the ruin of Britain'. Not a history as such; rather a savage diatribe on the corrupt and faithless men in authority over a once-noble people in a once-sceptred isle. The fifth-century Saxon invasions, thundered Gildas, were God's just retribution for sin against His holy benison. The glory had been utterly corrupted. It might have been a Moses railing against the wayward children of Israel. Indeed, this embittered theme became the stock-in-trade of churchmen haranguing the flock gone astray: men like St Wulfstan, made bishop of Winchester in 1062, who branded the Norman invasion 'a scourge of God for our sins which we must bear with patience'.

By Geoffrey of Monmouth's time, however, the oppressors were firmly in command, and the theme had to be subtly disguised if not ditched altogether.

Nennius is the name given to an eighth-century editor who collated the work of various anonymous chroniclers to produce an attempted survey of British history in the immediate aftermath of the Roman Empire's collapse around the beginning of the fifth century. His material ranges from native legend to serious essays at historical archive. The Kentish Chronicle, for instance, covers the early period of Saxon immigration, from 425 to 460. Nennius also lists twelve battles fought by Arthur. This may, in truth, constitute no more than a prose summary of a long bardic poem celebrating Arthur's great fight and victory over the foreigners. Insofar as the battlesites can be more than tentatively identified, the list appears to concentrate on the struggle with the northern Picts.

Gildas and Nennius may have been, at least by *our* lights, hazy about historical fact. Their highly wrought (overwrought, you might say) laments for a golden past turned into lead read more like fiction than history. Passion overrides objectivity. But, like all writers, they were doing no more than trying to make sense of their own melancholy at the plight of the people of their own age. It would be unfair to accuse them of being short-sighted or narrow-minded. Accurate records did not exist; and the flamboyance of their literary style cannot mask an intense sympathy with human woe. Like any writer worthy of the title in any era, they looked about them, those early churchmen, and, hating what they saw, wrote as if they were standing knee-deep in the rubble of a filthy charnel house that had once been a beautiful mansion. What's new? Reviling the ugly present is far from being the monopoly of Dark Age monks. It is the theme, perhaps the straitjacket, of most writers of all ages. We all hanker after something better.

Nonetheless Geoffrey, claiming – if not meriting – the status of objective historian, used his sources to compose an account of what really happened in Greater Britain's past. To what extent can we ascertain the historical facts which form the background of his book? But first, why did Geoffrey write his *Historia* in Latin?

THE ROMAN EMPIRE

Geoffrey's Arthur spoke Latin, with a British accent. From A.D. 43 when the Emperor Claudius arrived with his legions and elephants, Celtic Britain had been Britannia, province of the Roman Empire, governed by Roman Law, paying Roman taxes, all official business in Latin.

In 324, the Emperor Constantine, having repulsed the vanguard of barbarian invaders, built a new capital – Constantinople – on the site of Greek Byzantium. He had also experienced a celestial vision, they say – a fiery cross, emblazoned with the words *In hoc signo vinces* ('In this sign you will conquer'), later to become the Crusaders' motto. Not long afterwards, Rome having persecuted Christians for three centuries by law, by law embraced them. Britain, still under Roman aegis (though, by now, a federated state governed and policed by her own nobles and armies), received Christian missionaries. Latin became the language of God's law as well as that of the Emperor.

However, to the south, the nomad barbarians who had taken a fancy to a stable life in the well-organised purlieus of the Roman Empire streamed in from central and eastern Europe: Goths, Vandals (who settled what is now Andalusia in southern Spain) and the ferocious Huns. Alaric the Goth took Rome in A.D. 410 and the Roman Empire was, effectively, at an end. The outlying provinces were left to their own devices.

In Britain, a general, one Ambrosius, declared

himself Emperor, crossed the Channel to drum up support among sympathetic northern Celtic tribes (Alemanni, Franks, Burgundians), ran into an army loyal to the emperor in Rome and perished ingloriously.

Ambrosius' demise spurred a handful of lesser military commanders in Britain, Romanised Celts to a man, to launch their own bid for power. The old native instinct for rebellion, never fully extinguished under the Roman blanket, flared up once more and anarchy tore the province apart. Some of the inhabitants decided to get out while they could and the first determined migration of Britons to Brittany, across the water, can be dated to around this time. Here was a second Britain. In fact, some Latin authors referred to it as Brittia, or Lesser Britain. (Others called it Armorica, Celtic for 'Seaside'.) The *Asterix* books accurately celebrate the fiery Celtic independence of the ironbound peninsula which became second home to the displaced Celts of Greater Britain. And that traffic from beleaguered Cornwall and Wales to the north-west tip of France is vital to our story: it helped keep alive the old Celtic world wherein Arthur had his origin.

Meanwhile, in mainland Britain, one Romano-Celtic warlord was emerging ahead of the rest: Vortigern. He soon established himself as leader of the Celts against the scavengers flocking into the country.

The attractions of Britannia drew them as they had drawn the Romans before: undulating pastures and green meadows; space, too. Odd to think of this overcrowded isle as a source of elbow room, but thinly populated as it then was, the acres rolled empty of inhabitants. The foreigners observed grand towns, provided with elegant and sturdy buildings, well-stocked granaries and warehouses, fine temples-cum-churches, bequest of their predecessor invaders the Romans. Also fruit trees, vine-

yards, cattle, teeming fish. They liked what they saw of this Britannia: bags of room, everything sprucely kept and organised, groaning larders, and decided to muscle in on it. Eventually would come Frisians from the Netherlands, Saxons from eastern Germany, Angles and Jutes from Denmark, Irish; but the immediate threat came from the Picts whom the Romans had penned back for centuries in Caledonia.

However, Vortigern had limited manpower and, following standard Roman practice, hired Teutonic mercenaries, three keels of them. He quartered his belligerent Saxons, under the brothers Hengest and Hors, in the offshore island garden he knew as Ruoihm. They dubbed it Thanet and weighed in to bash the painted Irish scallywags back across the Cheviot ranges. Things went well and, relishing his job as Bouncer-in-Chief to the British, Hengest summoned reinforcements from home. They needed little inducement to join the fray and forty keels sailed up the east coast to snaffle the Orkneys and north Scotland. Vortigern had carelessly let in the first Saxon invasion of Britain through the back door. Worse. In next to no time, the Saxon and Pictish outsiders had found common cause, allied against the Celts, marched south and, in Holy Week, trounced an army of Cornovii in their homeland near Shrewsbury on the Welsh borders. In renewed panic, Vortigern did what he seems to have done best: he yelled for help. This time assistance came from Bishop Germanus, on a papal mission from Gaul to bolster the spiritual defence of Christian Britain against the heathen Picts. Germanus, like countless others a soldier turned priest, swapped his crozier back for his sword without a flicker of conscience, announced his battle-cry ('Alleluia!') and rode into action down the Vale of Llangollen.

As ruthlessly effective in the saddle as he had been forceful in the pulpit, Bishop Germanus knocked the pagans for six, reclaimed the lost territory for himself and, as an afterthought, for Christian Britain. Then, with a nice stroke of irony, he rechristened it the kingdom of Powys; *Powys* being the Welsh for 'pagans'. Shunted out of their homeland, the luckless Cornovii drifted south into Dumnonia (Devon), booted the Irish settlers back into the sea off Land's End and, at last, took up residence in the peninsula named after them – Cornwall.

Hengest and his Saxons fought back like wounded cats. Gildas recalls how, once the invaders had cried havoc 'the only burial was in ruined houses, the bellies of dogs or birds'. He also records the harrowing appeal for help sent by the beleaguered Celts to Aëtius, governor of Gaul, across the water:

> The barbarians drive us backwards into the sea;
> the sea drives us back into the barbarians. We
> have a choice of deaths. Either we drown or we
> have our throats cut.

> *De Excidio Britanniae* XX 1

Aëtius, himself overstretched, replied curtly that the Britons would have to fend for themselves. Unremittingly, the Saxons, wrote Gildas, pursued the stunned Celts up into the hills and cut them down. Droves of refugees took to their boats, meantime and, braving the Channel, sang in threnody for the lost homes and homeland that Psalm to which Geoffrey, following Gildas' book, refers in his own:

> *Thou hast given us like sheep appointed for the eating.*
> *And among the gentiles hast thou scattered us.*

> *Psalm 44 v. 1*

Surveying the pagan wreckage of lovely Britain a hundred years on, Gildas fastens the blame on

Merlin reads out a lengthy list of dire prophecies to King Vortigern. The King's Saxon girlfriend, the beautiful Renwein, much resented by his British subjects, eavesdrops.

Vortigern, calling him obliquely, 'Proud Tyrant', no more than the Latin for his Celtic name. Vortigern had invited the Saxons. Vortigern had encouraged them to stay. He rendered up Britain as a prize for their coming. The whole thing stank. Truly the glory *had* departed. But, on the eve of its going came another man not mentioned by Gildas in his orotund jeremiad: Arthur.

ARTHUR: DUX BELLORUM

After Vortigern, the Saxons had taken firm possession of most of the territory below the limestone ridge straddling Britain from Scarborough across the Pennine spine, through the Vales of York and Trent, over the Cotswolds to Lyme Regis. This was good farming land, generally flat and open, and largely cleared of forests by the Romans who had concentrated their presence there. The Celts withdrew to the north and south-west, on the rockier, thinner-soiled uplands of Cornwall, Wales, Cumbria and Strathclyde. Gradually they were pushed even further back, and only Cornwall and Wales remained to them. Here Ambrosius, son of the Elder Ambrosius, had begun to consolidate the tribes who banded together, calling themselves *Combrogi* (Welsh *Cwmru*), meaning 'Fellow-Countrymen'. Across the limestone peaks and wide rivers which acted as rampart and moat between them and the invaders they glowered at the heathen *Saesones* ('foreigners'). And now Arthur came.

Arthur was an archetypal Celt; that is overcharged with imagination and emotion, prone to large swings of temperament, from reckless confidence to utter despair. To his fellow countrymen, the Combrogi, he stood for complete victory even when victory had evaporated. On this his legend is founded. As Chrétien puts it, he is *the* King; when he has spoken he does not go back on his word. He leads the hunt; his court is the gathering place of good, brave and stalwart knights, of fair and noble daughters of kings. For, besides generalship and personal strength, Arthur boasts the peculiar virtue of the greatest Celtic heroes: charm or glamour, a magical power casting a spell of absolute loyalty and devotion.

Realistically, however, total victory over the whole of mainland Britain was beyond even Arthur's army of native Celts, every man jack of them as brave as a lion, as strong as a horse and as mad as a March hare, revved up to a fighting tourbillion. The Saxons were, by now, too well-established, too powerful and, the bane of all

freedom fighters, too well-integrated with the peoples they had conquered to give their recalcitrant British neighbours any hope of success in all-out war against them.

On the other hand, Cornwall, Wales, the Wirral, Cumbria and on to Strathclyde might possibly be cleared. Even the expertly drilled Romans had found these western tribal lands near impossible to subdue. Once we conceive of Arthur as chief of chiefs in *this* part of the island, that is Celtic Britain, as separate from the eastern part, now Angle-land, Geoffrey of Monmouth's claims for him begin to make sense: exaggerated but, at root, authentic.

Geoffrey records a great victory won by Arthur at Badon Hill, the twelfth battle concluding the war. The site cannot be located with any certainty, but there is a good candidate near Bath – Little Solsbury Hill – and geography favours the argument. Not far away the river Severn, broad as a sea at its mouth, begins to drive a long wedge up into the heart of western Britain. Along its line the Romans had built their great legionary fortresses to contain the Welsh. To the south extends the damp plain of Somerset, the soggy land that sets hard only in summer, as they say. Hummocky hills loom out of these western fens like tiny islands in a partial sea; often wreathed in mist, too, layering essential enigma on their natural oddity. To complete the impression that Severn divides Wales from the rest of Britain as emphatically as the Channel separates the island from Gaul, periodically a huge tidal rampart of water thunders down between its banks into the estuary: the famous bore, from an old Norse word meaning wave or billow.

If Arthur, then, won his victory *east* of Severn at the head of a Celtic tribal army mustered from *west* of Severn, the legend would match part of the fact: he had indeed cleared the Saxons out of Britain. That he had merely walloped them further back into the England they already owned and not off the island altogether becomes a trivial detail where the stuff of romance is concerned. The sea they retreated across was Severn, not the North Sea. Arthur pursued and beat them; and once more Celtic chiefs ruled from Somerset up the Welsh marches to Cumbria and beyond into Pictish territory.

Geoffrey of Monmouth's paraphraser Wace noted the savagery of Arthur's campaign in Pictish Scotland. It reveals an Arthur swift to punish, even vindictive. Such dispraise of a figure generally praised to the skies is telling. It proves that the folk memory of him retains a vivid clarity; it is no mere figment.

Wace describes a lull in the no-quarter fighting in Scotland, when the Irish king Guillomer, who had come to aid the Picts, had retreated home again. A number of the Scottish women approach Arthur, begging him to take pity on them, their people and their devastated land. Arthur's war had brought them worse distress than any visitations by the English. For:

These Saxons were pagan men. Thy servants are Christians. Therefore the heathen oppressed us the more mightily and laid the heavier burdens upon us, [but] thou hast done us the sorer harm. Theirs were the whips, but thine are the stinging scorpions.

Wace, *Le Roman de Brut* (Everyman p. 51)

That has the ring of true experience. The reference is to the second book of Chronicles ch. 10 v. 11, scorpions not being native to these shores; in Wyclif's translation: 'My fader beat you with scourgis, I forsothe schal beten you with scorpions.'

The restitution of Britain, following Arthur's great victory, was shortlived. The ageing leader (in the thirteenth-century *La Mort de Roi Artu*, he is

ninety-two), met defeat and died at Camlann, traditionally on Salisbury Plain. (Geoffrey locates it in Devon.) Whether he had overstretched himself or the Saxons had begun to press inland once more from the south coast, the calamity lead to what Gildas called 'the lugubrious partition of Britain among the barbarians'. Britain, as such, was finished. The glory had departed; and if Gildas, writing in about A.D. 540, cannot bring himself to mention Arthur, perhaps it is because he failed at the last and let slip the great treasure in his grasp. Here Gildas speaks of Britain before its ruin and spoliation by the vile Saxons; he might be speaking of Arthur's Camelot:

Everywhere you look sprawl pleasant fields and hills, fertile in their abundance; comfortably spaced, always within easy reach, mountain pasturages for flocks, where flowers of every hue grow, neither crushed by human feet nor gaudy-seeming or painted to human eyes, but as it were the jewelled necklaces bedecking a favoured bride; and everflowing crystal rivers stream over beds of silvery gravel, purling brooks bright in the sunlight burble lazily past their banks lulling us to sweet sleep, and icecold freshwater torrents spill over into lakes.

Gildas, *De Excidio Britanniae III 3*

Geoffrey places Arthur's death around A.D. 515. Up to the end of the sixth century, various chiefs in Cornwall, South Wales, Ireland, Strathclyde and the Wirral – pockets of British resistance which survived Cadwallader's departure – named their sons Arthur. That alone is significant proof that Arthur not only existed but that he was accorded hero status. However, no trace of the name appears again until the diffusion of stories based on the Arthur legends after the Norman conquest of

Britain in the eleventh century. This makes it virtually certain that Geoffrey, though he must have heard of Arthur independently from Welsh and, probably, Breton sources, was encouraged to record it by the new masters of England who brought with them their own accounts of him across the Channel.

ARTHUR: LITERARY HERO

There is evidence enough to prove that Arthur existed, even if folk memory of him outweighs historical fact about him. He was no king, though; rather an early guerilla leader inspiring fervent resistance to foreign invasion. His campaign may have been doomed, by remorseless, overwhelming odds, to failure; but its very mad courage ensured that memory of it would live, a twinkle of liberty in the gloom of oppression.

Imaginative reconstruction of the past – what *might* have happened – need not always conflict with fact – what *did* happen. Besides, fact is a slippery fish, not easily caught at the best-informed of times. If Geoffrey of Monmouth's historical sources were thin on verifiable fact, they were generous on passion for the old, lost Britain. And *that* is the story of which Arthur is the hero.

Geoffrey, a Celt himself, unquestionably relished the stories of old Britain told him or overheard from his boyhood on. From old men repeating stories they'd heard at their grandfather's knee. From diligent scholars comparing versions of the same legends. From garrulous monks, eager to impress from their poring over the books in the Irish monastery libraries, those compendious treasure troves of old lore and myth. No barbarians had ever invaded Ireland to sack that great storehouse of culture. Geoffrey will have listened, too, to quicksilver-tongued travellers who chose not to settle in one place but, instead, trekked from one private hearth or hostelry to the next, packing stories, riddles, poems into their already-teeming heads as they went – new gems to exchange for food and lodging. And there were the professional storytellers, many of them Bretons, who earned a good living at rich men's firesides, regaling the company at table with dramatic renditions of the ancient legends. Each storyteller added his own embellishments to the familiar tales, because on the richness of his invention and skill depended the weight of the purse he'd receive in payment.

No radio, then; no television, no films, no theatre, even, and precious few books available even to the minority who could read. Storytelling was all. It still is, of course; only the technology has changed. To write the *Historia*, Geoffrey applied twelfth-century technology – sharpened quill, oil-based lampblack and parchment – to the oral, or word-of-mouth tradition. He was no professional storyteller, though, nor yet a dry scholar. Perhaps a mix of both.

Let us, then, outline Geoffrey's version of the Arthurian legend, its first appearance in literature.

RÉSUMÉ OF GEOFFREY OF MONMOUTH'S ACCOUNT OF ARTHUR

1. Uther Pendragon is magicked into the likeness of Gorlois, Duke of Cornwall, by the wizard Merlin, so that he can sleep with Gorlois' wife Ygerna (Ygraine) in Tintagel and sire Arthur on her.

2. Uther dies. Saxon invaders are overrunning the island. Dubricius, Archbishop of the City of Legions (by the Usk in Glamorgan), is urged by the British chiefs 'as their king' to crown Arthur, now fifteen years old.

3. Arthur disposes his armies and generals, marches on York and besieges the Saxon leader Colgrin. (Baldulf, Colgrin's brother, trims his beard and hair and slips into York posing as a minstrel.)

4. Saxon reinforcements pour in from Germany.

Arthur withdraws to London and summons help from his first cousin Hoel, King of Brittany (also known as Lesser Britain).

5. Arthur and Hoel raise the pagan siege of Lincoln with great slaughter, bottle up the enemy for three days in the Caledon Wood (Sussex downs and northward) and finally, exacting hostages and promises never to return, pack them off home with nothing but their boats.

6. The Saxons embark, change their minds and land again, near Totnes in Devon. They sack and murder all the way to Severn Sea and invest Bath.

7. Arthur breaks off his foray against the Picts and the Scots, hurries south and hangs the Saxon hostages.

8. The Saxons are defeated at the battle of Badon Hill. Arthur kills at a single blow every man he encounters, dedicating each death to God. Colgrin and Baldulf are slain.

9. Arthur pursues and mops up the Saxon remnants. Cador, Duke of Cornwall, retakes Thanet.

10. Arthur returns to Scotland, cuts the Irish army to pieces and resumes his massacre of Picts and Scots. The Scottish bishops beg him to desist. Arthur takes pity.

11. Peace is restored throughout the kingdom. Arthur marries Guenever, a woman of noble Roman birth brought up in Cador's household.

12. Arthur conquers Ireland and Iceland: the king of Orkney pays him homage.

13. Twelve years of tranquillity follow, during which Arthur's splendorous court achieves renown throughout the world, and Arthur a reputation for courtliness, generosity and courage.

14. Foreign kings build castles, in dread of attack by Arthur. With cause: Arthur conquers Norway, Denmark, Aquitania, Gascony, Anjou, Neustria (Normandy).

15. To Arthur's court in the City of Legions come numerous kings to do him homage. The Arch-bishops place the royal crown (of holy Empire?) on his head.

16. Britain is prosperous and cultivated. Her women will not look at a man unless he has proved himself three times in battle. A time of plenty, jousts, tournaments and revelry.

17. Archbishop Dubricius resigns to become a hermit.

18. Legates from the Emperor Lucius in Rome scold Arthur for not paying tribute and summon him to answer in Rome. Arthur kicks them out.

19. Arthur rebukes himself for going soft and idle – he and his knights have lost battle fitness, skill and ardour.

20. Lucius' Roman army, augmented to huge size by contingents from the Kings of the Orient, leaves for Britain. Arthur commits the defence of the realm to his nephew Mordred and Queen Guenever. He embarks from Southampton.

21. Arthur dreams of a savage fight between a dragon 'flying in from the west' and a bear. The dragon wins. Royal advisers interpret the dragon as Arthur.

22. Arthur digresses to fight and kill the Spanish giant terrorising Mont St Michel, with the Seneschal Kay and the Cupbearer Bedivere seconding. Arthur compares the giant to another giant whom he had beaten, Retho, with his fur cloak made of the beards stripped from kingly victims.

23. Skirmishes in the vicinity of Dijon. Arthur plants his Golden Dragon standard, and encourages his Britons: thirty kingdoms already won, now Rome is the prize.

24. Gawain fights hand-to-hand with Lucius. Arthur plunges into the mêlée wielding Caliburn, his sword. The battle is tipped his way by the timely charge of Morvid, Earl of Gloucester. Victory.

25. News from Britain that Mordred, living incestuously with Guenever, has usurped the crown and brought in extra troops from Germany.

26. Arthur lands at Richborough. Fierce fighting. Mordred retreats to Winchester. Guenever flees to a nunnery in the City of Legions and takes the veil.

27. Bloody fighting near Winchester; Mordred escapes to Cornwall. Final battle at Camlann (Camelford?). Mordred's Saxons, Irish, Picts and Scots defeated by Arthur's British, plus contingents from Norway, Denmark and Gaul. Mordred dies.

28. Arthur is mortally wounded. He is carried to the Isle of Avalon and hands the crown to his cousin, Constantine, son of Cador, Duke of Cornwall.

GEOFFREY'S AENEID OF THE BRITONS

Geoffrey's *Historia* is, clearly, a sort of *Brutus* on the model of Virgil's *Aeneid*. For what audience did he compose his pseudo-chronicle? That he wrote it down at all proves that he was courting a posterity different from the vague timelessness of tradition. That he wrote in Latin indicates a bias towards the ecclesiastical hierarchy, baring a hope for preferment in the church. And that he wrote about kings testifies to his angling for the biggest catch of all: royal patronage and high authorial status. In the first aim and the last he succeeded. In his bid for material reward on earth he largely failed.

The new rulers of England had military power and legal tenure. They had yet to win unarguable authority. They yearned to be lords by born right, not achieved might alone. They longed, like any arriviste, for pedigree. So, quite simply, Geoffrey determined to bestow on the Norman kings of England the identical solid gold genealogy which Virgil had conferred on Augustus and his heirs. He made them ancestors, by direct descent, give or take a generation, of Brutus, great-grandson of Aeneas, prince of Troy, founder of Rome. To the Normans, like all bullies deeply insecure, Geoffrey

said: 'Britain/England is your birthright. Royal welcome.' And, in the allegorical style of his day, he peppered his quasi-historical text with colourful allusions to the living Norman conquerors. All allusions are flattering to those who ache to be flattered. Geoffrey's Welsh cunning told him that, sure enough. Even more astutely, he couched the flattery in the language of God and the emperors of Rome, Latin, thus elevating it to the rank of holy writ. For Geoffrey must have known that Arthur was the king above the rest of whom the Normans longed to hear. Had not the Breton storytellers long ago established Arthur's heroic stature in all the great halls of Normandy?

How much of its text can we trace to historical or traditional sources?

We do know that one version of the *Historia* was dedicated to a lesser member of the Norman ruling dynasty, Robert, Earl of Gloucester. Note, for instance, the decisive attack of Morvid, another Earl of Gloucester, which saved the day for Arthur in the battle with the Emperor Lucius. Morvid is an alias for Robert. The earliest known Morvid had been the fifth son of Ebraucus, king of England at the time when royal David, in whose dynasty Isaiah placed such hope, was king in Jerusalem.

Robert was the bastard son of Henry I, William the Conqueror's younger son. Henry, who died in 1135, the year before Geoffrey's *Historia* appeared, had been forced to spend much of his reign keeping his father's legacy intact at the point of a sword. Like Alfred the Great before him, he enjoyed intellectual pursuits; devoted himself to a study of Latin and the law; founded a Benedictine abbey at Reading and a famous zoo at Woodstock, a few miles from Geoffrey's home in Oxford. Unhappily for England, he fudged the most crucial emergency of kingship. Lacking a legitimate male heir, he had, at first, showered ample favour on his nephew Stephen, earmarking him for the succession, everyone supposed. Then, at the last hour, he designated his daughter Matilda heir to the throne. Stephen took the snub ill, contested the succession and the anarchy that ensued all but ripped England to pieces. At one point Stephen besieged Matilda in Oxford, which must have had the clerics of St George's twittering with alarm. On Robert of Gloucester fell the burden of defending his half-sister's title. Is Robert of Gloucester 'the Lion from the West' (he and Matilda drew most of their support from the west country) who takes on 'the Boar of Totnes'? (Mordred flees to the south-west and, like Stephen, brought ruination on the island realm.)

The legend of Brutus' stray arrow killing his father recalls the fact that Henry I had been in the royal hunting party on 2 August 1100 when his older brother, William Rufus, died from an arrow shot out of the cover. Had William Tirrel aimed the shaft or was it an accident? Geoffrey's assertion that Brutus shot blind seems to absolve his noble patron's family from conspiracy. That they did not reward him with advancement may be because they were too preoccupied with saving their own skins in the fight with Stephen.

Perhaps the most intriguing comment in Geoffrey's account of the court is his insistence that prolonged revelry and feasting induced a decline in military prowess. The contradiction between idleness at court – a quintessentially southern, hot climate trait – and the stern endeavour and taut-muscled exploit which obsessed the hard-bitten northerners, lies at the core of the Arthurian romance. The twin themes – chivalric action, cushioned enjoyment of courtly love – tug in contrary directions and tease out the vital drama of Arthur, the Round Table knights and their ladies.

The geographical divide should not be pooh-poohed, either. I dare say the average Norman myrmidon could gladly unbutton on the odd few days of furlough, just as the sun-basking Provençal relished an occasional gallant bout of arms. The difference lay in habit. The Normans, originating from icy Scandinavia, believed that excessive luxury (hot baths and the like) turned you soft, did you no good whatsoever. It was an article of faith with them, and they cordially detested those who believed otherwise – southern French, Saracens and Byzantine Greeks in particular.

The first Normans, tough customers from Scandinavia, had rowed their keels up onto the sandy beaches utilised by the invading allies in 1944. From the slender-necked prows of their open-decked longboats snarled dragon's head finials. Now, Arthur and his father, Uther, took the golden dragon as their fighting emblem (see chapter 9). But Geoffrey also mentions a bear in Arthur's nightmare about a savage fight between the two beasts. Arthur is a bear, too: Latin *Artorius*, *arctos* 'bear' and *Arcturus*, the brightest star in the constellation of the Ploughman who pushes the Plough or Great Bear. That is sufficient to make Arthur a *Norman* hero. But he cannot be dragon *and* bear, can he? Yet why not? Such elementary puzzles of identification pepper Geoffrey's and other versions of the story but should not be allowed to give us a sneezing fit.

ROYAL SUCCESSION

On the evidence Geoffrey declares an obvious interest in providing the legitimate Anglo-Norman line (Henry I – Matilda – her son, Henry-to-be-II) with something akin to an *Aeneid*, if only passionately to urge the vital cause of pure blood descent. Break the true line of inheritance he implies, and bloody internecine war follows – Henry I's death brought civil war . . . Augustus' accession put an end to civil war. Primogeniture, the idea of passing everything – wealth, lands, power – from father to eldest son, was by no means new. In Genesis 25,

Isaac's son Esau sells his own birthright to his younger twin Jacob for a mess of red pottage. In Genesis 27, Jacob cheats Esau out of their blind father's blessing by the hairy hands trick. Birthright there may have been but who was to uphold the right? The tribal kingdoms and clan dynasties of the Dark Ages – roughly from the fall of Rome in 410 to the first Crusade in 1098 – ran on the first come first served basis. Power ricocheted from one strong man to the next. And when nearly all the men of power were in some measure related to each other across the tribes and clans, however tenuously, it was quite often impossible to decide if one claim had greater right than another. A trial of strength was simpler and, to a class of warriors, vastly more congenial. It also impressed the people whom the ruler had to rule, and amounted to a free-for-all game of Feuding Families.

The Church did not like the game: it smacked of pagan barbarism and disorder *and* cut them out of the action. To regularise the transfer of power from rightful king to legitimate heir, the Church instituted a public ritual of royal matrimony (not yet a full sacrament), wedding king to queen, and thus staked claim to a share in their authority and that of their children. This authority they reinforced with a promise of divine right. Adapting ancient Gothic ritual, a benedictory ceremonial of coronation wedded king to power; thus advancing the claim of church ownership on the crown, too.

Problems arose when the king had no male heir. A daughter might, exceptionally, inherit. The Celts had queens, and Boudicca set a notable precedent of their effectiveness; but a woman's challenge in a ruthlessly male-dominated society had to be doughty to succeed. Moreover, in general, early mediaeval society knew no marriage ceremony as such: to sleep with a woman sealed betrothal, and this is the style of matrimony in the Arthurian romances. Arthur himself would, in the eyes of the

church, have been a bastard had not Gorlois' death in battle conveniently allowed Uther to marry Ygerna already impregnated by him. Geoffrey was a good churchman so he regularised Arthur's birth, even though it had been stage managed by Merlin's Druidic hocus pocus. In praise of the old-world Druidic contribution in the turn of events, Geoffrey added a long chapter some time after the composition of the main text called 'The Prophecies of Merlin'. The famous wizard had been born during Uther's reign and these Prophecies combine high Druidism – mystic imagery and obscure and dark utterance – with a very Biblical spin of warning and cryptic allusion booming across the florid language. Very Welsh and purple. Geoffrey dedicates this section to Alexander, Bishop of Lincoln, a former canon of St George's, and says that he has made it tuneful so as to persuade the listener as if he were playing a rustic reed pipe. That is a flowery way of saying he has dressed up his language in the style of David's Psalms and old bardic poems.

His reference to Arthur's whirlwind rescue of Lincoln from the abominable pagan Saxon horde surely marks a discreet bending of the knee in the direction of its present-day Bishop, a powerful ecclesiastic, lately his colleague, who might give the humble author some preferment. If so it didn't work, alas. Alexander died in 1148 and Geoffrey got no promotion till 1152 when he became Bishop of St Asaph's in Flintshire. But Geoffrey had already pulled other strings on his bow.

Geoffrey undoubtedly wrote a propaganda tract for Henry I and his grandson-to-be, Henry II, the Angevin king and founder of England's Plantagenet dynasty through his father, Geoffrey Plantagenet, Count of Anjou, Matilda's husband. By marrying Eleanor of Aquitaine, a central figure in the propagation of Arthurian romance, in 1152, the second Henry added that county to Normandy and England. Thus the lands supposedly acquired by

Arthur in Gaul reverted, once more, to a king of England. To round his history off, Geoffrey adds a thoroughly Virgilian touch. Britain has fallen, overrun by Saxons, just as the walls of Troy were breached by the Greeks. Her last king, Cadwallader, like Aeneas flees the ruins. Once across the water in Gaul he hesitates, wondering if he should perhaps return to Britain to carry on the fight. The voice of God forbids it, commanding him instead to press on to Rome, the centre of divine authority on earth, and there to place the holy treasures of the Britons in safekeeping until such time as they can be taken back home to Britain and the lost kingdom regained. Of Arthur's promised return from under the hill Geoffrey says nothing. As a cleric he could not dare advance the blasphemous theory that Arthur, having died, would, like Christ, come back to life. Geoffrey therefore transmutes Arthur's immortality into the safer idea of numinous reliquaries belonging to the lost kingdom. It is the relics, not the sleeping king, which lie under the hill. And the relics not only recall Aeneas' Trojan idols, but the treasures of Solomon, the holy things of the city of Jerusalem, hidden before the Roman sack in A.D. 70, abstracted somewhere and kept, so the legend ran, till they might be recovered and the kingdom regained.

Cadwallader, in Geoffrey's telling, had no doubt that the cause of Britain's misery was divine retribution: God's vengeance on them for neglecting his worship. God had tossed the Britons to the ravaging heathen like sheep meat to dogs, uprooting them from their native pasture, a calamity that Romans, Picts, Scots, Irish and Saxons had, severally, failed to inflict. Now, wept Cadwallader aboard his ship of exile, only a huntsman could survive in the desolation that Britain had become, shorn of crops and fruit; always supposing that a huntsman would choose to dwell in such a sorry wasteland. Gone the days but recently past when a

king of Britain stood heroically at the head of his army in defiance of the invading Saxon hordes, drove them back on their heels and preserved Britain free for the British. Gone the days when this Arthur, son of Uther Pendragon, born by the magic trickery of Merlin, had pursued the crusade against the heathen foreigners across the water into Europe, to crush the legions of the Roman Emperor, Lucius himself, a barbarian stoolpigeon, at the battle of Saussy.

And who was this Emperor Lucius? No such man existed. But Lucius is originally a Greek name, and the Normans, like the Romans before them, hated the Greeks, especially those Greeks in Byzantium (Constantinople) with a vengeance. Byzantium was Troy, near enough. In one romance, *Cligès*, Chrétien makes subtle play of this by having a Byzantine pay homage to the most illustrious king Arthur. The northern French must have enjoyed that, although Chrétien showed altogether too much sympathy for the Byzantine party.

From his beginnings in Geoffrey and throughout the romances Arthur is a northern prince. His nature, actions, stature are modelled on those of the northern princes, the Normans most of all, who took him for their own. He inspired them in their fight against devious eastern potentates, heathen or Christian, and their benighted armies.

One factor, though, in Geoffrey's telling is clear and unambiguous: Arthur's Christian piety. And Geoffrey's telling sets the tone for future versions of the story, remember, even if they vary widely in detail. The Arthurian romances, I believe, were written above all to promote the Crusading spirit in Europe. The leaders of the Crusades were French and Anglo-French, English. King Arthur plumped up their idea of themselves as mighty princes and monarchs. Pious Arthur consecrated their mission as Holy Warriors, for Arthur fights in the Christian God's name against pagans. Before battle, he and

An early mediaeval map of the world showing the Holy City Jerusalem, Bethlehem nearby, at the very centre of the round earth. Christ in glory with the rising sun beckons the Crusaders eastwards.

fore pagan, Merlin does not sully the pristine Christianity of Arthur and his company. Geoffrey, himself a lay canon of the Church and later ordained priest and consecrated bishop, plainly states that it is Merlin who persuades Archbishop Dubricius to summon the barons to press Uther whom to make king after him.

In Hoc Signo Vinces

The battle of Badon Hill, as described by Geoffrey, has a singular relevance for our investigation of the origin and popularity of the Arthurian romances. Before the battle, Arthur addresses his men. He vows personal vengeance on the pagon Saxons for their massacre of his people, Christian Celts. He concludes his oration: 'In the name of Christ our victory is assured.' That is to say: *In hoc signo vinces.* At this point, the Welsh bishop Dubricius harangues the army. 'Anyone who dies in this war and does not flinch from death', he says, 'will have served his penance and receive absolution for all his sins.' This is the exact formula of papal blessing to Crusaders who engaged to fight against the heathen in Moorish Spain or the Holy Land.

Another point of special interest is the first mention in literature of Arthur's sword, the fabled Caliburn, our Excalibur. The exact meaning of the word is not clear, although the usual 'Devourer' seems to be well wide of the mark. At root the word probably has to do with steel but there is a suggestion of 'sword in stone' also. The Welsh name for the sword forged in the paradisal lake island of Avalon is *Caledfwlch*, latinised by Geoffrey to *Caliburnus*. The spelling *Caledvwlch*, though common, is erroneous: Welsh had no 'v'. *Caled* means 'hardness' and is a synonym for stone; *fwlch* means 'gap', hence 'freed from the stone'. But *fwlch* often appears as *bwlch* which means 'notch' suggesting that the hardness of *caled* may be of steel. There is a

his knights, whether in company or alone, dutifully attend Mass. Their weapons and armour and combat are dedicated to Christ for the discomfiture of Satan and his unbelievers. In fact, Arthur is the archetypal Crusader king; the members of the Round Table fellowship, exemplary Crusader knights.

Even the lurking presence of the Druid, there-

hint of Greek *chalybs*: steel, too, so *Caledfwlch* may be translated as 'Hard steel'; which I prefer.

THE WRITING OF HISTORY

By our standards of accuracy in record, Geoffrey of Monmouth was a garrulous old fibber. By the standards of his day, such a mélange of fiction, rhetorical flourish and approximate fact as he wrote passed for history. Bards made their poems of battle and giant fighting at the day's end by fireside and table. Who was to say: 'No, it didn't happen like that'? Only a rival poet; and *his* account would come from the same source, ultimately, the imagination.

The Greek word *historia* comes from their word 'to know'; thus a historian is one 'in the know'. But early history consisted of stories (the same word) and was told by poets, storytellers who assiduously honed their memories and curiosity for the acquisition and retailing of knowledge. They were in the business of entertainment *and* keeping track of their own people's fortunes, good and bad. What happened in the past prepared you for what would happen in the future. No great distinction existed, either, between recorded fact and the storyteller's version of it, however elaborate. Homer's *Iliad* and *Odyssey* may read fancifully but they are as much history as the Old Testament. They have the sharp veracious edge of the best war despatches; their geography, sociology, mythography, anthropology and anatomy is vivid. They contain generous spoonfuls of fable, too, but so do the garishly coloured accounts of Christ's life in the Gospels, not one of them written by a contemporary observer.

The old cliché about truth being stranger than fiction actually amounts to a deliberate credo for writers like Geoffrey of Monmouth and the storytellers in the same, long tradition. To such people bald fact was useless, being isolated, shorn of moment, detached like a teasel seed on the wind. Fact had to be made memorable, in a story which fixed the deeds and achievements of the tribe and its great heroes for the delight and moral instruction of later generations. Ancient Greek education was based squarely on the Homeric poems. Calamitous or glorious incidents from the past inspire and encourage the future combatants against reverse and elusive triumph.

Geoffrey's *Historia* sticks to a rough chronology and, in truth, is no more high fantastical than the most gruesome excesses of Hollywood's dreamed-up reconstructions of the past, even those of recent date, all geared to box office demands. Geoffrey also had to please *his* audience, to be sure, but his audience, unlike most filmgoers, knew well the difference between what Chrétien de Troyes called *matiere* and *san*; that is the source material and the way the storyteller puts it over. All the stories they heard were, in one form or another, for the most part familiar – nothing new under the sun. The literary or narrative skill in purveying it *could* be new, fresh, unexpected. Above all memorable.

The mediaevals may have enjoyed exorbitant digressions, rambling disquisitions on the nature of love in their fanciful romances. They may even have demanded such material in their histories, but what pungent history, they'd argue, is worth the name without *story*? They had, generally, a simpler – but not simplistic – view of human nature and action, ordained by temperament, motive and the contrary interventions of Good and Evil. Our sophisticated, research-laden opinions, free of any subservience to those pantomime characters God and the Devil, are chary of the simple explanation where, so frequently, the simple explanation becomes almost impossible to dig out of the avalanche of fact beneath which it is buried. The twelfth-century audience relished a good story and Geoffrey of Monmouth served one up.

CHAPTER TWO

EMERGENCE: LESSER BRITAIN

Arthur held high state in a very splendid fashion. He ordained the courtesies of courts, and bore himself with so rich and noble a bearing, that neither the emperor's court at Rome, nor any other bragged of by man was accounted as aught beside that of the king.

Wace, *Le Roman de Brut* (Everyman p. 64)

The year: 1170. A dark winter's afternoon. The place: Troyes in France; the court of Henry the Liberal, Count of Champagne, and his wife Marie. Marie is the great-granddaughter of Guilhem IX, Count of Aquitaine and the first known troubadour, who exulted in the fact that he earned his bread as undisputed master in the art of love, selling expertise 'in every market place'. Her mother is none other than the celebrated Eleanor of Aquitaine: Queen of France by her first husband, Marie's father Louis VII; Queen of England by her second, Henry II Count of Anjou.

The banqueting hall has been fragranced with incense, aloes and myrrh. Twisted beeswax candles in holders illuminate the company of men and women seated round the long table. From its broad white cloth servants remove the platters of a sumptuous meal: venison in hot pepper sauce, roast heron, pike, perch, salmon, trout, bread and condiments, raw and cooked pears. Other servants recharge silver-gilt goblets of Chartres with mulberry or strong white wine. A kitchen boy puts fresh logs on the fire burning in the central grate. Spark and flame patterns dance on silk hangings. Marie de Champagne signals; a copper gong sounds three times. Maidens appear from a side door carrying thin glass vials in which glow soft lights of viscous aromatic balsam oil. A low hubbub round the tables and then silence, as the storyteller, one Chrétien (Christian) as he calls himself, steps forward out of shadow into the amber luminance and bows low to his patroness and to her guests in hall. She will pay for the entertainment – perhaps a small purse of gold bezants. Her husband has other things on his mind: religious and martial business which, eight years from now, will draw him away east with the Crusader armies to the Holy Land. At his elbow sits the Bishop of Troyes, encouraging his lordship's zeal and with more than half an ear open for wayward opinion in the rest of the proceedings.

He comes as a guest, but also as arbiter and custodian of what may and may not, by Church authority absolute, be said and listened to.

Chrétien draws breath and begins:

> My lady of Champagne bade me compose a romance. I undertook the task willingly, with all my heart, nor is that any flattery. I am hers to command: anything in my power, anything in the whole world.

He pauses to bow and starts his account.

> The countess herself told me the story; she even suggested in what form I should cast it. The rest was simple: I had but to concentrate on writing it down.

The flattery is polished, disclaiming it part of the trick of delivering it to his patroness, as adroit, indeed, as his storytelling. Chrétien will act out his scenes with movement and gestures as the story unfolds, for three hours or more.

He refers to his written text, propped on a reading stand, the pages turned for him by a page; but he knows long passages by heart, or rote, the name of the Celtic harp which frequently accompanies the insistent rhythm of the verse, its dulcet melody wooing the listeners into rapt attention. Into their trance steals Chrétien's magic.

> One Ascension Day, King Arthur held court in high splendour befitting his majesty. After the feast, the King stayed with the company, the Queen beside him. In the hall were gathered a throng of nobles and, so it seems, many beautiful, courtly ladies speaking polished French.

Lancelot or ***The Knight of the Cart*** lines 1 ff

Arthur and Guenever preside at a royal feast. A carver, knife in hand, waits to address the roast meat. A musician accompanies the kneeling storyteller on a viol.

Pausing pointedly on 'so it seems', will he scan the benches of simpering ladies, coaxing them to believe, each one, to imagine he spoke to her, his favoured Helen, and none other? And at Arthur's court they speak French. How come? Here the author, Chrétien de Troyes, makes a suave dig at cloddish Anglo-Saxon. 'You English,' he might drawl, 'or are you British? Or what are you? Ouf!

You may have claimed the first stories about this great Arthur – a real king, so he *must* have been French, it goes without saying. But what a wretched, vulgar job you made of cobbling the story. Listen, now, to its proper telling in mellifluous, in regal manner, in *French*.' The jibe was no snooty lie, either. When Chrétien composed his romances, towards the end of the twelfth century, the Plantagenet kings of England ruled vast tracts of France, too. Arthur, perforce, had made the early and swift transition from God's Latin (Geoffrey) to royal French (Wace, Chrétien) over a solitary bridge of plebeian English (Layamon). So Chrétien, employing what everyone who is anyone agrees to be the true language of romance, proceeds.

ARTHUR CROSSES THE CHANNEL

Within twenty years, certainly by 1155, part of Geoffrey of Monmouth's *Historia* had been adapted and loosely translated from erudite Latin into more readily accessible Norman French by a native of Jersey, one Robert Wace, canon of Bayeux. Accessible to the Norman conquerors, that is, if not to the English conquered. Wace had already composed a flattering verse chronicle for the Dukes of Normandy, the *Roman de Rou* ('Romance of Rollo'), nor was he the first to address himself to Geoffrey's subtle encomium to the new masters of England. An Anglo-Norman, Gaimar, had produced the *Estorie des Bretons* ('History of the Britons', or Bretons, proving that, for the time being, no one distinguished between Britain and Brittany).

The recasting by Wace and Gaimar of Geoffrey's *Historia* demonstrates three things. First, the immense, near-instantaneous popularity of the book. It was a best-seller. Second, the French-speaking rulers at Norman courts on both sides of the Channel clearly regarded it as a splendid propaganda vehicle for their young régime. Third,

and most significant, it was the figure of Arthur who was responsible for the book's huge impact on the Normans. Wace inscribed his poem to the Anglo-Norman Henry II (1133–89), titling it the *Roman de Brut* ('Romance of Brutus') after Geoffrey's putative founder of Britain and the Britons. However, he ditches most of the original text and focuses almost exclusively on Arthur. Wace it is who makes the first mention of the Round Table. He claims, too, that Merlin, in celebration of victory over the Irish, causes the building of what the Britons called the Giant's Carol; in the English tongue, Stonehenge.

Towards the end of the twelfth century, a Worcestershire cleric, Layamon, produced a version of Wace's poem in Middle English, an account remarkable for this novel description of Arthur's childhood:

> So soon as he came on earth, elves took him;
> they enchanted the child with magic most
> strong, they gave him might to be the best of all
> knights; they gave him another thing, that he
> should be a rich king; they gave him the third,
> that he should live long; they gave to him the
> prince virtues most good, so that he was most
> generous of all men alive.

Nonetheless, by the middle of the twelfth century, Arthur's story, in Norman, that is to say Anglo-French, had, metaphorically at least, crossed the Channel. It would be a long time before English writers reclaimed it. Arthur rapidly became the stock-in-trade of French poets.

The ancient British kingdom, Greater Britain, had, after Arthur, shrunk and been subsumed into the new Angle-land. Now that kingdom expanded via Normandy to embrace yet another conglomeration of duchies and counties across the Channel. Not strictly a kingdom but rather an appendix to one. Occupying the north-west corner of it lay what the old poets called the kingdom of Lesser Britain – Brittany. Brittany was home to the Breton storytellers, many of them with Cornish blood in their veins, descendants of the exiles who fled the Saxon invasion of Britain.

Arthur, the supreme king, the high monarch above all petty chiefs and princes, once Arthur of Greater Britain now emerged as Arthur of Lesser Britain, too. And French, being the *lingua franca* of European courts and culture, imparted to Arthur's story a universal appeal and majesty which parochial English or forgotten British would have denied it.

For Arthur in French above all stirred the pugnacious blood of the Anglo-Normans. Unhappily for that narrow-minded and rigorous warrior class, the chief of their tribe, Henry II, had married the ex-Queen of France, Eleanor of Aquitaine, princess of most *un*rigorous Provence. Arthur was beginning to stir rivalries which have *never* been laid to rest.

THE MATTER OF BRITAIN

So it was that a Frenchman, Chrétien de Troyes, at work during the 1170s and 1180s, composed the first, fully-fledged Arthurian romances. Almost at once his subject matter fired the imagination of audiences and other narrators alike. Geoffrey and his translators had paved the way, but Chrétien added the polish and emotional subtleties which lend the romances their enduring appeal. Soon, other versions of the Arthurian legend appeared; not only in France but throughout Europe.

The romances flourished, most strongly in France where native poets and storytellers (Chrétien was both) referred to the legends centred on Arthur collectively as The Matter of Britain. Whether they intended Greater or Lesser Britain,

the island or the peninsula either side the Channel, we cannot tell. Nor does it much concern us. The English kings had possessions both sides of the water. English laws were couched in French. The English King was married to a French Queen, Eleanor of Aquitaine, and the court spent much of its time in France. As there are English references in Geoffrey's *Historia*, so there are allusions in the romances to French kings and historical events. We have, therefore, now to consider French history alongside what was happening in England.

CLOVIS, THE MEROVINGIAN BEAR

In A.D. 486, at a time when Christian Arthur was quelling the northern tribes, Clovis I, pagan king of the Franks, met and defeated the renegade Roman general Syagrius at the battle of Soissons. For this victory he was rewarded, or, more likely, grabbed unbidden, the title *Rex Romanorum*, King of the Romans; achieving in fact what Arthur achieved in legend. Has Geoffrey of Monmouth muddled Arthur's Saussy with Clovis' Soissons? It's entirely possible, because certain aspects of Clovis' life and reign show how welcome the Franks, who had wrested Gaul from the Romans, found the story of Britain's King Arthur. As welcome, indeed, as the Normans, who later wrested England from the English, found it.

Ten years after Soissons, in the thick of battle against Alaric II, King of the Visigoths, Clovis swore to be baptised a Christian if the Christian God would grant him victory. His wife, patient Clothilda, the Christian princess of Burgundy, had long been urging him to kneel at the font. The fighting went Clovis' way, though Alaric managed to escape, and, on Christmas Day 496, in Reims cathedral, Clovis and 3000 Franks received baptism. Another ten years passed before Clovis emulated Arthur's feat at Saussy by slaying his foe in hand-to-hand combat. Alaric fell under Clovis' sword and the Visigoths were done for.

Thus, like British Arthur, the Frank Clovis defeated pagan barbarians in Christ's name to become sole king of his people. He even died at roughly the same time as his Celtic counterpart, in A.D. 511. Not surprisingly, the Franks, as bellicose and haughty a race as the Normans, regarded their Clovis in much the same light as William's countrymen, established in England, regarded Arthur.

The famously long-haired Merovingian priest-kings are said to have claimed descent from Troy, just like Geoffrey of Monmouth's British kings. Recalling Arthur's bear connection, they traced their origin even further, to the legendary founders of Troy, the Greek Arkadians, named after their hero Arkas, son of Kallisto the Bear. The Arkadians were pure Greek, as Arthur was pure Briton. The Frankish (Teutonic) Merovingians certainly couldn't claim to be pure Gaulish. They had invaded Gaul after the collapse of the Roman empire. A royal link with Troy glossed over that inconvenience, though: Clovis may have been *de facto* king of all the other Franks, but he needed to persuade them, by solid myth and legend, that he deserved to be.

Clovis' father, Childeric I, had laid some foundations to regal respectability, by adopting the white lily of the valley as a family emblem to replace the Merovingian black toads. The lily was the emblem of David's kingdom of Judah. Leaping toads, arms and legs spreadeagled, resemble, closely enough, the *fleur de lys* which became the symbol of French monarchy. Another account has it that Clovis himself adopted the emblem after a celestial vision in which an angel commanded him to conquer the pagans in the sign of the lily. *In hoc signo vinces*, again. And under the sign of the lily Clovis never did meet reverse. One pagan army was destroyed before even a blow was struck, crippled by the (Christian) god of battles.

The lily of the house of Judah symbolises God's church. In the *Song of Songs* Christ appears as 'the lily of the valley, the white rose of Sharon'. The stressed link with Judah reveals that the Merovingian Franks were reaching out to claims over the Holy Land as well as Asia Minor. These claims their descendants in France were to press with bloody determination five centuries later.

In old age, Clovis became devoted to the saintly memory of Geneviève of Nanterre, an early Joan of Arc figure who had stiffened resistance to his Frankish armies as they marched on Paris. After his conversion to Christianity he gladly embraced her installation as a virgin heroine of the new kingdom. There can be little doubt, either, that just as Arthur lusted after Tristan's Isolde, Clovis intended his embrace of Geneviève to be something more than political. At any rate, the murderous Merovingians seem to have inspired saintliness in others, and Geneviève had her reward in heaven if not on earth. But does not her name chime with Arthur's Guenever, the French form of the Welsh Gwenhwfar? We can draw no firm conclusion, but the two names are close-sounding and excite curiosity, knowing the mediaeval love of resonance in different words.

The apparently coincidental parallels between Clovis and Arthur eventually joined in a somewhat comic fashion. Sigisbert VI, a Merovingian king-in-waiting, a century after Charlemagne had robbed the family of power, pathetically declared himself King Ursus (Bear) and tried to win back the crown from Louis II. His failure led to exile in Brittany. Thence to England where, out of the blue, it seems, he founded an English branch of the lost dynasty called Planta . . . hence the Plantagenets. Which may be nothing more than pure romance, to give it the polite name.

Perhaps the story, like many others, goes to

show how widespread was the obsession with Arthur. All kings fed on his glory. All dynasties owed their stature to him. The poets and storytellers used the legends of Arthur as a guarantee of heavy purses and firm patronage. Arthur reassured them all. He possessed majesty, pedigree, grace, empire, power and, above all, glamour. Arthur charmed them all. The reason for that may lie in his essentially Celtic nature. However, the Middle Ages claimed him and made him their own: a mediaeval king *par excellence*, lodestone of ambition and inspiration in *their* age, not his.

For instance, the literary Arthur is credited with the subjugation of a vast European empire:

> . . . in addition to Wales, Scotland, Orkney and the outer isles, Arthur cruelly conquers Holland, Hainault, Burgundy [remember Clothilda] Brabant, Brittany, Guienne, Gotland, Grasse, Bayonne, Bordeaux, Touraine, Toulouse, Poitiers, Provence [Eleanor], Valence, Vienne, Auvergne, Anjou, Navarre, Normandy, Austria, Germany, Denmark, and all the lands from Sluys to Sweden with his sharp sword.

Morte Arthure (Penguin p.34)

Alexander the Great was spurred in his ambition by the exploits of Achilles recorded in Homer's *Iliad*. Arthur did similar duty for the grand vision of the mediaeval kings of Christian Europe.

MAHOMET AND THE RISE OF ISLAM

Roughly simultaneous with the bloody unification of Gaul under the Merovingian Franks, the scattered tribes of far-off Arabia were also drawn together to common cause. Just as in Europe victorious Christian warmongers prodded subject heathen to the altar at the point of their swords, the Arabs now began to pursue a similar line of persuasion on the Infidel, or Unbelievers. Thirst for empire went blade-wielding hand-in-hand with a sanguinary missionary zeal. The Europeans demanded death or baptismal oath to God's Son; the Arabs brandished death in the name of God's Prophet Mahomet.

The Middle Eastern world was already in ferment. In 627, against the will of the Christian population, the Jewish Patriarch of Jerusalem handed over the Holy City to an army of Persians. The invaders, Christians of the Greek Orthodox variety, spared the Jewish inhabitants, but massacred or sold into slavery the Christians of the Roman faith.

This news shook the rest of the Christian world, and Jewish complicity in the Persian sack of Jerusalem and murder of its people did as much as anything to boil up future hatred and persecution of the Jews in Catholic Europe. Their role in the Crucifixion of Christ, as minuted in the blatantly pro-Roman Bible, provided the reason for antisemitism; their cowardly opening of Jerusalem's gates simply capped the argument.

Five years later, in 632, occurred another momentous event: the death, in the Arabian city of Medina, of the Prophet Mahomet. His legacy: a book, the Koran. Its message: a directive to rule the world in the name of Allah, the only true God, by killing, if need be, all those who did not comply. 'Those of the Book', that is to say Jews and Christians whose faith was based on Holy Scripture (writings), might be spared.

Within ten years of Mahomet's death, the Caliphs, or Successors, had overrun the north African coast as far as Tripoli as well as huge tracts of Persia; within another hundred years the Empire of Islam extended into Spain as far as the Pyrenees.

The Islamic armies were composed of Arabs, who provided the brains and direction, and Berbers, Syrians and Moors (from Mauretania). For the sake of convenience we call them Moors, Arabs and Saracens interchangeably, Saracen being the Greek name for the desert nomads.

Spain conquered, the Moors pressed on north. An army under Abd-ar-Rahmân captured Bordeaux and surged on, stripping basilicas, churches, shrines and towns of anything worth taking. Its target was old Poitiers and the famous church of St Martin, the soldier turned pacifist-hermit who halved his cloak with a beggar. Outside the city the Arabs blundered into the Frankish army, led by Charles Martel, the Hammer. The armies nervously kept their lines a full week. Finally the Arabs lost patience. That October Saturday in 732, their light-armed cavalry charged pell-mell into what Isidorus Pacensis, a chronicler of the time, described as the 'immoveable wall' of Frankish infantry, standing firm and solid as a 'block of ice'. The Arab horse broke and were cut to pieces by the Franks wielding their famous battle axes; Abd-ar-Rahmân among them. Next morning, before dawn, the Franks dourly reformed their line to resume battle. But the Arabs had gone, leaving their tents, like their hopes for conquest in France, empty.

The Arabs never again ventured so far north, although they exerted incalculably rich influence, both cultural and intellectual, on all Europe; most evidently in the more relaxed and cosmopolitan society of southern France and in Spain which, for centuries, they ruled. Arab scholars, translators, doctors, astronomers, mathematicians, scientists, craftsmen, engineers, technologists were aeons ahead of their European counterparts. Such spectacular brilliance in so many fields endeared neither them nor the people who most enjoyed their influence, the southern Provençals, for example, to the backward, quarrelsome northern French. The enmity between the cultivated Arabs and the boorish Franks, which instilled such fury into the Crusades, had been struck.

CHARLES THE HAMMER'S FEDERATION

After Poitiers, Charles Martel instituted a Frankish military league of princes against the Moorish threat, which simmered, yet, across the Pyrenean mountain yokes. Every landowner had to swear a *foedus* or obligation to maintain fighting men at his own expense. In return they shared in the protection offered by the combined force. This *foedus* derived from the old Roman federation of tribal states which evolved as the imperial ties slackened. It meant that the underlings who worked the overlord's lands had also, at a moment's notice, to form an armed force under the overall command of the king, or local prince, for the defence of the realm entire or its lesser constituent units. The call might easily come for more selfish purposes, of course: the beating up of wealthier or pugnacious neighbours. In fact, it merely revived the old warrior caste network of warlord and carls which had been the pattern of early society, whether Celtic or Teutonic. From Charles Martel's *foedus* system developed the Christian feudal knightly code (see chapter 3) which finds its ideal expression in the fellowship of King Arthur's Round Table.

In A.D. 743 was born a man who exploited the new federation to the hilt and, as much as any other monarch, drew to himself the deathless mantle of King Arthur; an emperor indeed, whose vision of his own stature was grander than most; the man who can be said to have inspired if not actually launched the Catholic Crusades against Islam: Charlemagne (Charles the Great), successor to Charles Martel.

CHARLEMAGNE

Unlike Charles Martel, Charlemagne did not wait for Mahomet to come to him, so to speak. At the age of thirty-five he crossed the Pyrenees, captured the Basque city of Pamplona and marched on into Moslem-held Spain, only to meet a full-stop outside Saragossa. His pride badly snubbed, he was probably relieved to answer an urgent call back from the dusty peninsula to fight the detested Saxon invaders closer to home on the banks of the Rhine. He left behind a small rearguard under the command of Hruodland (Roland), prefect of the Breton March. As this remnant traversed the Pyrenean defiles, they were attacked and wiped out by Basques smarting for revenge but too weak in numbers to use any but Fabian tactics.

This unremarkable eighth-century chain of events, no more, really, than a sideshow, gave rise, in the eleventh century, to one of the finest heroic romances in literature: the anonymous *Chanson de Roland*. In its gloriously colourful pages, a local skirmish becomes an epic confrontation between Christian and Moslem armies. The Basque ambushers are transmuted into a numberless host of Saracens. The pass is clearly identified as Roncesvalles (Roncesvalles) which lay on the pilgrim route to the holy shrine at Santiago de Compostela. Charlemagne himself appears as a legendary monarch marching under the sign of the True Cross; his second-in-command, Roland, becomes the hero, betrayed to the Saracens by the Iago-like Ganelon.

Roland's central role in the drama suggests Breton authorship for this brilliant epic poem. The hitherto independent March of Brittany had joined itself to Charlemagne's kingdom as a protective measure against unremitting coastal raids by Norse pirates, the future Normans. The *Chanson* deliberately celebrates a Breton alongside the great Emperor and conjures a remarkable story out of a minor scrap. Did not exactly the same process apply to the literary glorification of Arthur?

At the age of eleven, Charlemagne was crowned heir to Pepin, sole king of the Franks and an empire that, like Arthur's, extended from France to Saxony in the north and Italy in the south. Malory records a similar occasion:

> And so anon was the coronation made. And there was he [Arthur] sworn unto his lords and the commons to be a true king, to stand with true justice from thenceforth the days of this life. Also then he made all lords that held of the crown to come in, and to do service as they ought to do.

Malory Book I chapter 7

Legend claims that Arthur saved the Eternal City, Rome, from the besieging Saracens. Charlemagne *did* save Rome, albeit at the Pope's request, from invading Lombards (Germans, kith of the reviled Saxons). Charlemagne's determination to scrawl his own glory across every chronicle in Christendom certainly matched the efforts of French romance to do the same for Arthur. Europe's first active involvement in the Holy Land is due to Charlemagne: he sponsored the establishment of pilgrim hostels there, to be run by Latin nuns. Tenth-century legend claimed that he had brought back holy relics from Palestine, but he never set foot in the place.

This Christian vigour he also turned on the battle-hungry Saxons lining his northern frontiers. It is important to remember that the Franks were, themselves, a Teutonic people who had invaded Gaul from east of the Rhine. They claimed kinship with the Alemanni and Saxons who remained behind. Thus Charlemagne's virulent hatred of the Saxons reveals not a little of the unreasoning

Saracens mounted on their light Arab ponies, with war drums (unknown in Europe till the fourteenth century), trumpets and elaborately decorated banners.

bitterness so characteristic of family feud, civil war, clan rivalry. Under Charlemagne, the Gaulish Franks became more Roman than the Romans in their detestation and brutal treatment of the Germanic tribes. And is this not why all the Arthurian stories, without exception, identify the godless Saxons as the first enemy, when it is a matter of preaching the doctrines of Christ with the sword?

In 800, Charlemagne stage-managed his own coronation as Emperor by Pope Leo III in Rome and was thus declared 'Charles Augustus, crowned by God, great and peace-loving Emperor of the Romans'. The Holy Roman Empire, rival to the Holy Greek Empire, had come into existence. If the Franks hated the Moors on religious grounds and envied them for being too rich, too soft, too good at everything, they seem to have detested the Greeks above all for being Greeks.

Years before, Charlemagne's father Pepin had signed a *Donation*, 'deed of gift', which guaranteed the Pope's territorial holdings in Italy. That is to say, the Pope ruled his lands by the grace and favour of the Frankish king. Now Charlemagne cooked up, through some deft and subtle-brained help of the clergy, a forged *Donation of Constantine* which affirmed the Pope's *spiritual* leadership over the whole earth. And from St Peter, the Pope in Rome inherited the keys to Heaven and Hell.

There can be little doubt that Charlemagne *was* the author of this spurious deed of right. Though nothing can be proved, he did quarrel violently with Pope Hadrian over its wording – hardly the act of a humble Christian monarch reverencing sacred writ. Interesting to note, in passing, that after Camlann, Arthur is said to have passed on the crown to his cousin, son of Cador duke of Cornwall, a boy by the name of Constantine.

These are two examples of what *we* would term manipulation of historical fact for political ends. Lies, in other words; though Charlemagne's fabrica-

tion has infinitely more serious consequences in the general frame than Geoffrey of Monmouth's.

Forty years after Charlemagne's death in A.D. 814, Pope Leo IV, in conscious memorial of the first soldier of Christ in the Holy War, promised reward in heaven to any soldier dying in battle for the Church against her impious foes. Charlemagne's greatest legacy was delivered: the Crusading principle had been enunciated; and Arthur's role in literature as the foremost king in Christendom embattled against the heathen was sketched out. Geoffrey of Monmouth's portrait of him, written thirty years after the capture of Jerusalem by Christian armies, is undeniably that of a Crusader king.

THE NORMAN CONQUEST

Charlemagne's kingdom, like Arthur's, did not last. A dissolute man, he married four wives, kept several mistresses, sired a number of bastards but no legitimate sons and bequeathed neither bureaucracy to manage the kingdom nor machinery to secure its title.

Across the Channel, Egbert, King of Saxon Wessex, who had grown up in Charlemagne's court and took more than one leaf out of his book, overturned the Anglo-Saxon kingdoms of England and then, with hardly time to draw breath, faced a new menace: the Danish marauders who swooped into the coastal inlets like swift birds of prey and as swiftly out again. The English called them Vikings, from their word *wíc*: a temporary camp. I am tempted to translate Viking, therefore, as early English for 'tourist'. No laughing matter, though. The Danes established themselves in what came to be known as the Danelaw: all England north of a line from London to Chester. Their seaborne raids continued to terrorise coastal towns, as far west as Exeter, until Egbert's grandson, Alfred, nicknamed the Great, burner of cakes, organised resistance and

Hell's portals depicted as the gaping jaws of a hideous monster.
An angel turns the key to lock; the condemned sinners are hauled
off by demons.

carried the fight to them. In 853, at the age of five he had been baptised in Rome by Pope Leo IV – in the very year of that Pope's offer of spiritual reward to soldiers of God. Later, as King of Wessex, Alfred built a fleet for his land-based Saxons to match the Danish pirates and, after some twenty years of fighting, this second great freedom fighter out of the west country decisively beat the foreign invaders and scattered them back across the sea.

Unhappily for Alfred's ghost, a hundred years later the Danes came back and reoccupied the Danelaw. King Canute mounted the throne of all England and, before his contretemps with the sea, became a Christian to boot. His stepson, the monkish Edward the Confessor, succeeded Canute's sons and, almost certainly, promised to hand on the crown in the same line to a kinsman by Harold Bluetooth, King of Denmark, one William, Duke of Normandy. Another Harold, this William's first cousin once removed, Earl of East Anglia, supported the Norman claim to begin with; then reneged and made himself king.

But the Normans were not to be trifled with. An old proverb warned: Have the Frank as a friend, *not* a neighbour. It might equally be said of the Normans; although they were notoriously danger-ous friends, too. The first Normans had arrived in France as pirates and pirates, at heart, they remained. When a Norman lord died, his firstborn son inherited the whole estate; any younger sons had to look elsewhere. Normandy being parcelled up from end to end, elsewhere might well be a very long way off. In the 1040s William Ironarm de Hautville had kicked the Byzantine Greeks out of Sicily and founded the Norman Kingdom of Lower Italy. On the same principle, if you can call it that, William Duke of Normandy might have crossed the Channel anyway. Rarely for a Norman, however, he pursued legal cause. He even got blessing from the Pope.

Into a large fleet, he packed a formidable army and specially prefabricated sectional wooden forts, to secure the bridgehead, and, at Battle near Hastings, secured his claim.

Like the good, hard-nosed Norman he was, William later set up a commission to measure just how much land he had acquired: nothing like sending hot word back to brag how well he had done for himself, and who wanted to live in stinking hot Sicily anyway? By 1072, to rub in his magisterial presence far afield in the conquered territory, he was building a castle way to the frozen north in Dunholme which, unpronounceable in his French, he called Duresme, our Durham. The Benedictine cathedral across the way followed in 1093 and both edifices still lower forbiddingly over the riverside settlement below, symbol and forcible-in-stone reminder of Norman might over the subject people. In the capital London, Gundulf, Bishop of Rochester, produced some architectural wizardry of his own, building the White Tower in 1078; the Church joining shamelessly in the subju-gation of the flock, by claiming neutrality of the Holy Spirit.

An old Welsh legend refers to:

Three Fortunate Concealments of the Island of Britain. The Head of Brân [Raven] which was concealed in the White Hill in London, with its face towards France. And while it was in the position in which it had been put there, no Saxon oppression ever came to this Island......And they were the Three Unfortunate Disclosures when these were disclosed....And Arthur disclosed the head of Brân the Blessed from the White Hill, since he did not desire that this Island should be guarded by anyone's strength but his own.

Quoted in R.S. Loomis, *Arthurian Literature in the Middle Ages* (p. 45)

It is tempting to think that Duke William knew exactly what he was doing when he approved the construction of a Norman keep in London, over and beyond fortifying a strategic position by Thamesside. Not only did the castle focus the power of England's new régime; it symbolised his possession of Arthur's lost kingdom. Fifty years later, Geoffrey of Monmouth would do for the Normans in England what Virgil had done for Augustus' family in Rome: hallowed the claim by tracing the line back to Troy.

England, then, had become well and truly Norman, and William, if only metaphorically, had identified himself with Arthur by disclosing Brân's head and building a Norman keep on the site. And with the Normans came the Breton storytellers, back to their old homeland, with their stories of that same Celtic Arthur, King of Britain, who presided over

the regal and highly-ranked of the Round Table
The champions of chivalry and chieftains of title
Prudent in practice, powerful in arms
And doughty in deed ever dreading disgrace

Morte Arthure lines 17 ff

ARTHUR OF BRITAIN - ANGLO-FRENCH HERO

Arthur's story heaves with contemporary, that is mediaeval, allusion to historical event and personage. No culture supports any myth entirely naked of religious, political, social or ethical point; no folk tale does not hide some, even the tiniest, primitive secret. Arthur's story is no exception. In the twelfth and thirteenth centuries his legend embodied *the* most popular theme in literature. French poets, who led the authorial field, put the Matter of Britain on a prominence of interest higher than all others. But why? How? Because they led the authorial field. But other factors helped. Arthur was all things to all kings. To all lesser nobles, too, he enshrined the noblest ideal; to all knights the truest virtue. He symbolised heroic resistance to dark forces, invading barbarians, for all the world minions of the Devil himself. Above everything else, Arthur provided a shining example to those Christian princes who journeyed east on their pilgrimage of blood to do combat with the pagans in the sign of the Cross. Arthur was the most glorious hero that any hero-worshipper could hope to emulate. Yes, all these reasons; but, knotting them together tight, a simple accident of geography. The Norman conquest reunited, in spirit if not in fact, the old, sundered Celtic kingdom of Britain. Greater Britain recovered its exiled portion Lesser Britain across the water. The interloper Teutons who renamed Gaul, France and Britain, England now gave way to the Anglo-French Normans who ruled most of both.

ARTHUR AND THE NORMAN KINGS OF ENGLAND

Welsh Geoffrey's *Historia*, written after seventy years of Norman occupation, ends with Cadwallader, last king of Britain, escaping to exile in Rome. Britain, an angelic voice tells him, will be restored to her rightful owners only when all her relics are gathered together and brought home. Meantime, the punishment of God lies heavy on the scattered people of the island ravaged by invading Saxons, Picts, Scots and their pagan kin, in retribution for faithlessness.

The Britons, as such, did *not* come back. The Normans came in their stead, however, and restored peace and stability to the reunited land. Does Geoffrey imply, then, that the Normans, being French and therefore, by affinity, if no more, related to Charlemagne, saviour of Rome, had fulfilled the prophecy given to Cadwallader? In his

'Prophecies of Merlin', added to the *Historia* some twenty years after its first publication, Merlin tells Arthur:

> The mountains of Armorica shall erupt and Armorica shall be crowned with Brutus' diadem. Kambria shall be filled with joy and the Cornish oaks shall flourish. The island shall be called by the name of Brutus and the name given to it by foreigners shall be done away with.

Britain, renamed England, will be Britain again. Kambria is Wales, with Cornwall a surviving relic of old Britain. Armorica is Brittany, whose Duke, Conanus, had led an unsuccessful revolt against Norman overlordship before the invasion of England by William.

> From Conanus shall there descend a fierce Boar, which will try the sharpness of its tusks in the forests of Gaul . . . The Arabs shall dread this Boar.

The Boar was the proverbial animal of unflinching valour, hunted in October, the year's 'fall' preceding wintry death. In his Metrical Chronicles 1297, Robert of Gloucester notes that, 'Cornewailes bor .. [that] was Kyng Arthure' (line 133). Richard, Earl of Gloucester, III of England had the White Boar as his device, according to Shakespeare who got it from Holinshed who leaned heavily on Geoffrey of Monmouth.

This boar is a king of England, so perhaps Geoffrey's boar is also a king of England: none other, surely, than Henry II, son of Geoffrey of Anjou (ally of Conanus), half-nephew of Robert Earl of Gloucester, Duke of Normandy, lord of Poitou, Guienne and Gascony? From 1154, the approximate date of Geoffrey's 'Prophecies of Merlin', he was undisputed king and, for the

moment, enjoyed the patronage of Pope and Church.

The voice of God interprets Merlin's prophecy to Cadwallader thus, saying:

> One day, in the fullness of time, and as a reward for keeping faith, the Britons are destined to take Britain back. This will not be until they gather up their old king's bones and bring them from Rome to Britain. And when, finally, they have shown the relics of *all* their saints so long hidden away from the clutches of the dreaded pagans, to the people, they will recover the kingdom.

Had not Henry II done something like that? His land holdings rivalled those of Charlemagne's too. Geoffrey's 'relics' seem, therefore, to have been a collection of royal titles. Henry II, married to Eleanor of Aquitaine, that ardent patroness of Arthurian romance, brought pedigree, title, land, prestige, amity with the Church in Rome. He, or his immediate heirs, extended Plantagenet interests to Ireland, Sicily, Castile, Toulouse and, most joyous prize of the lot, final revenge, Saxony.

Arthur has done more than cross the Channel. Like a dispossessed Norman son, he has gone in wide-ranging search of lands across the known world. The Norman connection is vital. Franks by assimilation, the Normans' conquest of England established their leadership in Europe and, most important, eventually reunited the two halves of the old Celtic world, Greater and Lesser Britain. This made the emergence of Arthur in full, heroic panoply not only possible; I'd go so far as to say inevitable. I have called the Normans pirates, *arrivistes*. Their progress to respectability resembles nothing so much as that of the outlaw cattle barons of late nineteenth-century America to pillars of society and politics, exorbitantly wealthy benefactors and upright patrons of everything worthy.

The more powerful the Normans became, the more attractive they found the trappings of kingship rooted in ancient custom, rather than tacked onto the walls of castle and dungeon masonry. Wealth and prestige they acquired in plenty. Like Augustus before them, they craved what he identified as central to authority: pedigree. Power without authority, that is power not vested in law or sacred writ, is short-lived. The Normans wanted a foundation dug into Time's deep bedrock and Arthur supplied it. Within two generations, the Normans had established themselves kings of England, formidable peers, rivals to the Frankish kings of France. Arthur substantiated their intrinsic belief in Norman superiority, if only by virtue of their vast Arthurian holding of land, from the Scottish borders almost to the Pyrenees.

So, then, was Arthur, of whom Chrétien and the other French writers spoke as 'the good king of Britain whose noble qualities teach us that we ourselves should be honourable and courtly', no more than a symbolic hero representing, say, the Merovingian king Clovis, sole king of the Franks? Or Charles the Great, hammer of the Saracens and Saxons? Malory heads chapter 11 in Book II: 'How the Saracens came out of a wood after for to rescue their beasts and of a great battle'. This might be a prelude to Roncesvalles; and, almost inevitably, after Charlemagne died they said he was merely sleeping until France required him and he would wake and to the rescue. They made similar claims in Denmark for their hero Holga Dansk. And for the heroes who sleep in Valhalla (see page 45). And for El Cid, the Spanish warlord whose struggles with ungrateful kings ended up tamely in a lawcourt, courtesy of church influence on an overbloodthirsty text.

And what of George of Cappadocia, the warrior of Asia Minor, destined to become England's patron saint, whose story the Crusaders brought home: a paragon of chivalry, rescuer of damsels, slayer of dragons, obvious reincarnation of Arthur of Britain? Where does *he* stand in the lists?

Arthur is too cunning, too full of ruses to be tricked into so ill-concealed a trap as clear identity. He provides much better game and sport than that lame quarry which 'professional storytellers', as Chrétien disparagingly calls them, the mediaeval equivalent of hack journalists, can chase to earth.

> Whither has not flying fame spread and familiarised the name of Arthur the Briton, even as far as the empire of Christendom extends? Who, I say, does not speak of Arthur the Briton, since he is almost better known than to the peoples of Asia than to the *Britanni* [i.e. Welsh and Cornish] as our palmers [pilgrims] returning from the east inform us? The Eastern peoples speak of him, as do the western, though separated by the width of the whole earth . . .

Originally attributed to Alanus de Insulis; now dated 1164–7 by G. Raynaulde Lage. Quoted R.S. Loomis, *Arthurian Literature in the Middle Ages*, (p. 62)

Arthur's story, in every telling, is dominated by Quests of one sort or another: to seek a saint, to hunt the white hart, to pursue love and worship of noble lady, to harry the black knight to his castle of villainy and death, the evil Fay to her Satanic lodge, to quest for the Holy Grail. All Quests replicating the Crusades, metaphorical and actual. All sparked, coincidentally, by the Norman Conquest ('quest achieved') of England and the Frankish Conquest of the Holy Land.

Chapter Three

City of God

Thou, hooly chirche, thou maist be wailed!
Sith that thy citee is assayled.

Romance of the Rose c. 1400

Castles in the Air

Travel through the south of France today, from Provence to the Pyrenees, and you will encounter dozens of hilltop fortresses, towers and *bastides*, fortified towns, built for the defence of their inhabitants during the years leading up to the end of the first millennium. It was a time of violent upheaval: petty rulers warring one with the other; land grabbing, reprisal raids, sheer brigandage in the name of supposed entitlement, all to the general misery of the unarmed citizenry. Indeed all France, particularly Normandy, is dotted with keeps and *donjons*, thick-walled towers the conquerors then built in England to use for prisons as well as forts. But the forts and barbicans of southern France are more numerous and, because of their lofty, iron-bound setting, usually more spectacular.

The Provençal masons put to good effect the gaunt, limestone parapets slung like stepping-stones between the mountains which straddle France's Mediterranean coastline, building on them as natural ramparts. A single curtain wall girdling the domed cliff top often sufficed to render the township packed inside it virtually impregnable. The one access road winding steeply up the arched and cullised gateway of the bastion offered little hope to any would-be intruder. His only recourse was to lay siege and pray for treachery or loss of nerve among the inhabitants of the town, a long-winded, costly business; also deflating to the morale of troops whose steadiness was questionable at best and who were edgily keen for a quick dose of havoc rewarded by a plunderous free-for-all. The *bastide*, unless it were an especially rich prize or strategically crucial to a larger campaign, like as not weathered all but a determined investment, holding out on thin commons – stale water, fusty grain and brined olives, maybe, perhaps no more than it had in normal circumstances.

From a distance, these fortified towns have an enchanted air: a cluster of roofs and turrets, pink-tiled, glowing in the sun, perched on a weather-bleached peak high above a valley; grey-green leaved olive, eucalyptus and pine trees crowding the steep slopes below. At sunrise, mist breathes up from the valley floor like breath from a slumbering giant to form a cloud about the lower walls of the town and the ribbed vaults of the church and the slim clocktower poke up in pale silhouette against the rinsed blue sky. The *bastide* appears to be floating magically in the air.

A familiar sight throughout Europe, these hilltop citadels, remote as eagle's eyries, appear in all the romances as places of danger, or mystery, or enchantment. We think of the Castle of Case (that is the Relic) visited by Lancelot in Malory's telling; or the Castle Mortal (Earth?), the Castle of Inquest (Purgatory?) and the Castle of the Black Hermit (Hell?) in the *Perlesvaus*. In the *Quest of the Holy Grail*,

The fortified bastide town of St Paul de Vence, in the Alpes Maritimes west of Nice.

Gawain and Hector visit a fortress-like ancient chapel 'deserted and apparently abandoned, on a high plateau between two crags'. Most intriguing of all is the Castle, in its various guises, which houses a holy relic whose importance to the Arthurian legend we shall come to in chapter 7: the Holy Grail.

To an age obsessed with holy relics, their collection, their excavation, their exhibition, their veneration, the Grail represented the holiest relic of all: the cup used by Christ at the Last Supper. However, like most conundrums thrown up in the Arthurian legend, that quest for the uncatchable, the riddle of the Grail, is not so easily summed up or explained. The Grail appears in many places, in manifold forms, in varying circumstances amid a variety of rituals and ceremony. Of all the castles where the Grail manifests itself, perhaps the most vividly drawn is that one located by Wolfram von Eschenbach in his *Parzival* atop Munsalvaesche, 'Wild Mountain', and described thus:

> No expense, no effort had been spared to make
> the castle impregnable. The masonry of the
> walls, smooth as if they had been lathed, offered
> no handhold. Numerous turrets and palaces
> stood inside the great battlements. Only an
> attack borne on wind or wings had any chance
> of success. The garrison could hold out for thirty
> years against the combined armies of the whole
> world.

Parzival

Sometimes the image is more peculiarly Welsh, damp mist steaming up from shadowbound valleys as if from a wizard's cauldron to swathe the hills and spill over into adjacent hollows. The Welsh tale of Gereint, son of Erbin describes the phenomenon.

Gereint asks a traveller the way:

> 'Say' said Gereint, 'which road of these two is it
> best for me to travel?' 'It is best for thee to travel
> that,' said the traveller, 'if thou go this, thou wilt
> never come back. Down below there is a hedge
> of mist, and within it there are enchanted games,
> and each and every man that has gone thither
> has never come back. And the court of Earl
> Ywein is there and he permits none to lodge in
> his town save those who come to him at his
> court'.

Mabinogion (Everyman p. 270)

There is enchantment here, as in the mysterious castle at the end of a causeway in the *Perlesvaus*, one of the earliest accounts of the Grail Legend. This is a stronghold on the remotest headland of the wildest islands of Wales, by the sea to the west, 'nought there save the hold and the forest and the waters that were round about it'.

Yet, whether in drizzle-swept Wales or sun-baked Provence, the *bastide* reminds us of Camelot, Arthur's castle, famously, and rose-tintedly recalled by Tennyson.

Camelot is at once the most enduring and the most celebrated castle of romance. King Arthur holds high court there. His Round Table stands in its great hall. Of this Round Table the *Quest* author says:

> The name, Round Table, brings to mind the
> round earth, also the concentric orbits of the
> celestial spheres, and the planets, the stars, all
> the heavenly bodies visible on earth. The Round
> Table is, thus, a perfect model of the universe.
> All knights be they Christian or heathen, who
> honour the code of chivalry, flock to the Round
> Table; and if, by the grace of God, they are

admitted to its fellowship they count that a prize richer than if they had gained the whole world. To achieve it, to fall under the spell of the love which binds its company of brothers, they will forsake father, mother, wife, even children.

The Quest of the Holy Grail, chapter 6

Not only is Camelot the most splendid of royal courts, though; the Holy Grail itself appears there, in celestial vision. Arthur's favourite home, therefore, seems, as do the Holy City Rome and Jerusalem the Golden, like a gateway from this mortal world to the heavenly bourne, Christ's immortal kingdom of glory, or else the Celtic Avalon, that paradise of the immortal heroes. Writers must always describe the delights (or torments) to come after death in vivid terms of life before death. Here is a description of life at Camelot one Christmastide:

All was happiness to the height in halls and chambers
For lords and their ladies in delectable joy.
With all delights on earth they housed there together,
Saving Christ's self, the most celebrated knights,
The loveliest ladies to live in all time,
And the comeliest king ever to keep court.
For this fine fellowship was in its fair prime
   Far famed
   Stood well in heaven's will,
   Its high-souled king acclaimed

Sir Gawain and the Green Knight (Penguin p. 22)

And that 'high-souled king' seated on a throne at the very centre of Camelot is Arthur. Should we interpret Camelot, first mentioned by Chrétien in his *Lancelot*, as a version of the Celtic paradise Avalon, or as a supposititious rebuilding of Jerusalem

in western Europe? Centuries later, Blake voiced that theme again:

And was Jerusalem builded here
Among these dark, Satanic mills?

For, if Christ had walked the streets of Jerusalem, the mediaevals asked, *and* He had loved all mankind, had He not also walked the damp pavements of the northern cities, in spirit accompanying those proselytising monks who preached his Gospel of light during the Dark Ages? Certainly Arthur the King's generosity, material and spiritual, recalls the liberal compassion of the Saviour; the splendour of his court reflects the bliss of the Paradise offered by Christ to all who believe in Him. When the Crusaders arrived in Jerusalem, they believed, as a matter of fact, not only as an article of faith, that they had stepped from the mire of their former life into a new, god-charmed existence. The romances embody such a duple view of life on earth, preparing for life in heaven. And Camelot embodied both: the ideal worldly castle and palace so rich in virtue and inspiration, so glorious, so utterly perfect as to be otherworldly. And here we observe a potent Celtic influence in the legend. The Celts, like the ancient Greeks, centred their culture on hearth and hall. The Celts loved to wander but wandering they also associated with trials and tribulations. Home stood for ease, for the holding of glory in the hand, rather than the wrestling for glory which precedes that joyous contentment. The Teutons had an altogether more restless attitude; their nomadic genes troubled them deeper. So, Charlemagne has no favourite or famous court. Arthur has Camelot, and a number of other lesser courts, and the magic of his name, for that and other reasons (Christ in Jerusalem, Christ in 'my Father's house'), worked a stronger pull on the imagination:

When Bors arrived at court in the city of Camelot from the faraway lands of Jerusalem, he was overjoyed

The Death of King Arthur, section 2

CITY OF GOD

To the European knights who, between the end of the eleventh and the end of the thirteenth centuries, went on Crusade, like the romance knights Bors, who returned, and Perceval and Galahad, who died, Jerusalem was the City of God on earth. It was *the* Holy City where Christ walked, preached and died; Sion the Golden, promised city of heavenly light, eternal spring, everlasting peace. St John, in the Book of Revelation (chapter 21), described his vision of a new heaven and new earth; and a holy city, a new Jerusalem, descending from God in heaven, decked like a bride for her husband. And John heard a great voice from the throne saying: 'Behold, God's dwelling place among men, where he will live with them and they shall be his people. And God shall wipe away the tears from their eyes, and death will be no more, neither will there be any grief nor crying out nor pain, for these will be banished first before all things'.

Arthur's Camelot, Jerusalem, old and new, the Celtic afterworld Avalon, the Christian heavenly Paradise – to the mediaeval imagination, attuned to read symbol as no different from visible reality, they might, simply, be all the same place. Terror of the unknown, devilish in its real grip on the mind, could not be explained away – the Devil existed, sure enough, didn't he? Terror had to be assuaged by Christian faith. Scientific explanation was more or less unheard of in a society where the Word of God, interpreted by His mediators, the priests, covered every baffling eventuality. Closer investiga-tion, probe or inquiry, was discouraged, even disallowed if the Church thought fit. It was an age in which use of the question mark, like the combination of a safe, was, so to speak, permitted only the trusted few. Spiritual truth, revealed truth, intuitive truth, that is to say *God's* truth, super-seded, made irrelevant all other knowledge. More-over, God's presence manifested itself in all things. Hence, symbol, God's *inner* message about Creation, equated with his *obvious* message, that is the evidence of the five senses.

Certainly, to listeners eager for stories of far-off Jerusalem and to pilgrims who had returned with minds cramful of wonder, Arthur's Camelot seemed as golden a city, not altogether of this world; Arthur the king resided there a king of kings, like the Pope in Rome, Christ's vicar on earth, and the Frankish kings in Jerusalem, Christ's lieutenant on earth. And was not Camelot, in later versions of Arthur's story, the city where the Grail appeared, like the tongues of fire at the first Pentecost, in holy Jerusalem?

If Jerusalem offered the Crusaders a stepping stone from the tribulations of this world to the rich glory of the next, from mortal life to the heavenly mansions, and was confused in their minds some-how with both, what of Avalon, the lake island to which the Celtic heroes went? And how did the Celts view mortality and immortality?

CELTIC LIFE AND DEATH

The Celts believed that death simply marked the halfway stage in a long life. This belief, and it was an aristocratic, warrior class belief not available to the commonality, is recorded, by the Roman author Lucan, as early as the first century A.D. and usefully promoted warlike courage in a fighting breed whose sole anxiety seems to have been a wild fear that the sky might fall on their heads. Asterix suffers from this neurosis: a curious tic which re-emerges in the children's story of Henny Lenny, the doomsday hen. Moreover, their otherworld being spacious and agreeable, the Celts looked forward, unabashed and eager, to life's second phase in the hereafter.

> Freedom and health come to the land around
> which laughter echoes; in Imchíuin [Very Calm
> land, one of the islands of the early Paradise]
> with its purity come immortality and joy.
> Through the perpetual good weather, silver rains
> on the lands; a very white cliff under the glare of
> the sea, over which its heat spreads from the
> sun . . . in the many-coloured land with great
> splendour they do not expect decay or death.

From 7th–8th century poem, quoted in
A Celtic Miscellany (Penguin p. 175)

Death bore no such dreamlike allure for the glum Greeks. They groaned that dying into eternal nothingness merely put an end to life's unrelieved misery. Greek heroes, alone, might strut their after-hours in the Elysian meadows of asphodel, but even that may be a final, sour twist of Greek scepticism; asphodel is a damnably prickly plant.

The Norse heroes, gloriously slain in battle, looked ahead to the jubilation of whooping it up in the roomy, light-filled Hall of the Slain with the god Odin, waiting for Doomsday, when they would march out at his side through the Hall's 640 doors to fight the ghastly giants. From this one can guess that Norse halls were generally cramped, smoky and dark. The less-than-heroes among the Norsemen gloomily resigned themselves to Niflheim: a cold, dank kingdom of mist, northward and downwards, presided over by the goddess of death, one Hel. (In Anglo-Saxon that means 'hole'.) A shore of corpses, a north-facing castle bedewed with snake venom, a blood-sucking dragon called Nidhogg . . . no wonder the promise of a celestial heaven, as light-filled and roomy as the heroes' Valhalla, brought the frost-bitten northerners to Christ in droves. When priests, warning them against the diabolic perils of not believing in Christ, said that the alternative was to roast in Hell, they must have chuckled and said: 'At least we'll be warm, then'. Hell or Heaven, they couldn't lose. Moreover, the same priests exhorted them to fight against the Prince of Darkness, meat and drink to a warrior race. They hated the dark, too, with a vengeance, enduring more than their fair share of it in the long, northern winter, full of ghostly-visaged creatures up to no good. This Devil fellow, Beelzebub, Satan, or whatever they called him sounded the very image, if not the blood brother of Nidhogg the dragon, down to his forked tail, gory teeth and sulphurous breath. *In hoc signo vinces* too, *and* hymns? Baptise me, quickly.

The Celts were equally content to swap Avalon for Heaven and, it seems, the pagans generally warmed to the Christian ceremony and ritual, having little of their own. These rituals had just enough flavour of the exotic east in them to appeal to the down-to-earth northerners. When St Patrick came to baptise the King of Ireland he accidentally drove his sharp-pointed crozier into the unfortunate man's foot. The king made no complaint and it wasn't till the holy man saw fresh blood starting out of the royal boot that he asked why he hadn't cried out. 'I thought it was part of the ceremony,' the king replied. One sole god to worship, instead of a whole warring pantheon, also made sense to such ingenuous souls. The British Celts, for example, could name 69 gods of war alone.

By chance, an opinion about the nature of Christ, voiced in the early fourth century about the time of Constantine by a bishop of Alexandria, one Arianus, helped boost the spread of Christianity among the northern pagan peoples. While it was roundly condemned by orthodox Church authorities, it was widely supported in Europe and based on what many held to be the original, Nazarene teaching of Jesus the Messiah.

Arianus claimed that Christ had not been the actual son of God, but was a flesh and blood man, God's son only by divine adoption, as it were – of similar substance as God but not the *same* substance. 'Just like *our* heroes,' said the Celts, 'we'll worship him all right'.

THE CELTIC PARADISE: GLASS CASTLES

We must be aware that whatever elements of Celtic myth we know about survive in a literature copied down by monks in the Dark Ages and originally intended for the heroic warrior class of Celtic society. Such élitism moulds most early myth. The legends of Arthur the King, the Round Table, Camelot likewise subscribe to an aristocratic, though not exclusively Celtic, tradition. Pauline Christianity may well have preached an egalitarian message but Christ himself was almost certainly of noble birth and certainly of élitist, scholastic and radical political leanings. The Celts responded to the Nazarene, freedom fighter Christ long before the Roman Church began to impose Paul's Greek-influenced sophistication of the Gospel on them.

So then, a Celtic warrior fought with no fear of death, perhaps even with haste to be clear of the cowardly, inferior, ignoble, unheroic elements in this life; not least the proximity of the hoi polloi. The afterlife offered all the glory imaginable to a hero (an impressionable hero, at that), with none of the debasing obstacles thrown in his path by malignant Fate. Consider, for example: a boulder falling onto and crushing his foot, thus incapacitating him before he had achieved hero status and epic

death in battle. Miserable. That malicious instrument of Fate whose sole joy it was to confound and thwart manly ambition was known to the Irish Celts as the Morrigan, our Morgan le Fay (le *Fate*). She turned life into a series of desperate adventures, a long voyage of danger, enchantment, wicked deception and rapturous prospect. A man had always to be on his guard against demeaning behaviour. So the journey was not imagined, but a real odyssey testing will, hardihood, courage, above all genuine nobility of heart and spirit. Fate would find out the flawed character. Celtic myth abounds with stories of journeys and voyage, as is natural among a people whose basic economy and *raison d'être* depended on cattle-raiding, cross-border tribal warfare, proud independence from oppressors, exploration, adventure. Moreover, because the Celts tended to congregate, or have to retreat, into sea-locked or sea-girt homelands (Ireland, Cornwall, Wales, and so on), not only does water figure largely in their myth but so, too, islands moated with water. Crossing the liquid element stood for, indeed flourished, danger; and the relief of landing must be tempered with the risk endured on the way. And islands might be real, platforms of land afloat in lake or sea or river; they might be illusory, hilltops looming up in a surrounding flood of mist.

Caílte, one of the Fianna (Fenians), Finn's warrior band, describes the finding of the Fairy Hill:

I cast about over the shoulder of the hill to the south, and as I gazed around me I saw a fairy hill, brightly lit, with many drinking horns and bowls and cups of glass and of pale gold in it. And I considered what I should so. And this is the plan I settled on: I went across into the fairy hill and sat down in a crystal chair on the floor of the fairy hill and gazed at the house all around me, and I saw twenty-eight warriors on one side of the house with a lovely fair-headed woman beside every man of them . . .

Anonymous 12th century, quoted in
A Celtic Miscellany (Penguin p. 164)

A word, here, about glass. The Celts thought of glass, a very rare commodity, as magical. Seas of glass, bridges of glass, walls of glass separated the living in this world from the dead in the other world. Indeed, primitive glass, full of impurities, thick and watery, distorts light in such a way as to make such an idea not wholly fanciful. The Biblical image of seeing as through a glass, darkly, records the same notion. In Celtic myth we read of crystal boats; of beautiful, shining (i.e. crystalline) islands; of seas and lakes of glass. Here, once more, reality fuses with symbol. Sunlight on the surface of water may seem to turn lake or sea to glass. Mist becomes opaque and vitreous as the sun's rays filter through. An island is transformed into what the Celtic legend calls a glass castle, girded by strands of green-blue water and a foamy herd of white horses; or else a star palace anchored in the moonlit,

royal-blue sky. Moonlight remains crystalline, magical even when the myth is long dead. And this draws us back to the *bastides*.

Imagine a hilltop citadel at dusk in the Welsh hills; see it twinkling with lighted windows, mantled with mist, that damp veil that a fourteenth-century Welsh poet called a loveless, unsunned crop, father of rain, homestead and mother of rain.

GLASS. GREEN. BLUE.

Now, here's curious, as the Welsh say. Welsh *glas* means 'blue'; but *any* shade of blue, dark or pale, from the blue of woad, used by the ancient Celtic warriors as war paint, to the steel blue of a sword blade; or the deep blue of Celtic enamel; or the light green of Roman bottle glass. But light filtered through crystal, enhanced by greenish, blueish hues, was pure enchantment to the poets of old

Brân's Fortress (Dinas Brân) on a high crag overlooking the Vale of Llangollen.

Britain. It is the origin of what came to be described, rather soupily, alas, by Yeats and others as the Celtic twilight. Better think of it as a penumbra of magic, the experience of which penetrates to the very depth of the psyche. Here I would instance the barge which looms out of the mist across the lake to carry away the dying Arthur to Avalon, to immortality. Bedivere has flung Excalibur back into the lake and the mysterious trio of Queens arrives to haste Arthur away from this life. In another story, a mysterious ship appears, uncrewed, in a creek below a cliff in Brittany. The hull is so perfectly caulked, inside and out, that no seam is visible in the planking. The pegs and deck-rails are made of ebony, the sail of costly silk. The wounded knight Guigemar steps aboard; whereupon it sails off unbidden on an enchanted voyage to bring him, who has always scorned love, to discover the true love of his life and, thereby, cure of his earthly wound. (*Guigemar*: the late twelfth-century Breton *Lais* of Marie de France.) And, in the *Quest for the Holy Grail*, the knights take passage on a ship whose sails, unassisted, fill with wind and drive the ship across the waves so swiftly it seems to fly.

Are not these all ciphers for the unquenchable nature of memory in the souvenir of great men and women; the exhilaration of romantic love; the intense exaltation of religious ardour? Above all, they stand for experience, emotion, understanding which transcends normal levels of human feeling.

Glass, therefore, stands in Celtic belief for separation, especially between living and dead ... which is the reason why you must never view the new moon through a glass window pane, the Moon goddess being the Death goddess. She is also the Love goddess, and so glass comes into romance; here marking the separation of lovers:

And one morning in the summer time, Gereint

and Enid were in bed, and he on the outer edge. And Enid was without sleep in a chamber of glass, and the sun shining on the bed; and the clothes had slipped from his breast, and he was asleep.

Mabinogion, 'Gereint, Son of Erbin'
(Everyman p. 251)

CELTIC PENUMBRA

They all talked of Arthur finding his last rest in the Isle of Apples, the lake isle of Avalon. Paradise, an old Persian word adopted by the Greeks, means 'garden', and many cultures agree that the final resting place of bliss and easeful death will be found in a garden. The Hebrew Eden leads, eventually, to our modern secular Garden of Remembrance. In his *Life of Merlin*, Geoffrey of Monmouth describes the Celtic garden, Avalon, through the Welsh poet Taliesin:

The Island of Apples, which men call the Fortunate Isle, is so named because it produces all things of itself. The fields there have no need of farmers to plough them, and Nature alone provides all cultivation ... Thither after the battle of Camlan we took the wounded Arthur ... and Morgan received us with becoming honour. In her own chamber she placed the King on a golden bed, with her own and noble hand uncovered the wound and gazed at it long. At last she said that health could return to him if he were to stay with her a long time and wished to make use of healing art. [Morgan was a celebrated herbalist.] Rejoicing, therefore, we committed the King to her, and returning gave our sails to the favouring winds.

Quoted in R.S. Loomis, *Arthurian Literature in the Middle Ages* (p. 92)

That accords closely enough with a Christian view of Paradise to occasion no great surprise that the Celts adapted readily to the new teaching. In Revelation, chapter 2 verse 7, St John writes:

> . . . the [Holy] Spirit saith unto the churches,
> To him that overcometh will I give to eat of the tree of life which is in the midst of the paradise [garden] of God.

It is a commonplace that church Christianity amounts to a sort of compendium of primitive beliefs gathered along the way, much as detritus adheres to a rolling snowball. Its festivals, customs, rituals, even its terminology are, almost without exception, pagan in origin. Christianity endured because it integrated skilfully with existing religions and borrowed, stole and learned from them. The Cross symbol, for instance, may be Egyptian in origin; but the Celts, too, used the cross well before the advent of Christianity as their own symbol for mortal life – mortality's two intersecting lines, ringed by the unbroken circle of immortality.

The writers of Arthurian romance, albeit working in a Christian ethos, plundered the continuing oral tradition for detail with which to embellish their own work. All writers are magpies, nor do they care greatly where the stolen bright objects to decorate the nest come from. The pagan colour of the old Celtic world added frisson, mystery, danger to the romances. Christian knights ride out to do battle with the spirits of darkness, minions of the devil. How more richly to charge that encounter than with borrowings from stories about heroes and giants, and strangeness, and wonder, and magic?

THE MABINOGION

The Celtic storytelling tradition certainly owed its longevity, at least in part, to the labours of Irish monks. Throughout the Dark Ages, roughly A.D. 500–1000, Ireland remained felicitously aloof from the ravages and barbarian invasions which flayed the rest of Christian Europe. Year after year, the shelves in the monastery libraries of Erin groaned under the increasing weight of lovingly illuminated and copied books, scriptural record of the bottomless treasury of Celtic legend into which the travelling storytellers, Breton, Welsh and Irish, dipped constantly. The monks often added a Christian overlay, but the stories did not significantly change. However, neither Arthur nor his knights figure in the Irish versions of these stories which, in one guise or another, were familiar, if only vaguely, to all Celts. For evidence of a direct link between the oral tradition about Arthur the King and the written romances, we must look to a Welsh text.

The *Mabinogion*, a collection of Welsh bardic tales, first appeared in the fourteenth century, although their true origin is clearly much earlier. There are echoes of known stories from the ninth century, and strong hints that the material came out of a common source: the oral tradition plied by Breton and British storytellers on both sides of the Channel, well before the Norman conquest. In all likelihood, the Welsh poets who wrote down the manuscripts which form the *Mabinogion* were doing no more than frame, in print, what had been passed on by word of mouth, to them and their ancestors for generations; at least as far back as the times of the historical Arthur. Geoffrey of Monmouth talks of a source book in 'the ancient British tongue', for example.

Was the tradition pure Celt? To begin with, probably; but other influences seeped in along the way, and Chrétien de Troyes produced versions of the Arthurian stories which appear in the *Mabinogion*, making them wholly French. There are Celtic clues scattered liberally throughout his polished and courtly writings though; as in his version of the story quoted above, where he renames Gereint 'Erec':

> With those I have mentioned came Maheloas, a great baron, lord of the Isle of Glass, an island where thunder is not heard, no lightning strikes or tempest blows, no toads or snakes stay, and it is never too hot or too cold. Graislemier of Fine Posterne brought twenty companions; and his brother Guingomar, lord of the Isle of Avalon came.

> Chrétien de Troyes, *Erec* lines 1895 ff

That is as close a description as any of the pagan Land of Earthly Joy. No snakes, notice – and didn't St Patrick himself drive the reptiles out of the Emerald Isle in the middle of the 5th century? None of Clovis' nasty toads, either, with their venoms of hell.

Guingomar is the Guigemar of Marie de France's Breton *Lais* who took passage on the enchanted ship. So, the strands of Celtic bewitchment weave in tightly across British and French tradition.

An obvious and charming example of this comes in Gottfried von Strassburg's marvellous romance *Tristan* (about 1210). The Celtic chimes ring loud, only because he is using the same material as the other writers, though making it thoroughly his own:

> In its greenness and firmness the marble floor [of Tristan and Isolde's secret hideout in the forest] is like Constancy. Constancy should be of the same fresh green as grass, and smooth and gleaming as glass.
> At the centre the crystal bed of Love . . . Love *should* be of crystal – transparent and translucent.

Three windows let in the sunlight to irradiate their cell deep in the rock. The windows symbolise Kindness, Meekness, Nobility. The blessed sun's rays betoken Honour, most luminous quality of all. Here in the cave, the lovers enjoy heaven translated to earth. Christian imagery and significance is superimposed upon primitive Celtic, but the origin is still clear.

CELTIC LORE – CHRISTIAN ALLEGORY

Without the injection of specific and more serious purpose than mere entertainment, old Celtic lore might have become no more than a quaint relic of a forgotten culture. Geoffrey of Monmouth embarked on the *Historia* with the deliberate intention of affirming the Norman kings in regal authority over their English subjects by giving them title deeds, as it were, to their conquered dominion.

Within a few years of the *Historia's* publication, the magic of Arthur's name pervaded all contemporary literature. Marie de France cannot forbear passing mention of him, a cameo appearance to put a seal of verity and pedigree on her Breton *Lais*. Arthur had undeniable star quality. So, equally, whether Geoffrey intended it or not, *his* written account of Arthur launched two grand themes which dominate the romances, those perfect vehicles for the fusion of symbol and reality: Kingship and the Holy War. Arthur, the paragon of regal glory. Arthur, the most Christian of kings inspiring the Crusade against the Church's enemies.

> Alexander, heir to the Greek Emperor in Constantinople, a courageous and proud young man, refused to be knighted in his own country. Instead, he sought this honour at the famous court of King Arthur the king, revered and celebrated throughout the world.

> Chrétien de Troyes, *Cligès* lines 60ff

TREASURE OF THE HIGH CITADEL

In the *bastide* town of St Paul de Vence, just north-west of Nice, narrow, crinkum-crankum streets are cobbled with small pebbles set in flower patterns or else paved with smooth, irregular flagstones. Low archways haunt entrances leading off the long flights of steps and shoulder-width vennels dart off sideways into the shadows like ghosts afraid of daylight. In the squat, polygonal church on top of the mound, lies a tomb, dating from 11 September 1077. In it repose the 'mere mortal remains' (*exuvias modo mortales*) of one Henricus Deguigues; generously, he left enough space for the bones of future occupants blessed with the same name. Carved at the head of the gravestone, set like a big paving slab in the floor, the family scutcheon, a pair of rampant lions squaring up for a fight, has been heavily gouged and defaced; perhaps by some resentful heir whose claim for entry was in dispute. Underneath the inscription a crudely hacked skull and crossbones has escaped damage; as the poet says, 'Death ties our hands behind our back' (Hélinand *Les Vers de la Mort* 13th century) so no monkeying with him. In a wall niche a few yards away stands a dusty, glass-fronted cabinet displaying a real skull and crossbones, yellow with age. A tattered label curling off the frame reads: St Clement. If these macabre relics do constitute the 'mere mortal remains' of St Clement himself, third successor to St Peter as bishop of Rome, St Paul de Vence no longer needs the tourist trade they might foster. The gift shops packed like stalls and sideshows in a fairground into the wynds – open turnstiles, little more – produce more than plenty already.

The story might well have been different in 1077, when Henricus Deguigues shuffled off his mortal coil. Holy relics were big business in those days and in 1077 plans were already brewing for the recovery of the holiest relics of all – those in Jerusalem, the Holy City. The year after Deguigues' death, Odo de Lagery, a minor French nobleman's son who had early in his career become prior of the great Benedictine monastery at Cluny, was appointed Cardinal Bishop of Ostia, outside Rome. Ten years later, aged only 46, he was elected Pope, taking the name Urban II. Rome being in the hands of an anti-Pope, Guibert, for several years Urban sought uneasy refuge in the Norman kingdom of Sicily. In 1093 he re-entered Rome, with considerable relief one imagines (the Normans were nearly as uncertain allies as they were truculent enemies); and two years later he returned in triumph to his native France, the undisputed master of all Christendom. It was not pure nostalgia that drew him thither, even if it might appear so: he went, first, to his old abbey at Cluny. But the Cluniac community pursued other interests besides St Benedict's rule of work, prayer and study.

The Holy War against the Moslems in Spain was going well, sponsored, originally, by the highly organised monks of Cluny in their determination to keep open the pilgrimage routes to the shrine of St James, Jesus' own brother, at Compostela. Under the abbots Odilo and his successor Hugh, who, between them, ran the house from 994 to 1109, the Cluniac monks more or less took over the Church in Spain as well as the administration of the military campaign geared to its stout protection from the infidel. In 1064, Pope Alexander took the unprecedented step of offering an indulgence (temporary guaranteed remission of sins) to all those who took up the sword for Christ in Spain. His successor, Gregory VII, gave absolution (total pardon from miscreance) only to those who died battling to make Spain's Moorish soil Christian once more. (Echoes of the bliss in Valhalla promised to the Nordic heroes who died a glorious death in battle.) Now Urban II summoned a Council at the hilltop

et austres sains lieux la environ.
Et les vpiens ysiditans z demou
rans. z que les austres par culx
tyranniquement z inhumaine
ment tuès . Ilz auoient resenes
en suscitense vie a fin que sur
culx en lopprobre du saint nom
vpien paissent continuer plus
sourement seurs Insaitables

multultes . Et comment Ilz
les tenoient en trop opprobrieuse
captiute z seruage . ou tressaint
deshonneur z opprobre de tous
les vpiens . Concluant z mon
strant par diuerses raisons tres
euidentes que se saint peuple
vpien ne deburoit plus souffrir
nendurer que ses saints sieruet

citadel of Clermont, west of Lyons, in November 1095 and there, to jubilant cries of *Deus le volt* ('God wills it') from the assembled clergy, he preached the first Crusade, holding out an assurance of redemption in the heavenly afterlife to those who would bring the Holy Land into the Christian (that is to say 'Roman') fold at the points of their swords, lances and two-handed axes.

BYZANTIUM INVADED

The invasion of Asia Minor by Turkish Sunni Moslems had sliced the Byzantine Empire almost in half and thereby set a huge tract of hostile territory between Christian Europe and the holy shrines of Syria and Palestine. The Emperor in Constantinople, now robbed of Anatolia, always a ready source of recruits for his armies, had appealed to Pope Urban for help in the restitution of Christian control in the east. This was no change of policy. Mercenaries from the west – most recently Anglo-Saxon warriors who could not stomach Norman mastery and had fled England after the Conquest – filled the ranks of the Imperial guard; they paraded alongside the freebooting Norsemen who had long been a permanent fixture in Constantinople.

The Holy Land itself was occupied by the Shia Moslems of Egypt and the Syrian Arabs, ruled from Damascus. Both loathed the Sunni Turks.

The Moors in Spain had yielded to Christian arms and been confined to the south, in the kingdom of Andalusia. The Pope now concerned himself with repeating this success of the old formula, *In hoc signo vinces*, elsewhere. The first millennium had passed without ushering in the widely expected and fervently prophesied End of the World. Yet, if Christ had *not* come a second time to His kingdom on earth, perhaps the next best thing would be for the rightful heirs of that kingdom – the Franks – to come to Christ.

The enthusiasm of the clerics gathered at Clermont, even granted the inevitable stage-management of popular response, quite surprised the French Pope. Before long, the call to pious arms was whistling round Europe into the ears of men to whom fighting – wherever, against whomever – ran deep in their blood. Perhaps, too, they had wearied of killing each other in trivial dispute, and saw the chance for more serious combat and richer booty. So the warrior princes of France, none of whom had been present at the Council, added their voice to the general clamour: Count Raymond of Toulouse, Marquis of Provence; Hugh of Vermandois; Robert II of Flanders; Robert, Duke of Normandy (son of William the Conqueror) and his brother-in-law Stephen, Count of Blois (who didn't want to go but was made to by his redoubtable wife Adela, daughter of William). All of them Franks, feuding differences buried for the moment. All swearing allegiance, for themselves and the men they would lead, to the French Pope. And all, doubtless, stirred by memories, ever green, of the legendary Charlemagne's hankering after the Holy Kingdom of Jerusalem.

Not only they came, but the German Emperor Henry IV's vassals, too: Godfrey of Bouillon, Duke of Lower Lorraine, and his brothers, Eustace III Count of Boulogne (a man of extensive wealth and property who would have preferred to stay and keep a close eye on his estates north and south of the Channel) and Baldwin, the youngest of the three, a churchman turned fighter who, with no inheritance in Europe to look forward to, leapt at the chance of a kingdom to be won somewhere in the rich east. Not strictly Frenchmen, by the terms of the day, but Franks all the same.

Pope Urban II preaching the First Crusade at Clermont to a Council of churchmen. Below, the fighting men, cruciform badges of cloth pinned to their shoulders, await papal blessing on the enterprise.

Other princes from as far afield as Scotland, Denmark and Spain made their vows to fight; and, if the sign of the Cross summoned them initially, it was the victory that the sign ensured which undoubtedly strengthened their resolve actually to turn up. Victory meant reward, spiritual and material. Recent scholarship plays down the materialistic motives of the Crusaders on the shaky grounds that most warriors of the Cross returned home empty-handed, if they returned home at all. A lame argument. If not every panhandler scooped a Yukon gold nugget big enough to retire on, the crowds who undertook the long trek out there were optimistic about their chances. Only a handful became millionaires, but there was still a gold rush. The conclusion must be that in the view of the Crusaders spiritual triumph was all fine and good but what counted was tangible gain: redemption in the next world, profit in this.

FIRST CRUSADE: In hoc signo vinces

After almost unspeakable difficulty, privation and barbarity on both sides, Turkish-held Antioch fell in 1098 and Arab-held Jerusalem in 1099. It is not our place here to record the chronological history of that great enterprise, though who can resist a few of the more bizarre episodes: the army raised by Count Emich of Leisingen in the Rhineland joined by a gaggle of pilgrims hot on the trail of a goose they firmly believed to have been inspired by God. (How could they tell?) The miraculous discovery, under the floor of Antioch cathedral, of the lance that pierced Jesus' side on the Cross. (Another such lance was on display in Constantinople.) Peter Bartholomew, the visionary who found the lance, submitting himself to an ordeal of fire to prove that he was no liar. (He died of burns.) The pigeon, killed by a (Christian?) hawk, which dropped dead outside the Bishop of Apt's tent, and was found to

be carrying a message from the governor of Acre calling on the Moslems of Palestine to resist the Frankish invasion. The many solemn testimonies that dead Bishop Adhemar of Le Puy had appeared fighting amongst the forward assault troops in the capture of Jerusalem. It is all the stuff of romance; but then so is real life the stuff of fiction.

However, there *are* details from the Crusade which are relevant to our investigation of the Arthurian romance. As we have seen, the eleventh-century *Chanson de Roland*, the most famous of the French *chansons de geste*, grew out of a historical verity. Arthurian romance, begun by Geoffrey of Monmouth only a generation after the capture of Jerusalem and properly defined by Chrétien de Troyes a further generation on, added the love interest which so occupied the Moorish-influenced eleventh-century Provençal troubadours; but, at root, the story of Arthur – whether he be of Britain or Brittany – is the story of a Christian king fighting against pagans. The tales brought home to France, and England, by Crusaders enriched beyond measure the stock of the professional storytellers in fireside seats and at candle-lit writing tables throughout Europe.

Many of the Crusader lords expressed their feelings before they left Europe on the great pilgrimage:

> *Sighing for my love I leave for Syria . . .*
> *A knight does well by winning paradise and honour*
> *And prizes and reputation and the love of his lady.*
> *God is beleaguered in his own holy city.*
> *Now we will succour Him who saved us from Sin's dark prison*
> *When He was nailed to the Cross that the Turks have stolen from us.*

Conon de Béthune (*c.* 1150–1219), **Chanson de Croisade** lines 9 ff

And King Arthur himself smarted with a similar grief. To Gawain, about to leave on the Quest of the Holy Grail, the king says:

> By your going you rob Camelot forever of its brilliant company of true knights . . . ah, God, that I should have lived to see the day when I and this fellowship by good fortune gathered here should be parted.

***Quest of the Holy Grail**, chapter 1*

QUEST AND JOURNEY

The journey the Crusaders made, some 2500 miles on foot, provides a rough parallel, perhaps even a stereotype, for what became the standard fictional adventure, or Quest, for the Holy Grail (see chapter 7). In Arthurian romance, this Quest is a trek through a perilous Waste Lande, beset by dangers natural, supernatural or human, to a region 'beyond the sea' (in French 'Outremer'), a region of plenty spoiled by a wicked overlord, where they would, ultimately, achieve joy, both spiritual and bodily. Outremer, contrary to belief, did not signify the Holy Land exclusively. It might describe any far-off place. Louis, later IV of France (921–54) when exiled to England, was known as Louis Outremer. The word, then, simply denotes a kingdom sometimes almost beyond imaginable reach, like the Roman island near the edge of the world *Ultima Thule*. Celtic myth deals much with the perils, and rewards, of the crossing of water (see chapter 6).

The difference with the Holy Land was that Christ had lived and not died there; so it became, in popular imagination fanned eagerly by the Church, a reachable Terre de la Joie, of romance, 'Land of Joy' or Earthly Paradise. But to achieve this destiny the Crusaders had to survive not only the fortunes of war but a long and rigorous odyssey.

In the *Quest of the Holy Grail*, Galahad and Melias arrive at a fork in the road. An inscribed wooden cross warns the travellers that none but the best knight in the world may hope to survive the journey down the left-hand fork to its very end; the right-hand fork promises even swifter demise to any but the worthiest. Even so late a book as John Bunyan's *Pilgrim's Progress* (seventeenth century) vividly reworks an image of Christian trial and endeavour which began with the Crusaders' long and arduous passage across the bleak Anatolian plateau and the barren passes of the Sultan Dagh mountains. Then they faced the wilderness between desert and mountain in blistering heat; the only available water that in salt marshes, the only vegetation thorn bushes which, nonetheless, they chewed, desperate for moisture. In agonies of thirst they struggled past the old Byzantine water cisterns by the roadside, every one destroyed by the Turks. After such an ordeal of desolation, the cool streams and luscious orchards and gardens of Iconium were milk and honey indeed. Would not celestial Jerusalem, still not far short of a thousand miles away and the grim Antitaurus mountains and worse in between, be that and far richer?

Here is the background to the exploits of Galahad in his story, translated by Malory out of the old 'French boke': the defeat of the seven knights (representing the Seven Deadly Sins) to destroy the wicked custom of the Castle of Maidens (Book XIII, chapter 15); his crossing of the forbidden water; his ride through the waste forest; his healing of the Maimed King (whose injury brings sterility – physical and spiritual – to the land) with the blood of the Holy Lance (Book XVIII, chapter 21); his kingship of the Grail City; his translation to heaven to the fellowship of Jesus and the angels.

We know that the Crusaders listened avidly to Arthurian romances read aloud. Here were stirring tales to encourage them in their great exploit;

indeed, tales which might have been inspired by that very quest to recover Jerusalem for Christ. They endured a long journey fraught with danger; did battle with pagan foemen, even, when occasion presented, single combat with Saracen warriors, all in their drive to reach the Grail city of all Grail cities. Swarthy Moor... Black knight? Fact and fiction became interchangeable, the excitement of one feeding the other and inseparable from it.

GODFREY OF BOUILLON – KING ARTHUR?

It was Godfrey of Bouillon who became first King of Jerusalem in 1099. He not only outlived the ambitions of many of the more powerful crusader leaders who all jockeyed for the ultimate honour of Christ's temporal crown. He even narrowly escaped becoming a Maimed King himself: hunting a bear outside Iconium, the beast turned and gashed him badly. He mended, however, though the hot, humid climate turned many a wound gangrenous seemingly overnight. Others aiming to crown their own ambition, if not that of the Crusade, had fallen by the wayside. Baldwin, Godfrey's youngest brother, plumped for Antioch early on but soon wound up in a Turkish prison; he eventually escaped. Eustace, his second brother, lacked the charisma of Baldwin and Godfrey, and yearned, anyway, to resume his tallying of accounts in Boulogne. Stephen of Blois, never much of a stayer, had scooted home long since, to the mortification of his wife, the bull-tempered Adela. Disappointed of the crown because of his arrogance and unpopularity, Raymond of Toulouse went home too. (The northern French could not abide the fay Provençals – they had truck with Arab books, if not with actual Arabs, and the sun had boiled their brains.) Robert of Flanders never intended to stay once Jerusalem was safe in Christian hands; the Sicilian Normans, Bohemond and his nephew Tancred, had little

support in the army and, though Robert of Normandy enjoyed considerable prestige as the head of the Norman people, he too was anxious to return to Europe, the job done. Only Godfrey of Bouillon remained of any stature: not a very efficient administrator, nor even much of a diplomat or wheeler-dealer in a world that absolutely required both assets. However, most of the Crusaders respected him for his personal courage, greatheartedness, devotion to the Christian cause, piety and chivalry.

This might easily be a list of King Arthur's virtues. Indeed, it may well have formed the basis of many portraits of the famous King of Britain: the Arthur whose inefficiency during the tranquil years of jousting and pageantry at Camelot (the holiday at Iconium, for instance?) leads to the peril of the whole kingdom, spurring him to ride out gallantly, at the head of his faithful knights, to save it; the great feudal lord in bold leadership of his liegemen. (Caxton's original choice for a hero was this Godfrey, not Arthur.)

HISTORIC DETAIL – ROMANTIC MATTER

This is far from being the only element in the First Crusade reflected in the Arthurian romances. Some chroniclers report that when the Sultan Kerbogha came to wrest back Antioch, at the end of a nine-months' siege, the Crusaders proposed a series of single combats to settle the issue of possession – a very Arthurian gesture. Some of the bloodiest fighting occurred in the Fortified Bridge leading into the city. This is reminiscent of those perilous bridges over water so common in Celtic myth; above all, maybe, the Sword Bridge – a sharpened blade spanning a turbulent flood, negotiated by Lancelot (in the Prose *Lancelot*). And Peter Bartholomew declared that St Andrew had told him in a vision that God would protect all the Crusaders, adding that all the saints longed to resume their earthly bodies to join in the fighting by their side. Is this a Celtic notion? Christian? A mixture of both? Or does it simply prove the influence of folklore, which is a watered-down version of ancient and religiously important myth, on later Christian belief, the subconscious tapping old imagery? I believe so.

Shortly after the Crusaders encamped outside the Holy City, the princes were advised by a hermit who lived on the Mount of Olives to attack at once, even without siege engines: their faith would bring them victory. The assault failed. Perhaps the Crusaders had too little faith. To put it another way, perhaps they did not truly *believe* as must any knight who faces the ordeals prior to achieving the Grail.

This was not the first time a hermit's advice had intervened to redirect the conduct of the armed pilgrimage. Peter the Hermit who, in an age when filth and body odour were reckoned to be next to godliness, stank like a stye of pigs, rode his mule, like Christ, as he led a bedraggled army of tens of thousands of weaponless peasants from Europe to routine martyrdom at the hands of the infidel Turks, armed to the teeth, in Asia Minor.

There had been hermits aplenty in Europe before the Crusades, solitary sages in the mould of eastern holy man and gurus. However, it was, in all likelihood, the visionary nature of the more prominent hermits' preaching of the holy war, mixed up with millennial menace, which imparted an extraordinary and vital impulse to the Crusading movement. The Church authorities might, officially, despise, even disown the apocalyptic rantings of these holy irregulars. Unofficially, they owed them much; not least their frantic energy in the pursuit of, and urging to, martyrdom and glory. The wilder hermits might embarrass the more sober faithful, but they were unsurpassed rabble-rousers. The romances preferred the less obtrusive, more contemplative members of the breed.

HERMITS

Arthurian romances offer many portraits of wild-wood solitaries, but perhaps the most rounded and sympathetic is Trevrizent in Wolfram von Eschenbach's *Parzival*. It is he who leads back the erring knight Parzival to his abandoned quest for the Holy Grail. Parzival is country-bred but noble-born: of the English house of Anjou, his great-grandfather a cousin to Uther Pendragon, Arthur's father; *their* grandfather, Mazadan, lured off, by love for the fairy Terdelaschoye, to the land of Feimurgan. Wolfram delights in the mediaeval sport of name-hunts: Terdelaschoye is Terre de la Joie, 'Joyous Land' or Earthly Paradise; and Feimurgan is Morgan the Fay, name of person and home swapped around. Parzival becomes a knight, against his widowed mother's wishes; he finds the Grail but does not achieve it, that is fails the test by not asking the requisite question: 'Whom does the Grail serve?' More and more disillusioned in God's so-called grace and support he abandons his faith and renounces Christ.

Trevrizent takes the young cynic in, feeds him on roots and herbs, fodders his horse on green fir tips and bracken. The simplicity of life and Trevrizent's frank piety recall Parzival, country innocent turned hard-boiled fighter, to his true nature. Instructed by Trevrizent, who turns out, after all, to be his uncle, Parzival spends two weeks in the forest grotto, confesses his sins, receives absolution (though the hermit is not a consecrated priest), and resumes his quest.

The Arthurian hermit, often a man of consequence who, like St Cuthbert, leaves a worldly life for contemplative solitude, tends what the Sufis call the 'secret garden' of his own understanding and wisdom. Often he combines isolated devotion with the care of a remote chapel or shrine. When life in the mediaeval town and village was crowded, unhygienic, claustrophobic, godless, noisy and permitted of virtually no privacy anywhere, the attractions of rustic peace and independence, even allowing for a bilious diet of roots and berries, were manifold.

Not that the pious man clad in homespun, living on nuts in his cave or hut, a charcoal brazier for warmth and fresh springwater to quench his thirst, always escaped the sceptical attentions of the rest of humanity. Certain elements in the backwoods of Brittany, sometime in the thirteenth century, took the shabbily dressed hermits, who emerged from the woodlands muttering strangely, for Saracens who had tunnelled their way from Arabia and popped up like a fifth column to betray the Christian west to the eastern infidel, and gave them a very hard time.

SALADIN AND ST BERNARD

The enthusiasm generated by the First Crusade waned, inevitably. The Holy Land gloriously won, it had to be, rather more dully, administered, defended, supplied. Managers took the place of conquerors; efficiency replaced dash and verve as the priority. The managers grew to love the country they administered for other reasons than its association with the life and ministry of Christ. A more ambiguous attitude to the Moors developed. Does Saladin himself, then, that byword for chivalry and magnanimity, emerge in Arthurian romance as the Saracen knight Palomides (in Malory) or else, perhaps, the noble Moor Feirefiz, Parzival's infidel half-brother in Wolfram von Eschenbach's telling of the story? It's entirely possible. The influence of Arab culture on European cannot be overestimated and it was immediate, vibrant, not the result of

slow seepage. The very fact that there exist, in Christian romance, sympathetic portraits of the hitherto loathed enemy shows how even brief acquaintance with them inclined those Crusaders who stayed on in the Holy Land away from the rabid odium that had drawn them thither in the first place.

There remained, of course, numerous vehement protagonists of Holy War to keep the fires of rage banked high, none more vehement than one of the fieriest religious leaders of the day, St Bernard, the Cistercian abbot. His preaching influenced not only the rationale of the armed pilgrimage – crucial when the Church had to square it with Christ's message of peace – but also the central narrative of the Grail Quest. Indeed, St Bernard made a central contribution to the theology of sacred war, and to the literature that stemmed from it. *The Quest of the Holy Grail* romance is wholly Cistercian (White Monk) in character, ritual and symbolism. As significant, in the intertwined history of Crusade and Arthurian romance, St Bernard drew up the religious rule for the Order of Templar knights, founded in 1118 (see chapter 7). It would be no exaggeration to call these warrior monks the Knights of the Round Table, fellowship of the Grail Quest, come to life.

This company of fighting priests were the inspiration of a knight from Champagne in France, Hugh of Payens. He persuaded Godfrey of Bouillon's brother, King Baldwin I of Jerusalem, to allot him and eight companions a wing of the royal palace in the Temples enclosure of the Holy City. The Knights Templar, who swore religious vows of poverty, chastity and obedience to the Pope, adopted a monastic rule drawn up for them by St Bernard of Clairvaux and made it their declared aim to protect, by force of arms, all pilgrims on their way to the Holy Places – and most of all those on their way to the Holy Sepulchre, reputedly Christ's tomb. Soon, however, the Templars were launching themselves enthusiastically into any military enterprise against any enemies of Christ, above all the Saracens, throughout the entire Holy Land. And, like all the great religious orders on oath to absolute poverty, the warrior monks in their three degrees of rank – the noble-born knight; bourgeois sergeants, the grooms and stewards of the community; and the non-military clerics – rapidly acquired immense wealth by pious endowment of land and money across Europe. Still, St Bernard, whose own entrepreneurial efforts had led to the significant aggrandisement and enriching of the Cistercian Order, wrote unctuously of the Templars:

> They are milder than lambs and fiercer than lions. They combine the meekness of monks with the fighting courage of knights so completely I do not know whether to call them knights or contemplatives.

Wolfram von Eschenbach's *Parzival* was dedicated to them, and their involvement with the development of the Holy Grail legend (see chapter 7) cannot be overestimated. The Knights Templar wore an ordinary red heraldic cross on a white tunic; the sergeants of the Order a black cross.

In 1147, St Bernard preached the Second Crusade at the ancient *bastide* town of Vézelay, the supposed home of Mary Magdalene's mortal remains. After Bernard's recruiting sermon, men shouted: 'Crosses! We want crosses!' Bernard had astutely prepared several bolts of red material for the purpose but not nearly enough. The cloth quickly ran out and Bernard stripped off his outer garments to be ripped into strips and run up as holy badges. The Cistercian sewing bee was still at full stitch when night fell.

The Second Crusade faltered and petered out in 1149 after fruitless attacks on Ascalon and Damascus.

St Bernard died in 1153, but his truculent message seared on. Fortune seemed to have turned her back on the Crusaders, alas, and in 1187 the Sultan Salah el-Din Yusuf, 'Saladin', defeated a thirst-ravaged Crusader army of Franks at Hattin, near the sea of Galilee, before moving on to capture Jerusalem. The Bishop of Acre died and many Crusaders with him; the rest were taken prisoner and the True Cross, which the Bishop had carried into battle to inspire the Christians, was lost.

Saladin treated the captured Frankish king Guy of Lusignan with exemplary courtesy. He seated him, with gallant ceremonial, at his table and offered him a goblet of rose-water iced with snow brought from Mount Hermon, fifty miles distant, to quench his terrible thirst. Another of the captives, Reynald of Châtillon, who had shocked the Moslems by sinking a pilgrim ship bound for Jedda and by other acts of impious brigandage, Saladin executed at once, striking off his head with his own sword. Saladin's reputation for gentle clemency to his noble captives and summary vengeance wreaked on the ignoble, and his fame as a chivalrous fighter, influenced Arthurian romance in Europe as a whole. Crusaders brought home stories of their high-principled foe, just as Arab poetry, filtering up into southern France via Spain, influenced the troubadour poetry. And troubadour poetry coloured the writing of Chrétien de Troyes and other Arthurian poets to a marked degree.

PEAK AND DECLINE OF THE CRUSADING MOVEMENT

In 1191, Richard I, the Lionheart, of England and Philip II of France commanded armies which captured Acre and, in the following year, Richard agreed an armistice with Saladin by which the Saracens gave up the coastal strip from Tyre to Jaffa to the Christians and allowed a right of pilgrimage to the holy shrines of Jerusalem. The City of God was lost, but access to it was given under licence.

The rivalry between Richard Lionheart and Saladin was accorded Arthurian status. Portraits of them jousting were common. It was as if, for a brief interlude, the whole spirit of the Holy War, the chivalry of action, the ideal of the romances had met in two opposed leaders. Certainly there was mutual respect between them; this marked the sunny peak of the Crusader wars, if so grim an activity as war can boast such a thing.

The Christians, having decided temporarily that Jerusalem was better left out of the fighting, decided to conquer Egypt, the ancient home of Christianity instead. After a near defeat of the Crusader army, one Brother Francis of Assisi bargained a temporary peace. He marched up to the Sultan's camp. The enemy guards were at first suspicious, but then concluded that anyone so naïve, dirty and malodorous must be crazy, and treated him with the respect due to a man who had been touched by God.

The Sultan at last agreed to surrender the True Cross in return for the city of Damietta, but the Crusaders went home bitter and empty-handed: when the time came to pass over the sacred relic, no one could find it.

In 1228, the German Emperor Frederick, heir to Charlemagne, finally yielded to the threats of excommunication laid on him by Innocent III for delaying his departure to the Holy Land. He embarked for Palestine and negotiated the repossession of Jerusalem, Nazareth and Bethlehem by treaty with the Sultan of Egypt.

Sixteen years later occurred two calamitous events which dealt the Crusading movement a death blow and, coincidentally, led, I conjecture, to the dwindling popularity of the Arthurian romance. In March 1244, after a ten-months' siege, the high

fortress of Monségur in the south of France capitulated and its citizens were massacred. This marked the last bloody act of the ferocious papal crusade against the declared heretical Albigensians of Provence. The Christian men, women and children, heretic and innocent together, of the beleaguered town were slaughtered. 'Kill them all,' said St Bernard's successor in Cîteaux, the Abbot Arnald Amalaricus, supervising the business, 'God will recognise His own'. Three months later, in June 1244, 10 000 Khwarismian Turkish cavalrymen swept past Damascus, through Galilee and on to Jerusalem. They took and sacked the Holy City which, thus, left Christian occupation and was never recovered.

Four years later, Louis IX of France made a forlorn attempt to reclaim the Holy City but he and most of his army were captured in Egypt and were ransomed for nearly a million bezants. (In 1200, 50 bezants constituted a generous reward to a knight for campaign service.) Louis returned, however, but, along with most of his army, died of the plague at Tunis. His last, pitiable words were: 'Jerusalem! Jerusalem!' the city he had never seen. In 1297, six years after the loss of Acre and the final abandonment of Tyre, Beirut and Sidon, the Church crowned Louis' pious enthusiasm and abject failure with canonisation.

Within a few years (1304) the great order of Knights Templar, guardians of Jerusalem, warrior monks, supreme incarnation of the Crusading spirit, had been murderously suppressed by the Church to whom they swore undying allegiance. Not coincidentally, the Arthurian stories which had been popular for so long, began to fizzle out (see chapter 7).

The legend of Arthur and his knights, and their Quest for the Holy Grail dominated European literature for roughly the same period as the pilgrim wars in the Holy Land preoccupied European

Wishful thinking: in a jousting duel Richard I, the Lionheart of England, unsaddles the great Saracen leader Saladin, here revealed as a scowling, hawk-faced ruffian with ogrish teeth.

churchmen and monarchs. Crusade and romance are inextricably bound up together, real life inspiring legend, legend glorifying real action. As the motivating ideals of the one became discredited, the enthusiasm for the other waned. It was, I believe, no unrelated coincidence.

FEUDALISM

The Crusades were a feudal enterprise, King Arthur's Round Table a feudal company. But liege lord? Vassal? Feudal service? What do they mean?

The Arthurian romances abound with examples of knights undertaking adventures to rescue those in peril. People come to the court of King Arthur to ask for his help, usually armed help, against some oppressor, some invader of their territory, some unruly baron who has got it into his head that he is nobler and therefore more powerful than the king.

Wasting no time, Cligès sets out on the long and arduous journey to his uncle's Arthur the King's court. There he denounces his uncle the Emperor who has disinherited him by taking a wife having sworn to his own brother, Cligès' father, that he would never marry.

King Arthur promises to set sail against the

61

Emperor in Constantinople with an army of sworn knights in a thousand ships, men-at-arms filling three thousand more. . . .

The king's preparations for war dwarfed any made by Caesar or Alexander. At his bidding mustered the armed strength of all England, all Flanders, Normandy, France and Brittany, and all the southern territories as far as the Spanish passes.

Chrétien de Troyes, *Cligès*, lines 6552–84

(Note the record, there, of Frankish detestation of the shifty Greeks in Constantinople: they just itched to get their hands on old Byzantium and teach the Asian Christians a lesson in orthodoxy, not to mention the itch for Byzantine treasures. The Crusaders believed that they had arrived in Asia as saviours and read the cautionary tactics of a series of Greek emperors as no better than duplicity. The Greeks, for their part, had scant regard for the loutish Europeans, and this mutual dislike soured the Crusading enterprise at its root.)

This passage from Chrétien's romance no more than describes a common occurrence in an age before well organised and widely supported central government. The king or noble was the font of law and might. Individuals had to protect themselves much of the time, hence the building of fortified towns and manor houses all over Europe.

Charles Martel can be reckoned to have fathered what became the feudal system when he marshalled the defences of France against Moorish invasion. Feudalism was not, however, invented by one man on one day. It evolved naturally from the old warrior caste framework, wherein kingship and the paternal role that implied, and the loyalty of subjects depended on strength of arms (might) not the sanctity of law (right), into the acknowledged supremacy of monarchs who expected and, by and large, enjoyed the loyalty of their people as a matter of course and holy inheritance, succession.

Before this, smaller divisions of the kingdom – duchies, counties, marches – were ruled by lesser lords who might or might not, depending on their own strength and bellicosity, swear allegiance to the king. The March ('Borderland') of Brittany rarely threw in its lot with the rest of France throughout its history. And Clovis, first king of all the Franks, had to bully and bludgeon the subordinate princes into submission. Feudal law, then, systematised a process whereby the king drew together the lords of the realm under his own leadership for the mutual benefit of all. The lords, in their turn, drew in their own men to consolidate the power at the roots.

Although feudalism affected non-combatants too, it is the military aspect, and therefore the aristocratic level of the arrangement, which most concerns us, if only because the Arthurian story records most vividly the military necessity which gave rise to the feudal pact.

KNIGHT'S FEE

The origin of the English word 'feudal' cannot be pinned down precisely, though it has nothing to do with 'feud' as in vendetta, which derives from the Anglo-Saxon *feod* meaning 'hatred, enmity'. The basic currency of the feudal bargain is the *feu*, or, more commonly, *fee*. *Fee* means (1) livestock, cats and dogs to pigs and cattle and thence wealth, just as Latin *pecus* ('a flock') became *pecunia* ('money'); (2) land or property given to someone in exchange for service as long as the vassal was alive to render that service. Thus the bargain amounted to: 'You fight for me, here's a farm to keep you supplied and I'll call you my man,' or, to a lesser man, 'I'll make you over some land; in return you give me most of what you grow, to keep *me* supplied.'

A knight's *fee* of land, sometimes called a *fief*, varied in size but if a *hide* of land could be reckoned to support one family and dependants for a year a knight in 1494, for example, received 8 *hides*. The opposite of this tenure for life was the *allodium* where the same bargain was struck but transferred, by right of inheritance, from father to son.

This parallels the old Roman system of patron and client, master and slave. The Teutonic races, however, were prouder than to accommodate themselves to anything that smacked of bondage. Their very name Frank means 'free' and in Frankish Gaul no man could boast freedom unless he belonged to or had been adopted into the dominant race. The Franks boasted a noble pride in the muscular service of their lord, honouring him by the very fervour of their devotion; they, in their turn, were honoured by the greatness and reputation with which their strength and valour endowed him. They were *his* riders, his knights.

The knights became the lord's vassals, a word of Celtic origin denoting the men who ate at the King's table and, like Sir Kay in the Arthurian romances, served his meat. These men were by no means common servants. They went through a formal act of *homage* whereby the lord acknowledged the vassal to be his man (Latin *homo*).

The Romanised Franks who invaded Gaul refined the homage ceremony. The vassal knelt before his lord and offered his hands pressed together. This may be interpreted as offering the wrists for manacling, but the lord turned the symbolic gesture of submission into one of prayer by enfolding the hands in his own. Then the vassal swore fealty, or allegiance, to his liege ('sworn') lord and each kissed the other full on the mouth. After this, the vassal received ceremonial investiture with his fee: a deed of property, perhaps, or more likely a sod of turf, symbol of land, a glove, symbol of the fighting strength and so on.

King Marsiliun when he sees Baligant
Calls up two Spanish Saracens.
'Take me in your arms, sit me up.'
In his right hand he takes one of his gloves.
He says, 'Marsiliun . . . I have lost
Myself and all my people.'
And Baligant replies: 'I'm sorry for it.
I cannot speak long with you, Charles
Does not wait for me but even so
I take your glove.'

La Chanson de Roland lines 2827 ff

Vassalage

Thus the fighting man became a member of the lord's household, his retinue, his vassal – a Celtic word meaning 'retainer' (kept man). The vassal was expected to keep himself in arms and armour – either by purchase or by stripping a slain enemy. Requirements varied but the Franks insisted on their knights being self-sufficient, even to the extent of supplying their own horses – a costly due which led to considerable friction on occasion. The knight, though, received land which was worked by his own tenants, and he could depend on his lord to ransom him from captivity, just as Christ ransoms souls from sin. (The Church adopted the language of the people to secure *their* allegiance.)

In battle he fought under his lord's banner, entirely at his lord's bidding. This made the leadership of big armies a chancey business. The Crusading expeditions, generalled by committee, did remarkably well in the circumstances, their differences glued together by shared reverence for the co-travelling Churchmen. If a man's lord died in battle, he was released from any obligation to fight and often quit the field.

For his part, and in tune with the bargain, a lord

was expected to fight conspicuously hard and bravely, leading from the front as Alexander the Great always did, otherwise his men would lose heart to the consequent shame of both sides of the feudal unit. It behoved the men to fight valiantly, too, in protection of their lord, if only to avoid the expense of a bill of ransom for him if he was taken.

At the apex of the feudal pyramid stood the king, taking allegiance from his lesser lords as they took a similar oath from their underlings. And, as the momentous gathering in the Thamesside meadow at Runnymede proved, being at the top might simply show that, at one turn of Fortune's wheel, the king might just as readily slide to the bottom. The lesser nobles of the kingdom swore fealty and made their act of homage too but an ambitious lord at the head of a strong private army (the usurper Mordred) might, unlike the cat in the adage, do a lot more than look at a king.

Much else could be said about feudalism but for our purposes this sketch will suffice. Between the gathering of Celtic warriors about their warlord's fire, in a circle so as none should have obvious precedence, and the high ceremonial of belted earls in attendance on the anointed king there lies a difference perhaps only of perspective. The uncomplicated rituals of the pagan feast or banquet give way, eventually, to the sophisticated rituals of heraldic decorum, but the ethic does not alter: the bargain is loyalty, mutually sworn, between fighting men and their king, for the safety of the kingdom and all the people. If the king thrives, the kingdom thrives. The greater the lord the more illustrious his men, and the Knights of the Round Table most illustrious of all.

Is it any wonder that Arthur was reckoned to be immortal since, if he remained alive, so did the allegiance to him as the chief king of Christendom, thus ensuring the continued prestige of those who swore him loyalty?

POETIC INSPIRATION

The Homeric poems had celebrated the heroic exploits of the ancient Greeks, particularly their capture of the great city of Troy. The Crusader knights, and the formidable women who cajoled and encouraged them in their chivalric enterprise, inspired and demanded florid accounts of *their* great exploit, namely the recapture of God's holy city on earth for western Christianity. Chronicle histories were written by writers who joined the expeditions, but it was the Arthurian romance, that novel blend of the old war song or *chanson de geste* and *fin amor* ('pure love'), which so captured their imagination and fixed the glory in their minds. To such men, and women, some of whom joined the armies, faced with separation from their loved ones, a gruelling long journey, hard fighting, furnace heat and freezing cold, disease, even bankruptcy, that lure of imagination was crucial. Here was a quest for the Grail indeed. Here was the ultimate proof of knighthood; the supreme ordeal of faith. Going to the Holy Land for love of fair damsel and in pledge to the ideals of Christian virtue, they could *be* the Knights of Arthur's Round Table; their royal leaders could *be* King Arthur himself. They would all win that immortal Paradise which the Celts had always known as the lake island of Avalon.

The mediaeval romances glorified real action. To this end they deliberately blurred that distinction between supposed fact and imagined fiction upon which the modern world strains to insist. In one account of the Arthurian story, the treacherous King Mark of Cornwall (fair Isolde's husband), ' . . . because King Arthur loved Camelot all his life above all other cities that he owned, destroyed it utterly and razed it to the ground after the death of King Arthur'. That account, in the French prose cycle known as the Vulgate, coincided with the news brought to Europe of the final loss of Jerusalem. Camelot was no more.

CHAPTER FOUR

PROUD CHEVALIER:
NOBLE HEART AND WHETTED STEEL

Who so myght take ordere of chivalry moste
in evry wise be a gode knught.

Merlin c. 1450

Father, if you would favour me then give me
ermine and grey vair, silks and fine horses.
Before I am worthy to be dubbed knight, I
would serve Arthur the King and learn my skill
with arms at his court.

Chrétien de Troyes, *Cligès* lines 137 ff

In the Welsh *Mabinogion* Wrnach the Giant can
never be slain except by his own sword and he will
not give it to anyone neither for price nor for
favour, and no one can compel him. Three of King
Arthur's knights set out to the Giant's castle to win
the sword: Cei (Kay), Bedwyr (Bedivere) and
Golden-Haired Gwrhyr (Gawain). They journey till
evening until they see a great fort of mortared
stone, the greatest of forts in the world. They make
their way to the gate.

Quoth Gwrhyr, Interpreter of Tongues: 'Is there
a porter?'

'There is. And thou, may thy head not be thine,
that thou dost ask.'
'Open the gate.'
'I will not.'
'Why wilt thou not open it?'
'Knife has gone into meat and drink into horn,
and a thronging in Wrnach's hall. Save for a
craftsman who brings his craft, it will not be
opened again this night.'
Quoth Cei: 'Porter, I have a craft.'
'What craft has thou?'
'I am the best furbisher of swords in the world.'
'I will go and tell that to Wrnach the Giant and
will bring thee an answer.'
The porter came inside. Said Wrnach the Giant:
'Thou hast news from the gate?'
'I have. There is a company at the entrance to
the gate who would like to come in.'
'Didst thou ask if they had a craft with them?'
'I did, and one of them declared he knew how to
furbish swords.'

'I had need of him. For some time I have been seeking one who should polish my sword, but I found him not. Let that man in since he has a craft.'

The Porter came and opened the gate, and Cei inside came all alone, across three baileys to the inside of the fort. And he greeted Wrnach the Giant. A chair was placed under him. Said Wrnach: 'Why, man, is this true which is reported of thee that thou knowest how to furbish swords?'

'I do that,' said Cei.

The sword was brought to him. Cei took a striped whetstone from under his arm. 'Which dost thou prefer upon it, white-haft or dark-haft?'

'Do with it what pleases thee, as though it were thine own.'

He cleaned half of one side of the blade for him and put it in his hand. 'Does that content thee?'

'I would rather than all my dominions that the whole of it were like this. It is a shame a man as good as thou should be without a fellow.'

'Oia! good sir, I have a fellow, though he does not practise this craft.'

'Who is he?'

'Let the porter go forth and I will tell his tokens: the head of his spear will leave its shaft and it will draw blood from the wind and settle upon the shaft again.'

The gate was opened and Bedwyr entered in. The furbishing the sword was done, and Cei gave it into the hand of Wrnach the Giant, as though to see whether the work was to his satisfaction. Said the Giant: 'The work is good and I am content with it.'

Quoth Cei: 'It is thy scabbard has damaged thy sword. Give it to me to take out the wooden side-pieces, and let me make new ones for it.'

And he took the scabbard, and the sword in the other hand. He came and stood over the Giant as if he would put the sword into the scabbard. He sank it into the Giant's head and took off his head at a blow. They laid waste the fort and took away what treasures they would. To the very day at the end of a year they came to Arthur's court and the sword of Wrnach the Giant with them.

Mabinogion 'Culhwch and Olwen' (Everyman pp. 121–3)

This story, offered here in what I consider one of the best translations of a mediaeval text available, contains several points of interest. The world it describes appears to be Celtic. Cei is the Welsh, old British form of Kay, Arthur's seneschal. Yet, the location, Arthur's court, the grand styling of the Giant's castle, irresistibly imply a mediaeval setting, too. From a superior vantage we can tick off five or more centuries yawning between those two worlds. The writers of Arthurian romance adverted no such chasm; the mediaeval storytellers observed no absolute distinction between past and present. What was true and vivid once remained forever true and vivid. Arthur was once king and would be king again. That was all there was to it.

But here we encounter stock items of folklore: a sword of jealously guarded virtue; its owner a Giant; a ritual of passage into his castle; the esteem of a craftsman's skill; a hero; his courage housed in cunning as a sword is sheathed in its scabbard; and the defeat of a powerful and dangerous enemy. This sequence of elements, brought up to date, would readily transfer into any adventure story of any age. Let us examine how what appears to be a fundamentally Celtic story assumes a mediaeval character.

ARTHUR'S COURT

A twelfth-century audience, as contemporary painting and illustration prove, would see any king as a twelfth-century monarch, with all the trappings. Allusion to 'Arthur's court' would, therefore, conjure up a contemporary image of tapestry-hung halls, massive stone keep, crenellated curtain walls, a stoutly guarded double-towered gatehouse. The audience would no more think of a villa of Roman brick (the real Arthur's probable dwelling), or a timber barn wreathed with the fumes of applewood fires (as twentieth-century romances might depict it) than they would question the existence of Giants.

GIANTS

In that tyme were here no hauntes
Of no men but of geauntes.
Geaunt ys more than man
Lyke men they ar in flesch and bone
Of members have they lykeness
The lims all that in man ys.

R. Brunne, **The Story of England** *c.* 1330

Arthur himself and alone fought and slew giants; among them the most odious, inhuman monster, kin, it must be, of the Homeric cannibal Polyphemos, who carried off Helena, Duke Hoel of Brittany's niece, to Mount St Michael.

The mediaeval age believed wholeheartedly in giants; not as a throwback to a Celtic prehistory, nor, further, to a race sprung from the loins of Goliath the Philistine. Sir John Mandeville (in all likelihood a deskbound monk's alias) in his curious pseudo-travelogue (1356) speaks of a valley near the Ganges river in India called, variously, the Vale of Enchantment, the Vale of Devils or the Vale Perilous, all good Arthurian romance names. Beyond this valley, he writes,

> is a great isle where the folk are as big in stature as giants of twenty-eight or thirty feet tall . . . they have no house to live in and they will more readily eat human flesh than any other.

Travels (Penguin p. 174)

It was an age where 'Here be Monsters' inscribed on a map was no quaint foolery but meant what it said.

SKILL AND CUNNING

Ingenuity was much esteemed by the Celts. The exquisite metalwork and jewellery, the glorious illuminations which survive attest handsomely to the breathtaking skill of their artisans. The nimble riddling, the deep-dyed language of their poets can leave small doubt as to their intellectual wizardry either.

And what of mediaeval craftsmanship? Kings and noblemen in the Middle Ages valued and patronised the best work of the best artificers. *Their* skills, however, were more likely to have been copied from or modelled on the work of craftsmen from the Arab culture than learnt at home. The barbarian invasions had extinguished many sources of native skill. Cei's skill in furbishing swords, polishing of rust and tarnish to make the steel glint bright, would, I contend, prompt a mediaeval audience to look to the Moorish east of the present for analogy rather than to a Celtic past. Nonetheless, from admiration of a beautifully wrought sword of blue-iridescent steel, costly, richly chased, well-balanced and keen-edged, to the belief that it had magical properties inherent in it was a short step. The Celtic tales harp much on heroic weapons fashioned expressly and fit only for heroes.

HEROES

The hero exists in all ages; all ages shape him to their own ends. Jung rates the hero as a timeless archetype spurring the passage from young manhood to maturity through the tribal initiation of ordeals testing prowess and courage. The attributes and virtues of the Celtic hero fitted snugly those exalted by the Crusaders, centuries on; namely, physical strength, magnanimity, skill at arms, a noble aura, luck. For luck the Celts would probably have substituted magical power, but it amounts to the same thing. The hero was superhuman in almost every respect. And no superhuman being could be reckoned to die. The Celts enshrined immortality in their scheme of things; the Crusaders regarded immortality as the specific gift of God the Father and Christ the Son.

CHRIST AS HERO

The Celts of the old kingdoms outside the Roman frontiers had received baptism within two centuries of the Empire's collapse. The Christian Church in Ireland, particularly, grew strong very rapidly from the start, and stories of the Irish Celtic tradition survived through the careful offices of the monkish scholars who, nonetheless, at once superimposed on them a Christian gloss as they copied down, translated, illuminated them.

The Celts responded warmly to the Christian gospel, in no small degree because they so eagerly identified Christ as a hero in their own mould. Christ was also craftsman, poet, scholar, magician, hero, warrior. Yes, warrior prince. It was St Paul who invented the picture of meek, non-combatant Christ, God made man by the virgin birth, Spirit rather than flesh. To his early followers, Jesus had been the royal Messiah, descendant of the warrior prince David, who would lead his people to freedom from the Roman oppression. The early Celtic Church, moreover, saw Christ as living man, born of woman, his immortality lodged in the memory and actions of his heirs, *not* as a theological abstraction. Entirely unmystical, in a way, though rooted in Celtic hero-worship. From this tradition came such as the fictional King Arthur and *his* Celtic forebears, like handsome Lugh who could walk on a bubble just as Christ walked across water.

CELTIC ROLE MODELS

Lugh was the old Celtic Sun god, who could set a cauldron of cold water boiling by leaping into it; famous, too, for his charmed spear which thirsted for his enemies' blood, spat flame or roared loud in battle. Lugh first rode a horse to war and was celebrated as the divine hero who drove out from Ireland the mysterious race of Formorians who had earlier conquered it. A foretaste of Arthur and the invading Saxons? Hint of his voracious spear? His dragon crest like the flame of a comet bedimming the sun?

Another story is told of Golden-haired Lugh of the Long Arm when he arrives to seek entry at the great king of Ireland's hall in Tara. The porter, in the time-honoured fashion of the Celts, locks the door against him. I'm a carpenter, he says. They have one. A blacksmith, too. They have one. Also a warrior. They have several. A musician . . . a scholar . . . a poet . . . a magician . . . a hero. They are well-supplied with each and every one. But do you have a man who is all eight in one? says Lugh. And the porter lets him in.

THE PORTER AT THE GATE

This custom, refusing admission to the king's hall once the feast has begun except to a man with practical or intellectual skills beyond the ordinary, is probably Irish in origin. It may have a hard-headed rationale, working as a check on strangers, to ensure that ne'er-do-wells, spies and criminals didn't worm their way into the community. Myth would translate so logical a form into a more arresting account: the porter becomes the guardian of the gate between this life and the Celtic Otherworld to which entry is allowed only to heroes. From the warrior paradise of glorious reward, all lesser mortals are barred. Celtic society, remember, was highly élitist, its ruling aristocracy a warrior class. Its priests and poets had charge of the mythmaking essential to the building up and maintaining of self-belief of men committed in fealty to the whims of glory. Mediaeval society, for a host of reasons, some of which I hope, in this book, to clarify, was very little different. And, if Christ satisfied the need for a divine hero, there can be small doubt that Arthur drew to himself the mantle of secular hero celebrated, as Caxton wrote, for his 'noble acts, feats of arms of chivalry, prowess, hardiness, wonderful histories and adventures' (Preface to *Morte d'Arthur*).

That fame made Arthur a hero for all ages and all countries. As a hero in Celtic mould, he must be fitted for the warrior's paradise; as a hero in Christian terms, he must win entry to Heaven. And, thereby, immortality.

Immortality

The knights of Arthurian romance enjoy perpetual youth, even at advanced age. According to the *Chanson de Roland*, the age of that thoroughly Arthurian prince Charlemagne at the battle of Roncesvalles is 200 years; and when will he tire of fighting? says the poet. In *The Death of King Arthur*, Arthur is ninety years old and still meeting opponents head-on, man-to-man. Naturally, creeping time and creaking joints argue cogently against perpetual youth and its corollary eternal life. Unless, that is, the mind, charmed by dreams of heroic record in the collective memory, can persist joyfully against the more melancholy approach of that other grim reality, extinction. Indeed, many myths say that death was not, formerly, our ultimate fate, but was visited upon us after a fatal error. Thus, in the Australian Aborigine story, Moon kills Possum and, as he lies dying, Possum breaks the silence which holds the secret of immortality: 'After me and forever,' he says, 'men will die.' Had Moon spoken first, death would have been unknown. (How Possum can die, therefore, is unexplained.) To drill in that terrible loss, the Moon visibly wastes away, dies and is reborn each month.

Merlin tells Arthur that Excalibur will cut through any steel but that its scabbard will preserve him from injury. The scabbard (Latin: *vagina*), therefore, represents feminine intuition, *mémoire de sens*, deemed to be more potent, more magical, than the naked and visible sword of masculine reason. It is far more wayward and tricky, too, because it is hidden, devious (hence Morgan le Fay and the rest). The periodic flow of menstrual blood from the woman's dark cavern proved that something was amiss with her. Merlin asks the king which he values the more. Arthur gives the male answer: sword, reason, attack, to Merlin's utter fury. Merlin depends, more than a little, for his own wizardry, on the supralogical thinking enshrined in the special powers of the sheath. Arthur quite simply lacks the vision and audacity required to plumb the blacker depths of nature in her every aspect. Merlin denounces his stupidity and Arthur is, thereby, doomed to a sort of failure: the glory of his kingdom will be destroyed before his eyes, even if he himself survives it in the everlasting record of memory.

Royal dynasties – Merovingians, Capetians, Plantagenets – overrode Time. The crown passed out of death's reach along the pure bloodline, a bloodline which included David, king of Jerusalem, Aeneas, king of Rome, and the mediaeval king of kings, Arthur, saviour of Britain from the infidel Saxons. Arthur lived on but was denied, in the church-dominated world in which he had been recalled to life, the ultimate seal of immortality: canonisation as a saint. This privilege had been accorded to battling Crusader King Louis of France, in 1297. This placed him where Arthur could never officially go, in company with St George and the Archangels, Michael – patron of a British order of Knighthood, and Gabriel, the Angel of Death.

Unofficially Arthur *did* go there, but his days were numbered. The church had marked him out for removal from this exalted plane. The overt lionisation of King Louis, giving him the ultimate accolade of sainthood, was, amongst other things, I suspect, a surreptitious move to scotch any fanciful ideas about the immortality of this Arthur with his pagan folklore and his popularity amongst the hairier breed of Crusader. Louis had at least had the pious decency to court a peaceful conclusion to the holy war by failing to win it.

Arthur's double potency, as old-style warrior given new-style badge of rank (Christ's cross of victory), bears out the Greek definition of hero as demigod. And just as classical demigod heroes, like the Greek Achilles or the Trojan Aeneas, could not stoop to standard issue weapons from the common armoury but required spear, sword, shield forged on a divine anvil, so too did the Celtic heroes. The mediaeval heroes needed the same, but the Church equivocated, inevitably, about the appropriateness of such a myth to their Christian god who enjoined peace and anathematised killing. However, St Bernard, following St Augustine, argued the loophole cleverly. Had not Christ, the mild Saviour himself, declared: 'I bring not peace but a sword'?

HEROIC WEAPONS

And just see what havoc Yvain wreaks with his sword, slicing corridors through the enemy ranks wider than Roland cut through the Turks in Roncesvalles.

Chrétien de Troyes, *Yvain* lines 3229–33

Irish legend spoke of an axe 'sharp enough to cut hair against the wind'; and in the same story (*Bricriu's Feast*) Cuchulainn throws 'three fifties of needles into the air one after the other; each needle went into the eye of the next so that they all formed a chain'.

No mere mortal could perform such a feat. Only a hero of enduring sinew, full to bursting of unwearied vitality. Only a warrior whose green

God's word . . . God's sword. Bishop Odo encourages the young soldiers of Duke William's army to fight their good fight.

salad days of youth never lose their sap in withered decrepitude.

In the *Mabinogion* we read of Gwiawn Cat-Eye, who could cut a haw from a gnat's eye without harming either (the haw being the inner lid); and Bedwyr (Bedivere of the Round Table), to whose every thrust of his spear the spear made nine more thrusts of its own. This reminds us of Cuchulainn, whose many spear-thrusting feats had their heroic names, such as the *gáe bolga*, 'lightning cast', which sliced through water and struck out his enemy's innards at his feet. In the Arthurian romances, Arthur alone is allowed to have weapons of divine forging: the famous sword *Caledbwlch*, his spear, the Killer Lance *Rhôngomyniad,* and *Wynebgwrthucher,* the shield which enveloped him like the darkness of the night.

If they did not wield divine weapons (Gottfried's Tristan is an exception), other heroes of the romances might, however, exhibit preternatural skill at arms. Chrétien's Perceval, whom Arthur's knights at first write off as a tiresome, uncouth, stupid lad, 'a typical Welshman', has much the better of them in skill of arms. With his javelins – Celtic throwing missiles rather than the weighty Frankish thrusting spear – he can hit birds on the wing and fleet-footed beasts on the hoof, while the armoured knights can only move as fast as their horses (probably about 12–15 mph) with spears far too heavy to throw. In the Welsh *Mabinogion* where, needless to say, Peredur is *not* written off as a Welshman 'more stupid than a grazing beast', he can outrun deer. This prejudice against the Welsh gives some insight into how the French regarded their source material: good, but flawed. On the other hand, it does indicate the Celtic origin of the sources.

In the *Mabinogion* we also hear of Culhwch, Arthur's cousin, who had a hard job convincing the porter that he was worthy of admission to the royal hall, even though he cuts a very knightly dash:

> . . . on a steed with light grey head, four winters old with well-knit fork, shell-hoofed, and a gold tubular bridle-bit in its mouth. And under him a precious gold saddle, and in his hand two whetted spears of silver. A battle-axe in his hand, the forearm's length of a full-grown man from ridge to edge. It would draw blood from the wind; it would be swifter than the swiftest dewdrop from the stalk to the ground, when the dew would be heaviest, in the month of June. A gold-hilted sword on his thigh, and the blade of it gold, and a gold-chased buckler upon him, with the hue of heaven's lightning therein, and an ivory boss therein.

Mabinogion (Everyman p. 97)

Of course the sword of gold, just like the Druid's golden sickle, would be useless, gold being far too soft a metal to carry a cutting edge; the meaning must be 'gilded' or bronzed and polished to such a lustre it seemed like gold. For, even in the early days of smelting and working metal, the blades could certainly cut: the romances abound with descriptions of men being cut in half, from helmet to thigh, of arm and shoulder lopped off with one stroke, of two legs severed at the knee as if they were fennel stalks. Wild exaggeration? Apparently not. Graves of fighting men have revealed wounds similar to these, although romance certainly coloured the grim reality from a jewel-encrusted paintpot. Grim reality, in the early days of fighting, also dictated that when it came to pitched battle, the side with the more advanced weapon technology enjoyed a considerable advantage.

BLACKSMITHS AND HEROES

The Celts discovered how to forge iron early on. It gave them a marked superiority which their fiery temper and reckless courage sustained when the slower folk caught up and had smiths, anvils and hammers of their own.

The Greek smith-god Hephaistos (Vulcan) was lame. This suggests that Greek tribes maimed their ironworkers as a matter of course. The man who could melt and work the black metal – iron, alloyed with carbon to make steel, as opposed to the white metals, silver, gold, copper and so on which are so much easier to work because they melt at a lower temperature – was far too valuable to risk losing to any other tribe.

This Vulcan, 'the celebrated and ingenious master craftsman, fashioned a peerless sword and hauberk for Tristan with his own hands' (Gottfried von Strassburg *Tristan* p. 109). His was a sacred, god-given art, kindled in the mystery of the flame: transforming ore to pure, therefore soft, metal; hardening it by alloying it with other metal impurities; and, from a thick steel billet, say, hammering out the fine-edged blade, tough to drive the cutting edge in, whippy to resist shock.

The nomad Arabs were famous for their steel – the silver and gold-inlaid blades of Damascus (damascene), the finely tempered razor edge of Toledo. Europe had its experts, too, producing, for example, the blue-green swords of Vienne, which cleave through bright helmets in a cough of sparks [Chrétien *Erec* p. 79].

NOMADS. TRAVELLING SMITHS

Blacksmithing, farriery, were skills developed, initially, by nomad tribes whose economy depended on the wellbeing of their animals, whether grazing herds or horses. Their interest in metalworking, bound up with the vital need to press on unhindered from exhausted pasture to fresh, seems to have been fired by the contingent need to care for and shoe their mounts. Horseshoes came late, comparatively – not till the ninth century in England – but the nomads had been making the tools required for the treatment of unshod ponies and horses long before that.

Constant travel spurred the nomad's curiosity. *Wanderlust* kept them alive to adventure, invention *and* one step ahead of the disasters they'd previously overcome or evaded. When King Arthur and his knights stay too long in one place they get lazy and, as in Geoffrey of Monmouth, things go badly wrong. The King, therefore, holds court at Winchester, Carlisle, Caerleon and so on, as well as at the elusive Camelot. Even in the French romances the English locales are kept, as well as a sprinkling of continental names. So, king, knights and ladies up sticks and progress (the original meaning of the word) from one court or household to the next: a way of policing the kingdom and of spreading food resources more evenly. In several of the romances reference is made to what are clearly trestle tables – standard in the Middle Ages; this indicates just how moveable the court was, and how the feudal system represented a triumph of nomadic lords who did not have to work to maintain themselves but relied on vassals, pastoral and arable farmers, to provide for them. This harks back to the royal, military caste system of the old Celtic society, of travelling courts and a wealthy warrior class whose life was devoted to prowess in battle.

I call it the old Celtic society but might as well have called it mediaeval society, for all the difference it makes. The romances were composed in the twelfth and thirteenth centuries in contemporary modern dress. There was no firm distinction drawn between past and present. Heroic was heroic and an end of it. King Arthur inspired mediaeval warrior princes not because he was a Celt, but because he was one of them: he shared the same ethics, enemies, gods, bloodline. All that had changed was the emergence of a Roman Church, ahead of its rivals – Greek, Syrian, Celtic and so on – to monopolise approved doctrine and ratify kingship where the old sovereignty had been secured by force of arms.

HEROISM AND THE NOBLE ART

To the ancient Celts, skill at arms was a matter of honour, a mark of virile courage in the face of odds, often overwhelming odds; the warrior's strong right arm was incomplete without the garniture of a sword. In the Middle Ages, the accomplished handling of weapons was a stamp of nobility, spiritual *and* actual, setting the armoured knight apart from the common rout of soldiery. When his Clerk advised him to caution on the battlefield, Richard the Lionheart said: 'Stick to your writing and leave matters of chivalry to us'. There was no reputation to be won fighting plebeian rabble like archers, and the Franks didn't employ *them*: a nasty Norman idea, killing from an ignoble distance, copied from their vile Norse ancestors.

In short, skill at arms made one of the chief tests of chivalry; and chivalry amounted to a strict code of behaviour observed by men of noble rank. Such men inherited wealth, even if not huge wealth, enough to live without concern for money. They could, therefore, spend every daylight hour from their birth, very nearly, in dedicated training for the ultimate proof of their manhood, in battle.

Because their social status was defined by the status they enjoyed as fighting men the code was, primarily, a fighting code. However, as in ancient times, warfare marked the summit of manly activity, so what a man did off the battlefield was only another aspect of what he did on it.

Chivalry may have begun in Greece and Rome, as Chrétien de Troyes claims at the beginning of *Cligès*, but it certainly did not proceed direct to France. Once again the Middle Eastern flavour is unmistakable, courtesy of the Arabs – horsemen *and* a high-caste warrior society.

To many writers of the day, prejudiced by that worst of terrors, ignorance, the Saracens were 'as black as boiled pitch', fonder of 'treason and murder than all the gold in Galicia', as the anonymous *Chanson de Roland* poet puts it. Some Moorish princes excite admiration in the romances, however, for their nobility of spirit and chivalrous behaviour – Feirefiz in *Parzival* and Palomides in Malory, for instance. This is not token praise, either. Why applaud an enemy if all he is capable of is wanton cruelty? The living witness of Saladin proved the contrary. What is more, the Franks themselves were not a race conspicuous for trustworthiness or magnanimity. Their conduct of the Crusades, their duplicity and ruthlessness in dealings with their supposed allies the Greeks, all indicate they learned more about gracious attitudes to the beaten victim from the Moors than vice versa.

A story is told of the Moorish king Marsilus taken prisoner and brought before Charlemagne. He is offered baptism or death. He looks round:

'Who are those fat men, clad in furs, seated at your table?' he asks the Emperor. Charles replies, 'The bishops and abbots'.

 'And who are those thin men, clad in black and grey?'

'The mendicant friars who pray for us,' replies the Emperor.

'And beyond them,' says the pagan king, 'what of those people squatting on the ground, feeding on the scraps from your table?'

'They are poor people,' says the Emperor.

'If that is the way you treat your poor, God's people, in dishonour of His love and charity, then kill me; I have no wish to be baptised into *your* faith'.

Mediaeval legend quoted by Gautier in
Chivalry (p. 25)

The essentials of a chivalric code *did* exist in Europe but they reached back to the old Celtic warrior spirit: literally 'never say die', courage and bigheartedness in everything, the valiant gesture supreme. The Franks still showed strong traces of a more pinched and barbarous hostility of spirit, less emotionally self-possessed. The Celtic bigheartedness was blended with a spiritual duty which evolved from the practical obligations of feudalism enjoined by birth, namely *noblesse oblige*. The new aristocratic feudal lord was expected to set a noble example, never behaving in base or cowardly fashion; deserving honour and respect from those lesser men, the commoners. Of course the whole business had to be conducted publicly – the very word noble, 'well-known', requires just that, and there was no earthly point in a good deed performed in secret. Style was all. It not only mattered how you comported yourself in the fight – bravely and honourably, face to face with the enemy; it also greatly counted how you comported yourself away from combat, either peaceably occupied or at warlike preparation, in exercise yard, at tourneys or lists. The feudal vassal was tilling your land to provide you with food and income: your time, like that of the English amateur sportsmen of

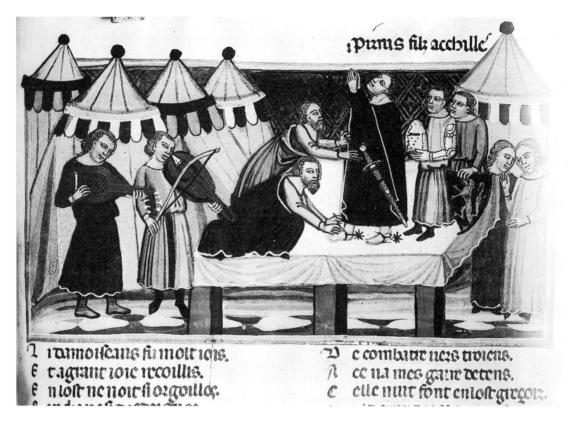

The illustration contains the labels: *:prius fil; acchille* and lines of medieval French text:

I damoiſaus fu moit iois.   D e combatir ucrs troiens.
E t agiant ioie rccoillis.   A ce na mes gaire detens.
E n loſt ne noirs ſi orgoillos.   C elle nunt font en loſt gregot;.

The order of chivalry. A new knight, in attitude of prayer, receives his accoutrements: sword, spurs, helmet, shield.

the nineteenth and twentieth centuries, was your own. Glory, chivalry, the possession and handling of fine weapons dominated the nobleman's every thought and action.

King Arthur's Knights of the Round Table swore a solemn oath which sums up the code of honour:

> . . . then the king established all his knights, and to them that there were of lands not rich, he gave them lands, and charged them never to do outrageousity nor murder, and always to flee treason; also, by no mean to be cruel, but to give mercy unto him that asketh mercy, upon pain of forfeiture of their worship and lordship of King Arthur for evermore; and always do to ladies, damosels, and gentlewomen succour, upon pain of death. Also, that no man take no battles in a wrongful quarrel for no law, nor for no world's goods. Unto this were all the knights sworn of the Round Table, both old and young. And every year they were sworn at the high feast of Pentecost.

> Malory Book III chapter 15

The endowing with lands is important: it placed a knight beyond financial need, which might impair his ability to act chivalrously, that is without self-interest. And material wealth encouraged spiritual largesse: everything with flourish.

So, the new European nobility, a mixture of Celtic and Teutonic bood, perhaps only codified an old Celtic notion and gave it new purpose and meaning within a Christian context, where the ultimate, the supreme feudal lord was God. The Celtic warrior hero fought elemental dark forces in the shape of giants and mysterious powers, dragons and demons. Feudal knights fought demonic powers, too, but principally in the shape of godless, swarthy-skinned Saracens.

'God help me when they make their warcry/For cruel are the Saracens,' wrote Guiot de Dijon in his Crusade Song (early 1200s) where Crusaders armed to the teeth are called 'pilgrims'. More will be said of dragons in the last chapter, but it must not be supposed that dragons and others were exclusively Celtic monsters. The Bible speaks much of dragons. To the Crusaders, that beast, symbolic of evil, might as easily prey on them in a Saracen desert as in a pagan cavern nearer home. The Round Table oath in the extract from Malory quoted above is taken at the feast of Pentecost, notice. This commemorates the descent of the Holy Spirit in tongues of flame onto the disciples in Jerusalem. The oath, therefore, is solemn way beyond any military pledge; it is a pious vow combining noble duty, martial commitment, religious bond.

In *Lancelot of the Lake*, the Lady of the Lake (young Lancelot's gardienne) outlines, at considerable length, the considerable burdens of knighthood. She is quite firm on one responsibility above all, in her catalogue of the chivalric virtues: 'The knight was established exclusively to protect the Holy Church'.

CAVALRY

The word chivalry is French in origin, derived from *cheval* (a horse), and, therefore, carries the brand of Frankish prejudice: a proper fighting man like Arthur rode a horse, just as the Celtic sun god Lugh had done. Arthur had been an old-style Celtic horseman and the Franks were nothing if not devoted to the pull of ancient rank and station.

Whatever the advantages and disadvantages of cavalry warfare, and this is not the place to enumerate them, the code of chivalry was based squarely on the notion that noble birth sat more estimably on horseback than slogging it out on foot with what later generations resignedly called the 'poor bloody infantry'. Horse troops cut speed and dash.

> No animal is more noble than the horse since it is by horses that princes, magnates and knights are separated from lesser people and because a lord cannot fittingly be seen among private citizens except through the mediation of a horse.
>
> Jordanus Ruffus, thirteenth-century Italian 'vet', quoted in R.H.C. Davis, ***The Mediaeval Warhorse*** (p. 99)

(Usually, of course, mediation was the job of priests.) By the time the Frankish kingdom had been organised for its own defence as well as its own internecine strife of prince against prince, in a feudal chain of counties and duchies, a large part of the available fighting force was mounted. Perhaps the Franks yielded to the lure of social status – knights in pomp on horseback. Perhaps they, like Alexander, were convinced of the usefulness of cavalry having seen it skilfully deployed by the nomadic tribesmen of the hot countries. Whatever the exact reason the chevalier was born; and by the early ninth century, Charlemagne could call on the feudal service of about 36 000 mounted knights throughout his kingdom. Each one, he stipulated, should be armed with and skilled in the use of: shield, lance, long sword, short sword, bow, quiver and arrows. Bows and arrows later became very *infra dig.*, used only by slyboot ruffians like the hit-and-run English, who got the idea from those worse recreants the Normans. Uncouth bumpkins like Perceval, the Welsh oik, stoop to bows and arrows not gentlemen. Cavalry was the thing.

In 864, Charles the Bald published an edict imposing the death penalty on any Frank who ransomed himself to the invading Northmen with 'coat of mail, any sort of arms *or a horse*' [my italics]. The Northmen came to do great damage to the kingdom 'because of our sins,' he went on, 'exposing Christianity to the heathen and perdition'. The language of the Crusades was already firmly entrenched. So too were the Northmen, whom we now know as Normans. Their later conquests in Sicily brought them into contact with Arab horses and horse-breeding methods. They discovered that the hard, limestone uplands of Sicily and southern Italy were ideal for nurturing toughness and stamina in their steeds, an excellent strain of horses for the Norman cavalry. The Mediterranean trade routes brought them other famous breeds: the Baktrian horses from Central Asia (Alexander's Bucephalus had been a Baktrian); the products of the old Roman studs in Asia Minor, once Trojan; and the Numidian and Spanish thoroughbreds.

The Franks and Normans, therefore, not only procured Arab horses from the eighth century on; by the eleventh century they had the Arab stirrup, as well. Without stirrups a horseback charge with levelled spear – essential to the Arthurian combat – is much less effective since one rider or both are likely to topple backwards off the saddle on impact. Stirrups meant the rider could brace himself,

virtually standing up, and keep his seat, if he were strong enough.

Cost

The cost of being a fully-fledged knight was high: every mounted warrior required at least one riding horse, a palfrey, to get him across country *to* the battlefield; another, the destrier or warhorse, to ride *into* battle; and, more than likely, a couple of spare mounts, including one for his squire (literally 'horse servant'), a young trainee to the profession of arms.

Comparative prices are difficult but not impossible to gauge, roughly. In his excellent study *The Mediaeval Warhorse*, R.H.C. Davis quotes figures current between 1250 and 1350. This is some time after the first period of Arthurian romance (late twelfth century) but must offer some kind of clue to scales of wealth:

Destrier (best warhorse) £50–100+
Rouncy (for non-knightly man-at-arms) £5–10
Hobby (used by light infantry to and from the battleground) £2
Palfrey (all-purpose knight's riding horse also capable of elegant ceremonial performance) £10–50

In contrast:
Packhorse, military and non-military 35–40p
Carthorse 12½p

So, a good warhorse cost 800 times as much as a workhorse affordable, even then, only by the better-off peasants. And the English bowmen at the battle of Crécy in 1346 received 2p a day, compared to the daily cost of 3½p to quarter and feed a warhorse. The popular notion of the flower of French chivalry amassed on prancing steeds ready for the great charge is woefully short of the reality: armies simply could not sustain the heavy financial burden. Arthur's Camelot may have had bottomless coffers of gold and silver bullion; most kings and princes, relying on the taxes squeezed out of overburdened subjects and the haphazard profits of battlefield ransom and confiscation, were more stretched.

SINGLE COMBAT

Contrary to popular belief, most fighting was done on foot. The nominal cavalryman more often dismounted and fought with lance, sword, mace (a spiked ball swung on a chain), or, harking back to Celtic tradition, the battle-axe. The horse was cheaper as a symbol of chivalric ideals left out of the fighting than as a vulnerable charger, needing to be fed and stabled. The celebrated charge of the pick of French chevaliers on St Crispin's Day was, in fact, something of a minor, and tardy, event, in a grim and bloody fight by footsloggers, heavy-armed knights, in the gluey mud of a late October ploughed field.

Alexander the Great led from the front, in the thick of the fight always. Thus Arthur, too, plunges into the mêlée alone to hearten his wavering troops at the battle of Saussy. This revives the old Celtic idea that what distinguished the hero was the defeat of a noble foe in hand-to-hand fight. According to Geoffrey of Monmouth, at the battle of Bath against the Saxons, Arthur flies into a rage after a long day of inconclusive fighting. He draws Caliburnus, calls upon the name of the Blessed Virgin (and is it a coincidence that Roncesvalles is, supposedly, fought on the Feast of the Assumption of the Blessed Virgin?) and charges alone into the barbarian army. He hews his way through their ranks, slaying four hundred and seventy of the enemy with single blows. This, needless to say, reverses the impasse of the battle and victory sways decisively to the British side.

The feudal lord led his vassals by example, conducting himself valorously because honour required it.

To many lands has he [Charlemagne] ridden in person
Many blows has he caught on his buckler
Many rich kings has he reduced to beggary.

La Chanson de Roland lines 540 ff

The feudal lord also wished to avoid the costly and humiliating process of surrender − giving up his right gauntlet to his vanquisher as a sign of submission and offering ransom, the price fixed by his social rank. This would leave him standing in the prisoner's command, minus helmet, removed to show that he was *hors de combat*, and his captor's vassal.

The solid wall of Frankish spearmen who broke the Moslem charge at Poitiers reverted to the old Greek and Roman practice of line fighting. However, the Romans, although they invented the highly drilled professional army, relied on every soldier fighting for himself even in the thickest press. The code of chivalry revived the principles of honour adhered to by the barbarian tribes who, if they never really matched the Roman armies, were never wanting in individual bravery.

MAGNANIMITY

The code also required magnanimity of the chivalric knight. King Arthur typifies the quality. To the two Senators who kneel in surrender after the great victory over the Emperor Lucius at Val-Suzon (or Saussy, or Soissons) Arthur says:

I grant it by my grace . . .
I allow you life and limb

Morte Arthure lines 2320 ff

Magnanimity, largeness of spirit, had to be substantiated by material generosity, *largesse*, as in the Breton *Lai* of Marie de France *Lanval*, where Arthur makes lavish gift of land and marriage settlement to his knights. But to emphasise the full depth of generosity vouchsafed those who merit it, Arthur exacts swift and terrible punishment from those who do not. The traitor Mordred, for example:

'By the Rood,' the royal man raged, 'revenge shall be mine.
He shall promptly repent all his pitiless acts.'

ibid.

It affords another insight into the vast and penetrating influence on Christian culture of Arab civilisation, that, perhaps, the warrior prince who personified two-handed justice was the great opponent of the Crusaders, Saladin.

Saladin typified the generous Arab *imam* or leader. In a eulogy to another leader, an Arab poet of the tenth century, writing in Cordoba, wrote:

By God, if equinoctial rains were like him
Despair of famine would never arise in the world.
In the light of his person Time made appear
An empire free from weaknesses and baseness.
An imam *just and honest in every respect*
Such as a just imam *should be and is expected to be.*
He surpassed in glory all past and present eras,
Like a necklace whose centre excels its ends in worth.

Ibn Hani' Al-Andalusi,
quoted in Nykl **Hispano-Arabic Poetry** (p. 29)

Hyperbole fitted to Arthur? Or does it merely demonstrate how universal his heroic qualities were, how easily they stepped beyond the narrow confines of Frankish caste-consciousness?

Saladin, the great Saracen leader whose name means 'Honouring the Faith', became a by-word for chivalrous gesture and dealing, to the chagrin of Christian clerics who were hot against all things Moslem.

When Saladin began his siege against Raymond of Châtillon's fortress Kerak and learned that Raymond was holding a wedding party, he ordered his artillery, already hurling giant boulders at the walls, not to batter the quarters where the honeymoon couple were abed. On another occasion, a Crusader prince, Balian of Ibelin, asked for and was granted safe conduct from Saladin to bring his wife and children out of besieged Jerusalem. He was allowed 24 hours, but, once inside, the clergy and Templars (see chapter 7) begged him to help organise the defence. Balian, in a fine quandary, wrote to Saladin, explained the problem and Saladin not only released him from his vow to leave the city, but escorted his wife and children under armed guard to a Christian port.

When Cligès sets off for Arthur's court, his father stresses the value of generosity: it is the mistress and queen which imparts lustre to every other virtue. By the same token, meanness vitiates every good quality. Liberality enhances a man's worthiness five hundredfold; nor does liberality come from chivalry, courage, beauty, command, it is of itself, and, for that reason, essential to the nobleman.

RANK

The old warrior caste determined rank largely by merit. Noble birthright came later, though a bunch of hero-class antecedents made famous in legend didn't go amiss. Chrétien de Troyes, as the other writers of Arthurian romance, continued the old oral tradition, handed on to them by the Breton storytellers, dating back to when the Celtic warriors gathered in a circle round the fire to hear their bard recount heroic exploits of the fighting. Not all bards, we must assume, could weave the same magic of words. Getafix in the Asterix stories may be a horrendous exception but probably not without equals: a few of the Arthurian romances are pretty dull fare. Chrétien and his heirs again and again emphasise the nobility of the knight's calling in a world where a slave owned nothing save by his rightful lord's permission. As Cligès says: 'A serf is obliged to do anything his lord tells him'.

Aristocratic knights did not fight with non-knights: there was no reputation to be won. Archers, for instance, were outside the chivalric system. Thus Malory's Gareth has to be dubbed knight – tapped on each shoulder with a sword – before his apprenticeship is complete, to enable him to undertake an adventure in King Arthur's name, as his man.

Low birth equated with evil looks, moral depravity and social inferiority; and vice versa. When a misshapen dwarf strikes a handsome noble, man or woman, it offends the laws of creation as interpreted by the mediaeval Church, as well as aristocratic dignity; not that one could expect any better of so deformed a creature:

> When he saw the girl coming towards him, the dwarf raised his whip and made to lash her across the face. She held up her arm to protect herself and took the blow full on her bare hand. The scourge bit into her flesh and raised an angry weal. She recoiled from the dwarf in terror and ran back to the queen, tears streaming down her face. Witnessing this assault on her maidservant, the queen was beside herself with grief and rage. 'Alas, Erec, good friend,' she said, 'How dare this ugly dwarf strike my maid. How ignoble this knight to allow such a monster to strike so lovely a creature'.

Chrétien de Troyes, *Erec* lines 179–200

Determining rank was an important matter. Chrétien de Troyes lists the Round Table Knights in order of merit: Gawain first; Erec, son of Lac, second; Lancelot of the Lake, third, and so on. At the bottom of the list, but 'not to be forgotten', he includes Bedoiier the Marshall, a chess and backgammon expert, Letron of Prepelesant, 'whose manners were so refined' and the Count of Honolan 'who had such a fine head of hair'. Curious.

Nobility, of manner, behaviour, birth, exercised the mediaeval mind greatly. There lay no merit in the worsting of social inferiors; the trouble, though, arose with those opponents whose outer mien, of noble chevalier, belied their inner villainy.

EVIL KNIGHTS

> Meliagant looked every inch a noble: frank expression, physically well-proportioned and handsome. Helmet and shield hung from laces round his neck. He cut a striking figure . . . However much the father helped me, his son Meliagant, malicious through and through, did the opposite, treacherously ordering the doctors to apply deadly poultices to my wound.

Chrétien de Troyes, *Lancelot* lines 3540–44

The evil knights in the romances were evil precisely because they wickedly shortened the odds in their own favour by unnatural (black magical) tricks; or had been sired by less than pukkah parents.

Reasonably, one might object, what about Arthur's sword Excalibur which could cut through any steel? His scabbard which rendered him invulnerable? Did that not give him unfair advantage? Ah, but Arthur already had the priceless advantage of being a hero, in the stamp of Culhwch and the rest; and, besides, didn't his wicked sister Morgan, like the evil hag Morrigan who tormented Cuchulainn, scupper him by stealing away Excalibur and scabbard, leaving him dud copies? As the King, Arthur must not be party to any baseness, deception or high-handedness. His exposure to evil merely underlined the pervasive nastiness of its minions. It was *his* duty, as any mediaeval monarch's, so Arthur affirms to his knights in *Erec*, to safeguard right and reason, his business as a true king to uphold the law, truth, good faith and justice. Not all kings came up to snuff. Tristan's Isolde, in Gottfried von Strassburg's *Tristan*, deems her lover so noble, so handsome, that 'it is a topsy-turvy world where so very many thrones are filled by men of second rank but none by Tristan'.

Armour

Arthurian knights did *not* wear plate armour, though the illustrations in later manuscripts show them so. In fact, they wore chain or ring mail, invented in the east: a loose fabric of interlocking steel links, each link made of thick wire looped and riveted. The skill and craftsmanship expended on the artefacts of war never ceases to astonish.

A suit of mail consisted of hauberk (coat), chausses (leggings), ventail (hood), mufflers (gloves), and overshoes; underneath a thick, padded jerkin of leather or fustian (cotton, wool or flax) to reduce bruising. For added protection, the mailed knight carried a shield of wood (or ivory, in one of the romances) reinforced with metal bands. When plate armour came in, largely to match the greater

A crusader of rank, welcomed safe home by his coroneted wife, removes helmet, shield, sword and belt, and the hauberk (mail coat).

penetrative power of the newly improved cross-bow, shields became redundant, except in tournaments.

The overall efficiency of mail is proved by its widespread use, especially in the beating sun of the Holy Land where the knights persistently wore it, although they must have been poached alive in what amounted to a loose-knit oven. A mail suit was, moreover, supple and not impossibly heavy – about 60 pounds, the same as a modern infantryman's accoutrements but, being distributed all over the body, far more manageable. An expert at the Tower of London, who has worn the armour, told me that you can do almost anything in it: hop, skip and jump. Indeed, the French romances talk of a favourite trick performed by knights to show off their zeal and vigour. They would leap from ground to saddle without support. This became a Frankish trademark and, clearly, predated the advent of stirrups. It also has a Celtic bravado about it. Cuchulainn could perform the hero's salmon leap, springing up from the ridge pole of one house to the next. And, in Thomas' version of the Tristan story, the hero executes a similar jump called the Welsh leap (Penguin p. 337). So, the fit youth, even mail clad, could well perform the Frankish leap 'lightly' as Malory claims.

For, contrary to popular belief, the mediaeval knight did not have to be winched into the saddle: that is just one of many absurd Victorian fictions. How they can have imagined a man who could hardly stand under a weight of iron and steel could then raise a sword and fight amazes me.

Plate armour, as we know it, did not supersede mail until about the first quarter of the fourteenth century, when greaves (shinguards), knee defences and thigh protectors, as well as flat discs to shield the elbows, were fastened to existing mail. By about 1360, plates encased the whole arm and, by degrees, the entire body. Once again, the image of the stiffly lumbering armoured knight has to be dispelled. The plate armour suit is as comfortable and well-articulated as an armadillo's crust. It would have been useless had it not been. Plate armour might well have arrived earlier: the technology of metalworking was equal to its manufacture, but prevailing opinion favoured the suppler mail. The only plate in general use had been that of the helmet, rounded in surface to deflect a sword or missile blow, but varying in shape from conical to cylindrical; either as a steel hat or a bowl encasing the whole head with neckguard and noseguard sometimes added. Armourers hammered the best helms from a single sheet of steel.

ARMS

A knight wielded various weapons. The mediaeval 'hand and a half sword', that is for one- or two-handed use, weighed about three pounds. Malory and the others talk of combats lasting whole days, where the reality is that most ancient battles, depending on the stamina and strength of men fighting with hand-brandished weapons, were of fairly short duration. A heavy sword would, naturally, impair staying power. From horseback, or on foot, the knight used a thrusting lance. Indeed, a knight and his retinue (mounted man-at-arms, page/squire and archer) formed a basic military unit, the *lance*. An army would consist of a number of such *lances*; and a mercenary soldier, with no feudal obligations tying him to one lord, was called a *free lance*. Not popular, either: their fickle loyalty hung slenderly by purse strings.

Kings and noblemen endowed their own weapons with royal virtue, the mediaeval equivalent of the old Celtic magical power. Poets emphasised the regality of the lord's armaments just as the old poets praised the heroic spear of Cuchulainn, the axe of Culhwch, Arthur the King's first cousin.

In the *Chanson de Roland* we read:

The Emperor has lain down in the meadow,
The baron lays his great spear by his side.
This night he will not disarm;
He wears his blue-bordered silver hauberk,
He laces his helm of jewelled gold,
He girds on Joyous his peerless sword
That thirty times daily changes its colour.
And we know the lance well
Which pierced our Lord's side on the cross;
Charles has its blade, thanks be to God,
Set in his gilded sword hilt.

La Chanson de Roland lines 2496 ff

A determined thrust of the knight's sword pierces tunic, hauberk and flesh. The original caption records this as a 'Victory of Humility over Pride'.

TOURNAMENTS

Mediaeval knights honed their fighting skills and steeled themselves for the unnerving experience of lethal conflict by jousting and fighting in the tournament lists. This artificial arena of war further allowed them to let off steam if there were no real slaughter on the go at the time. A tournament, or tourney, familiar in the pages of every Arthurian romance, consisted of combats between two parties armed with blunted weapons, in various bouts, on horseback and on foot. Strict rules governed the engagements, just as every mediaeval battle was observed by heralds from both sides, to agree on the result, naming of the battle and disposal of prisoners. The tournament's Ordinance and Form would decide the prize awarded, like the Victoria Cross, 'for valour'.

The Lateran Council of the Catholic Church in 1179 called these events 'detestable', as much, probably, because of the gratuitous violent and godless behaviour they spawned out of the arena as for the apparently aimless mayhem they required in it. The just war had to be fought against legitimate targets; pretend warfare was morally repugnant. The Church had no control over it. The tournaments were vainglorious, their prizes empty and self-seeking, like copulation without procreation. The knight's true role was that of ardent soldier in Christ's great army where individual glory was outshone infinitely by the greater glory of God and His Son.

Christ's teachings – love thy neighbour as thyself, blessed are the peacemakers and so on – did not, maybe, sit well on the belligerent teachings of the Church militant; and not all clerics were war-crazy. But, responding to St Augustine's definition of just war, there were many princes of the Church hell (or heaven) bent on the imposition of holy orthodoxy by sword or by cross. The Greek Byzantine Church had a divergent view. Any soldier of the Byzantine army who killed an enemy on Byzantine soil, even in a battle, was refused communion for three years. The western Christians invariably said mass before going into battle, as do Arthur and the Round Table knights. But unease about the activities of knights away from the authorised field of conflict grew, steadily.

There is no doubt that the tourney was, to the Middle Ages, what football matches have become to ours: a gathering of footloose hooligans, a potential army, skilled and bloodthirsty, on the doorstep, spoiling for a rumpus.

In the joust, heavily armoured knights charged at each other at top speed either side of a fence barricade, the list, with spears levelled, or couched (the old word is 'fewtered') in a purpose-cut niche in the shield, so as to 'tilt' or knock the opponent off his horse. Hence 'full tilt'. There were also sword bouts, on foot, singly and severally.

Another aspect of the tournament which almost certainly aroused clerical opposition was that although the European tourney started in France (English writers called it the 'Gallic conflict'), it had reached Europe from the east, being a refined version of the competitive horse-riding practised by the hated and feared nomad tribes of Asia. The Afghans still play Buzkashi, originally a Mongol pastime, where professional horsemen play a sort of mounted Eton Wall Game with a headless calf. Polo came from similar roots, so, too, *chota peg*, piercing a ring with a lance from a galloping horse. Similarly, in romance, all combat is undertaken for dash and display; for glory and favour.

CHAPTER FIVE

LOVE

Loue is a selkud wodenesse
That the idel mon ledeth by wildernesse,
That thurstes of wilfulscipe and drinket sorwenesse
And with lomful sorwes menget his blithenesse.

(Love is a strange madness
That leads the idle man by wilderness,
That thirsts of wilfulness and drinks sorrowness
And with frequent sorrows mingles his happiness.)

early thirteenth century

Early morning, Easter Monday. A tournament. Parchment bills tacked to trees, gates, doors in towns and villages within a wide radius have announced the day a long time since. The tournament field stands ready, an oblong section of the meadows outside the castle walls, fenced off with stout palisades known as lists. Centre field, a lengthways barrier divides the ground; down either side will charge the armed knights at joust. For the moment they wait, those young stallions of chivalry, outside the painted pavilions which line the foursquare road cordoned off beyond the lists' perimeter with another, flimsier barricade. The knights pace nervously or loll in feigned disregard of any fear, any apprehension, any feeling at all. An obligation of rank and *noblesse*, never to be stirred as the common soldiery. The field stands quiet as an empty church; the road agog. Armourers busy at anvil and forge, last-minute work, squires and pages, those young aspirants to the exalted rank of knighthood, bustle fussily about their high-mannered masters' errands; ostlers curry, soothe, cosset the sturdy warhorses, big-bellied, heavy-rumped chargers schooled to the brutal shock and turmoil of mediaeval battle. Heralds in glittering coats prowl and strut, officiously checking names, blazon, nationality, rank of the competing knights, some of whom come across foreign borders to compete.

Suddenly, in a pant of noise and ostentation, across the road a procession of ladies makes for the huge wooden grandstand erected for their comfortable viewing of the jousts. Some on foot, others nonchalantly cock-legged on white mules. Here ambles the noble audience, attended by a small presence of lords for whose elderly delectation too this young man's day is organised. And the ladies, like a mews of richly plumaged falcons, come to the show to show themselves, in dresses of gorgeous ciclatoun and sendal and the rich silk known as samite, the weave often interthreaded with gold; and capes of vair and ermine; and muslin caps; and shoes of glossy soft leather; and gems and trailing scarves.

The common folk, crowded against the outer barriers, with a long sight of the field, watch, mouths agape, as the finery arrives. And the waiting knights see them, too, their blood pumping suddenly harder like the throb of adrenalin and lust, both of which this provoking sight of amorous ladies excites, as they troop by, hips swaying, into the grandstand. More than one of the combatants has already been singled out by a maiden, long hair spilling over her shoulders, a present of one of her detachable sleeves tied round his lance shaft. With it she gives her promise to sigh and gasp for him alone when it comes his turn to match his manhood against the rest. In receiving that token of her favour he will fight to deserve it as well as her gasps and sighs with a stalwart display of fighting mettle. And this is the business of his entire life: whether at hunt, tourney or war he fights with deadly earnest in all three, to the death if need be.

A flourish of trumpets. Sinews tighten; nerves fizz like flame at tallow and, inactive so long, the knights can move at last. They swing into the saddle with a ring-jingle of mail and tugged bridle. The horses neigh and snort, flanks shiver at the prick of spurs and the mounted parade swerves out along the dew-dampened turf of the road and round into the arena to muster below the stand. Roars from the ill-bred crowd jostling for a better view, but that is their coarseness. Mark the pedlars amongst them, the chapmen, the hucksters and hoydens milking the crowd for trade; and the jades, too, offering their own version of ringside favour. The genteel ladies of the lofty gallery do not roar. They simper and glance and whisper and hiss and chatter gossip and sharp retort to rivals, and flutter eyelashes. As a favoured champion catches their eye, the younger, less discreet among them, will allow a blush to pink their white-farded cheeks. Silly girls, only. The cooler hands let slip no sign of tumbling affection.

The parade salutes the stand before wheeling off and dispersal to the appointed lines. In the arena it will be lance to lance, blade to blade, bones broken and blood spilled, sometimes *à l'outrance*, to death. There may be romantic engagements before and after, but the tournament's mimicry of war differs little from the practice of war: as thrilling in its pomp and colour beforehand as it is sickening in its pain and finality afterwards.

The heralds summon the first competitors. A buzz of excitement about the field as the two opponents canter out to either end of the central barrier. A signal. They lurch forward in the high-backed saddle. A swelling thunder of hooves; jarring collision of lance on shield. One man down. The long day begins, to end by lamplight, with feasting and dancing for those combatants left exultantly unscathed to enjoy the second, hotter swap of favour. That reward the wounded miss out on; as do the dead and the dying.

The tournament, though, has three days to run: more prizes to win, more favours to enjoy. As Chrétien says, in *Lancelot*:

> Knights and ladies would return next morning
> to the tournament: the knights to fight for
> honours; the ladies to seek husbands.

lines 5726–30

The ladies' business was serious, too.

FAVOUR

If the tournament enjoyed royal or princely patronage, as did Arthur's, naturally, it became

The royal wedding night. Guenever's handmaidens modestly avert their gaze as she slips into the nuptial bed to join an expectant Arthur.

an affair of great pomp and pageantry, witnessed by the stars of the court, above all the ladies. Henry VI's Queen says to William de la Pole, about the time Malory was scribbling away:

I tell thee, Pole, when in the city Tours
Thou ran'st a tilt in honour of my love
And stol'st away the ladies' hearts of France
I thought King Henry had resembled thee
In courage, courtship and proportion:
But all his mind is bent to holiness . . .
His study is his tilt-yard.

Shakespeare, **Henry VI Part 2**, Act 1
scene iii line 50

Enough said. Not kingly behaviour at all. No wonder there was a civil war on.

At the tournament noble ladies offered their favours – coloured silk scarves tied to lance tips – and with favour often their heart.

Lancelot said: 'Fair maiden, I will grant you to wear a token of yours upon my helmet, and therefore what it is, show me'.
'Sir,' she said, 'it is a red sleeve of mine of scarlet, well embroidered with great pearls': and so she brought it to him.
So Sir Lancelot received it, and said, 'Never did I erst so much for no damosel'.

Malory Book XVIII chapter 9

The erotic significance of flimsy token offered to favourite knight and twined about his helmet or else slim weapon shaft was not lost on the mediaeval audience, either. Nor, assuredly, on the clerics who condemned the tourneys as stews of corruption; which they partly were. Guenever eventually goes to bed with Lancelot, her champion, but for years she had done no more than expect him to wield lance and sword blade in her exclusive behalf. In simple allegorical terms that is as close to adultery positive as you could get: sexual wooing of a frank order. And that provides the basis of the unique blend of highly charged war song and emotionally taut love ballad which Chrétien, and others after him, produced in the Arthurian romance. The late romance *Gawain and the Green Knight*, written in a Lancashire dialect of fourteenth-century Middle English, fairly sizzles with eroticism.

COURTLY INFLUENCE. THE WOMAN'S TOUCH

Towards the middle of the twelfth century, the kings and queens of Europe acquired, and began eagerly to display, a new self-assurance. Feudal hierarchy, divine ordinance, even if covenanted by an envious Church, strengthened throne and crown. Conquest in the rich East, with its great nexus of trade routes, supplied a material bounty never before enjoyed in the poorer north and west.

In fact, Europe itself was in a ferment of expansion and industrialism helped generate more wealth. In a remarkable passage in *Yvain*, Chrétien describes a factory where three hundred maidens are employed at gold and silk thread embroidery; but they are pale, thin, ill-clad, hungry, overworked and underpaid. A sweatshop, in other words. The owner grows fat on the exploitation of skilled labour.

Prosperity bred an appetite for self-advertisement. The courts flourished and became centres of pageantry, artistic pursuit and ceremonial – lavish displays of wealth as vital to royal image as exorbitantly costly sets to a modern musical. Wealth attracted culture – poets, painters, musicians, to add the lustre of their genius to the gilded magnificence of the patrons they served. For the nobles who thronged the courts there were but two occupations: war (preparing for, engaging in, reminiscing about); and entertainment, which fed the appetite for the first. And in the late eleventh century had come the added zest of the Crusades to the Holy Land. From now on war became a pilgrimage, too. The old hero donned his blood-red cross and, with it, a new image. Fighting glory, a lust for conquest and rich booty could, henceforward, be justified in the heroic quest to liberate the sacred earth of Palestine from the pagans.

With their lords either absent on Crusade, or, like Eleanor of Aquitaine's first husband, Louis VII, drily occupied with administration and law, the ladies of court began to exert a powerful and illuminating influence on its life and pastimes. Eleanor herself imported to grey northern France, and later England, the polychrome brilliance of her native Provence, a fertile ebullience of literary activity and stylistic novelty hardly even sniffed by poets shivering along the Channel coasts. Above all, she introduced the work of the troubadours (including the first of them, her grandfather Guilhem IX of Toulouse), who took as their all-consuming theme *fin'amors*, or romantic love.

Early Celtic literature dwells hardly at all on love. Heroes meet women, for sure, but they tend to be enchantresses from the Other World. A woman's beauty cast a spell and of spells beware. It was from the Arab poets of Spain that the troubadours of southern France learned their craft: love poems characterised by heady, intimate emotion. The woman-wary Celts had reserved their emotional heat for heroic, that is to say masculine, enterprise: war. The Moors were franker about sexual engagement:

She could not visit me because
She feared the spy and the envious one
Who knew her by three things:
Her radiant brow,
The chink of her gold and silver adornments,
And the amber-like fragrance of her body.
Her brow she can cover with her sleeve;
Her adornments she can remove;
But her fragrance? Nothing can be done about that.

Lines written by a lover, disappointed of nocturnal rendezvous, one Al-Mitamid, Arab ruler in southern Spain during the eleventh century. When living in the palace at Seville, his wife, yearning for the old footloose life of the desert, complained that she could no longer find anywhere to walk barefoot in mud. Al-Mitamid ordered his servants to spread the tessellated marble of his courtyard with a slush of musk and sugar and bid his lady paddle up to her slim ankles to her heart's content. (The kohl-eyed

Sheikh of Araby is no mere fiction.) And of such a woman Guilhem IX wrote:

Joy of her will cure a sick man
Sorrow of her will topple a fit man
A wise man turn into a fool
The handsome man lose his looks
The courtliest man become a churl
The churl put on courtly manners.

The Moors studied and theorised on the art and practice of love just as they investigated every other enigma of human experience. To treatises on medicine, optics, astronomy and a host of scientific subjects was added an enquiry into love by the Andalusian poet Ibn Hazm. In his *Tawq al-Hamama*, 'The Dove's Neck Ring', published in 1022, he dilates at great, and rather tedious, length on such central issues as: keeping the secret, divulging the secret, loyalty, betrayal, tell-tale signs of love, falling in love in dreams, breaking up, and so on. His chapter headings might almost make a catalogue of twentieth-century popular song titles, omitting, of course, the chapter on 'the supremacy of chastity'. Herein we see the basis, the rules, even, of that complicated passion which crossed the Pyrenees to inflame the southern French troubadours and, finally, to scorch all European literature with its heat. As Marcabru, the Provençal poet, writing between 1130 and 1150 described it:

Love is the cinder
That feeds the flame in the
Soot and burns under
Wood and straw. Listen!
He knows not which way to turn
Whom that fire begins to burn.

How very unEuropean, how turbulent this was.

Immoderate? Complicated? Passion? Not at all what you'd associate with a dour Frank. The Celts, though, of wilder temperament, needed little persuasion to embrace this new theme in their poetic vapourings. The Celts adored excess.

However, the Moorish taint did not please chillier morals. The authority of the Roman Church had begun, even in the eleventh century, to fasten a controlling grip on every aspect of social and intellectual custom across Europe.

So, all very well in theory this true love which transcended marriage and convention and brought a hectic rosy flush to cheeks pallid with despair: smouldering glances and furtive brush of clothing; trysts along the rose-scented walks on musky summer evenings; deliberate chance meetings in the echoing stone passages where lighted tapers licked at shadow.

In practice it came badly unstuck: hotbreath dallying in fragrant garden walks led, inevitably, to arbour or bed; and that could lead to pregnancy. Big trouble. Sartorial fashion – décolletage and codpiece – didn't help. Hence the chastity girdle. But, as every lord and master due to return home from long absence at the Holy War knew, there was no wisdom below the girdle nor any clasp made that an expert locksmith could not be persuaded to unsnap. For biological rather than purely spiritual reasons, therefore, poetic *fin' amors* ossified into Courtly Love, the elaborate science of how to inch to the brink of uncontrolled release but not over. An eccentric scheme of things which pondered long and hard on such conundrums as how may lovers lie naked together yet deny themselves gratification of fleshly desire, needed, and got, its own courts and canon law to rival that of the Church, whose theologians would soon be debating such precious twaddle as how many angels could balance on the point of a needle.

A priest, Andreas Capellanus ('The Chaplain')

published his seminal *De Arte Honeste Amandi*, 'On the Art and Practice of Honourable Love', in about 1185. This extensive manual of Courtly Love, written for a Christian readership yet owing much to the *Art of Love* and *Remedies of Love* by the pagan Latin poet Ovid, furnished the mediaeval poets and court dilettanti with a legal codex and theology combined of romantic love. Here they found, in schematic form, chapter and verse for the appreciation and understanding of falling in love, falling out of love, conducting an affair, salving the wounds of unrequited love, and so on. Love has its thirty-one Laws, as the Christian faith has its Ten Commandments. One of Andreas' allegorical examples tells how a knight, through pious obedience to Love's laws, wins the Hawk of Victory at King Arthur's court. Already that great king has been installed as the arbiter in matters of the heart as well as the paragon of majesty.

The one circumstance fatal to love, says Andreas, is marriage: 'I cannot overstate the absolute truth that love is incapable of growing between lovers who get married.' Such an opinion would inevitably turn out to be the cuckoo in this particular nest. Imagine what St Bernard and that crowd made of it. They were from the outset wholly unconvinced of the virtues of sex within marriage let alone without it. Andreas offered other counsel which might be described as contentious. If a nobleman has the misfortune to fall for a peasant woman he is advised that, because the lower classes, being short on mental refinement, are known for their bodily vigour, some force will be needed, and permissible, should an opportunity arise to press the suit. Up against a tree, for instance? There are other absurdities which reflect accurately the febrile nature of romantic love:

> If a lady is courted by three admirers and she listens to one, but squeezes the hand of the

second and touches, with her toe, the foot of the third, which of the three does she favour most?

Andreas' treatise, which followed on behind 'The Dove's Neck Ring' exerted immense and wide influence on mediaeval literature. The subject was comparatively new and writers of prose and verse revelled in it, as had the troubadours before them. Not the least enthusiastic were the writers of Arthurian romance. With the old theme, what men do to each other: War, they amalgamated the new theme, what men and women do to each other: Love.

REAL-LIFE ROMANCE

If the wars and political events of the day supplied the romances with the stuff of action, court intrigue certainly helped stimulate the amorous content. The woman who sponsored Courtly Love in Aquitaine, and the Arthurian romance throughout the Plantagenet kingdom of England and France, Eleanor, wife of Henry II, was at the centre of a real life romantic drama of her own. Malory calls lovemaking 'to have ado'; the same phrase he uses for knightly combat of arms. He might have been thinking of the turbulent relationship of England's king and queen.

Henry (1133–89) and Eleanor (1122–1204) lived and reigned when the literary Arthur burst upon the European scene, from origins wreathed in Welsh bardic mystery. Their interest in the romances, Eleanor's in particular, cannot be in doubt. They seem even to have lived as if their life had been ordained in romance.

Eleanor of Aquitaine, a known beauty, vivacious, cultivated and sparky, was married at fifteen to the saturnine, dull Louis, king of France, and escorted by him from hot, bright Provence to a damp castle by the Seine, there to sit and be bored to death. Fifteen years passed. In 1151 there arrived on a visit to the French court the eighteen-year-old heir to the English throne, Henry Plantagenet, of red hair and piercing eye: fighter, hunter who rode horses till they foundered under him, scholar and wit. Within two years she was divorced and they were married: king and queen of England, Anjou, Maine, Touraine, Normandy. Poets sang her praises:

> *Were all the world mine*
> *From the sea to the Rhine*
> *I'd give it all away*
> *If England's Queen lay*
> *In my arms.*

So wrote Bernart de Ventadorn, who added, indiscreetly, that he thought her the most beautiful woman in the world and trembled like a twig in her presence. Henry II forbade him the court, as Eleanor's first husband had banished another troubadour, Marcabru. Marcabru became a Cistercian monk.

And Henry fell in love with fair Rosamond, the daughter of his baron, Sir Walter Clifford. To hide her away from the jealous snooping of Queen Eleanor, a great beauty in her prime, now past, who knew as many venomous and deadly recipes of pestilential brews and concoctions as Morgan le Fay nor shrank from using them, the King gave orders to be built a house of wonderful working in Blenheim Park, near Woodstock, so that no man or woman might come to Fair Rosamond. This house was named Labyrinthus, and was wrought like unto a knot in a garden, called a maze, sweet with roses, too, as Fair Rosamond was a rose in all the world. But the Queen was crafty beyond all women and came to Fair Rosamond, undoing the secrets of the concealed bower, winding her way by a clew of silken thread, wherewith she entered and came out like night in a shadow, unseen. And there she so dealt with Rosamond, by a poisoned chalice, or

Lovers seal their love with an oath under a briar. He ungirds his sword to betoken submission; her pet dog bespeaks devotion; the rose and briar symbolise the entwined beauty and thorny trials of love.

some say a bowl and others a dagger, that Fair Rosamond lived not long after but withered and died. And King Henry, in his grief, caused her to be buried at a house of nuns by Godstow, in a tomb before the altar, hung with silk and perpetually lit with lamps and tapers. The tomb was adorned with intricate stone weavings decked with roses, green and red; and cut into the side this verse; to show the vanity of human wishes, that all flesh comes to perish, even that fair flesh beloved of kings:

Fair Rosamund goes
To her last repose
Her scent no longer fragrant,
The rose no longer rose.

Adapted from the account of a Chester monk,
Higden, *c.* 1350

Henry and Eleanor as Tristan and Isolde? Or Eleanor as the herbalist/enchantress Morgan le Fay? Geoffrey of Monmouth had made Arthur's steward Kay an Angevin. The historical connections are planted deep. Perhaps Eleanor saw herself as Guenever, rather. A nameless author may have thought of her as such, though not in any way that she would have welcomed. In an exact parallel to the Fair Rosamond case, Queen Guenever is accused of administering a dose of poison in an apple. It carries off a good knight Sir Patrise at a feast given by the Queen to show that 'she had as great joy in all the other knights of the Round Table as she had in Sir Launcelot.' When Sir Patrise had eaten the fruit he 'swelled so until he brast and there fell down suddenly among them'. Suspicion lighted on the Queen, though in fact the apples had been enpoisoned by one Sir Pinel out of hatred for Sir Gawain. Sir Gawain it is who voices the outrage:

'My lady the Queen,' said Gawain, 'wit ye well, madam, that this dinner was made for me, for all folks that knowen my condition understand that I love well fruit, and now I see well I had near been slain; therefore, madam, I dread me lest ye will be shamed.'

Malory Book XVIII chapter 3

So, Guenever proves that the business of women and apples is by no means settled.

Were there Englishmen wary of this French Queen Eleanor? Did gossip about skullduggery harden into outright accusation? And does Henry's Labyrinth at Woodstock, not so far from his father's zoo, recall the marvellous tower made by Cligès' servant, John, where Fenice his lady goes into hiding?

Do you imagine you have seen all the delights my tower has to offer? It contains secret places no one could search out. However hard you look, however closely you examine it, however cunning, however astute you are, you will never find them unless I show you . . . if you notice, the tower widens at its base below ground level, but you won't find an entrance anywhere. The craftsmanship is so ingenious that the outline of the door in the hard rock is quite invisible.

Chrétien de Troyes, *Cligès* lines 5502–26

Chrétien's patron, remember, was Eleanor's daughter.

Mediaeval princes and kings, princesses and queens, lived at the centre of attention. Their lives were rich and influential at the peak of the feudal hierarchy. They expected to be flattered as a matter of course, and they paid the best poets to do the flattering, dressing up historical record as romance and vice versa. Rulers inspired romance just as they had the shaping of historical events in the grand style characteristic of Arthurian literature.

Eleanor of Aquitaine may well deserve to be called the 'onlie begetter' of Courtly Love. Certainly Andreas first enunciated its principles during her reign, though it was at the direction of her daughter, Marie Countess of Champagne, that he wrote his book. He was, too, a friend of Chrétien de Troyes. Thus a cleric with a nose for romantic storytelling and sententious cataloguing of varying states and degrees of amatory bliss and anguish, sexual and non-sexual, leads the way. Don't be too surprised at that. For many centuries, most of the best-educated minds in Europe were churchmen, precisely because the Church exercised a strict monopoly on formal education and regarded any other sort with deep suspicion. Andreas himself boasts of his skill in the art of soliciting the favours of nuns because he has 'an experienced knowledge of all things'. The secrets of the confessional put to good use, you see. He even admits to one particular escapade with a coiffed sister. He led her on but, threatened either with her surrender and devotion, or dire punishment in the ecclesiastical courts, turned her down at the last minute. Ignorant of full participation in the expression of love, his theories on its art and practice, nonetheless had, and continued to have, wide currency amongst writers who applied their imaginative and intuitive skills to the embroilments of love. Around this emotional drama Chrétien de Troyes and others following his lead, shaped the Arthurian romance.

Courtly love is *amor de lonh*, love-at-a-distance, hole-in-corner, look but don't touch. It amounts to a chivalry of romantic devotion with a sexual etiquette as complex as the rules of the tournament. It is a feudalism of the heart, where the impassioned knight is vassal to his liege lady, a soldier fighting under Cupid's banner:

> The Queen took Lancelot's hand and said: 'Stand up, dear sir. I have no idea who you are; but if you were born of noble rank it is not right or proper for you to kneel at my feet.'
>
> 'My lady,' said Lancelot, 'if it would please you, I would be *your* knight, solely in *your* service.'
>
> 'It does please me,' she replied.
>
> 'Then by your leave I will ride out on quest straightaway,' he said.
>
> 'Go, in God's name, my own dear knight.'

> 'My lady,' he whispered, 'for that name you give me, I thank you.'

Lancelot du Lac , section 165

For his true love the courtly lover aches; for love of her shrinks from no danger; in her name undertakes any mission, however doomed or hopeless . . . in fact the more doomed and hopeless, the better to wring heroic deed out of him; for his mistress' sake he endures all manner of torment and disappointment, perhaps the acutest of which, by the strict rules of Courtly Love, being that he is not allowed to join her in bed. His, and her, one solace has to be spiritual: dandy for the inspiration of perfervid literature if not much good for the peace of mind.

Two love stories brought to prominence in Arthurian romance have stood high in European literature ever since: of Lancelot and Guenever; of Tristan and Isolde. The love between Lancelot and Arthur's queen is central to the sprawl of fiction generated by that great name.

LANCELOT AND GUENEVER

Lancelot and Guenever fall hopelessly in love at the very beginning of the story, when the young Lancelot receives his sword belt of the Queen. They contain their mutual yearnings, keep them secret, somehow, but the passion smoulders unquenchably. How Arthur misses the signs of their besotted attachment, we can only guess: perhaps, like Eleanor's Louis, he was too busy with state affairs. Perhaps he was blithely engaged with undiscovered flirtations of his own. One thing is certain: Guenever's loyalty to him wavers in every version of the story. Geoffrey of Monmouth even has her taken incestuously to bed by the usurping Mordred, as *his* Queen, when Arthur is in Gaul. Mordred slain, Guenever retires to a nunnery.

Eventually, having managed to stay at arm's length, sexual frustration sternly held in check, Lancelot and Guenever kiss; an event so momentous, so charged with emotional electricity that when Dante's lovers demure Paolo and Francesca read the description of it in *Lancelot of the Lake* their desire, so long suppressed, overwhelms them and *they* kiss; alas, before they can repent of so heinous a crime, they die and spiral straight down to the second circle of Hell where:

The carnal sinners are condemned, in whom
Reason by lust is swayed.

Dante, *Inferno* Canto II lines 39–40 (trans. Carey)

Lancelot and Guenever go further than an illicit kiss: they make love. Their adultery is discovered and they run away, in double betrayal of King Arthur – husband and best friend, liege lord to both. Faith is broken; the kingdom is rent by civil war and the golden age of King Arthur and the Round Table comes to an end. That, at least, is the earliest version; in *Lancelot of the Lake*, thanks to Church benediction, the faith is healed, divisions closed up and all is right with the world. A better sermon, a much lesser story. Tragedy, as lovers, should be, in the Welsh phrase, 'naked as a needle', like the unhappy story of Tristan and Isolde.

The tragic story of their passion, at once exalted and doomed, is *the* great love story of Arthurian romance. It draws in many of the profounder aspects of Courtly Love and deserves summary here. Of the tale's many versions, I refer to the remarkable account by Gottfried von Strassburg, published in about 1210.

TRISTAN AND ISOLDE

Tristan is a fine and noble knight; a peerless huntsman; musician and poet (like Eleanor and Henry's son, Richard the Lionheart, who whiled away his time in a German gaol composing troubadour songs); a champion, loved and respected by all, 'as one rightly treats a man whose thoughts tend only to excellence and one who is averse to all unworthiness'. His uncle, King Mark of Cornwall (a villain in Geoffrey of Monmouth's history), sends him on a mission to Ireland to escort back Queen Isolde's daughter, the Fair Isolde, to be Mark's queen.

The girl's beauty is widely known:

Wise Isolde, Fair Isolde,
She shines out like the dawn.

However, the Queen, like Morgan le Fay, a skilled herbalist, is sadly aware that beauty alone may not ensure a loving marriage, mixes a love potion and entrusts it to her niece, Brangane, who accompanies her princess cousin. Her instructions are secretly to pour out the philtre as wine for Mark and Isolde after they have been united in marriage. Gottfried is keen not to offend against the sanctity of Christian marriage so the philtre has to be drunk *afterwards*. He was, in all probability, employed in some capacity by the Church.

On the sea voyage back to Cornwall, Tristan goes into Isolde's cabin to discuss 'various matters of mutual interest' and calls for a drink. Brangane is absent; only young chits of girls remain in attendance. They see the flask of special brew (oh why had Brangane thoughtlessly left it untended?), and one of them serves Tristan from it. Tristan offers it courteously to Isolde. She is not thirsty and, besides, nurses a grudge against him. Tristan, she has lately discovered, is now revealed as the hitherto unknown killer of her uncle, the pitiless Morold. However, Tristan presses her to drink. Out of courtesy she takes a draught, then passes the glass to him. He drinks. Brangane re-enters the

Et pins si laues fait plus riche q̃ le w̃ li auiez
conne tout le monde. Coment al. lancelot beula

la roune crenieur la premiere fois.

nsi fait elle loctroy ie que bien
que il soit tout nnen et ie toute
sienne et que par wus soient
amenbes tous les meffais et
les trespas des connenances.
Danie fait galaot gñt meras
avais ore y connient conmencement de seurte
wus nen teurseres ia chose fait elle que ie ne

Lancelot and Guenever kiss for the first time. A trio of chaperones
look away. Lancelot's companion gives warning, too late.

cabin, recognises the flask and turns pale as death with the shock of realisation. She dashes up on deck with the bottle and flings it into the sea, lamenting: 'Ah, Tristan and Isolde, this drink will be your death'. Death, yes, but ecstasy, too. Of course she is too late. Down below decks Love, waylayer of all hearts, arch-disturber of tranquillity, had stolen into the cabin. In the Middle English retelling of the story *Sir Tristrem*, even Tristrem's dog, Hudain, laps up some of the elixir and devotes himself, like a romantic Greyfriar's Bobby, to the lovers for life. But Gottfried's love philtre (in French *potion* from which comes English 'poison') excuses from the outset all subsequent, and strictly reprehensible, behaviour of the besotted, blighted pair. Their passion, over which they have no control, can be seen to have its origin in the manipulation of Nature, a bewitchment that diminishes blame and responsibility.

Love still conquers all, but only thanks to trickery and deceit. Isolde has to marry King Mark, but she and Tristan persuade Brangane, much against her will, clandestinely to take Isolde's place on the bridal night. Custom required visible proof – an issue of blood – that the bride came to bed unbreached. Brangane is a virgin; she does her duty (as a servant and vassal), quits the bed to be replaced by Isolde; and then Tristan, the loyal champion, enters the freshly illumined chamber to serve wine to the newly-weds, as another custom required.

Later, the jealous steward Marjodoc lays a trap to reveal Tristan and Isolde's adultery to the King. The couple outwit him and Isolde soothes away the King's suspicions in bed: she 'took him in her arms, kissing and embracing him and pressing him close to her soft, smooth breasts and resumed her verbal stalking by question and answer'.

Eventually gossip, rumour and suspicion hammer so insistently on Mark's peace of mind that Isolde agrees to submit herself to trial by ordeal as proof of innocence. Gottfried's *Tristan* dates from about 1210 and at the Lateran Council in 1215 trial by ordeal – a test of oath by physical duress – was condemned; hitherto the clergy had given their blessing to it.

Isolde's trial is to be held at Caerleon. Tristan disguises himself as a pilgrim and when Isolde's boat docks she calls to him, shabbily dressed and unrecognisable, to carry her from the gangway to the harbour. She whispers in his ear, telling him to stumble and catch her as they sprawl on the ground. Then, having attended Mass in hair shirt and woollen robe, she confesses her sins and swears, in the presence of the King and judges, that:

> No man has enjoyed my body or lain with me or
> between my arms but you. Except, of course,
> the pilgrim beggarman, but you saw him with
> your own eyes lying in my arms.

She grasps the hot iron bar and her flesh remains unburned: she has sworn nothing but the truth. It is another strange interpretation of the pilgrim's role.

Mark does, at last, open his eyes, if reluctantly, to the truth and banishes Tristan and Isolde in a remarkable, a royal display of tolerance, considering the pain and humiliation he has endured:

> Take each other by the hand, leave my court,
> leave my kingdom. If you must betray me I wish
> neither to see it nor to hear of it. The friendship
> we three shared is over.

In their forest refuge, Tristan and Isolde sleep side by side with a naked sword between them: a sword of Fate on which they eventually fall. Absolute love knows no fear, it gives them courage to weather all storms. The sword blade stands for naked desire, too, but now their great love has scaled greater

vant gifles voit que
faire li couient. sire
uient arriere la ou les
pee eſtoit ſi la pzent ꞇ la recomê

King Arthur, mortally wounded after the final battle, orders Sir Bedever to hurl Excalibur
back into the lake whence it came. A hand appears above the lake surface to catch it.

Above: Charlemagne, like Arthur blessed in his regal power by the Church, is crowned king and emperor. The pagan Ostrogoths probably introduced the anointing of kings, but biblical authority — Samuel's consecration of David with oil — confirmed it.

Opposite: Jerusalem two centuries after its loss to the Turks. Minarets crowd the city. The goldfoil Dome of the Rock (the Holy Sepulchre) is prominent. A ruined Crusader fortress by the seashore makes a forlorn memento of the departed glory.

Within the illustration:

S fez y ferr et
furtar·
Et mainteffore
le efcoutar

front reliufant fourez voustre
Lentreoeul fi neftoit pas vne
Ane fut affez maney p mefme
Lenez eut bien fait a droiture

Previous page: A tournament mêlée. Gaudily caparisoned knights with men at arms.
Judges watch from a pavilion beneath the legend Deus est en vous. One knight offers his
sword for favour to a lady in the other stand.

Above: Ladies and gentlemen at ease in a garden. Music, poetry, birdsong, a chattering
fountain. Two lovers talk urgently in front of a locked door, to which the lady has a key.

Above: *St Mark as a monk in a* scriptorium. *His lion symbolises the resurrection. (A carved lion at the feet of a Crusader's effigy shows that the knight died for the holy cause.)*

Below: *Perceval arrives at the Grail Castle. The Maimed King presents him with the sword of the Dolorous Stroke. Inside, the Holy Grail and Sacred Lance are carried in procession towards the banqueting table.*

The hunt is up. The quarry sighted way off in the dark interior of the forest, dog-handlers let slip the chasing hounds. Horsemen rein back and swerve in pursuit.

heights than mere physicality; it has quelled appetite, yearning, even irrelevant thought:

> Their high feast was Love, who gilded all their joys; she brought them King Arthur's Round Table as homage and all its company a thousand times a day. What better food than Love could they have for body or soul? Man was there with Woman, Woman there with Man. What else should they need?

A Celtic echo audible here. In the ninth-century story of the Irish chieftain Finn mac Cumaill, Diarmaid is his trusted nephew and Grainne his young wife. Grainne is compelled by a magic spell to love Diarmaid, but he spurns her in loyalty to Finn. Grainne works another enchantment which forces Diarmaid to run away with her into the forest. Finn pursues the couple; but Diarmaid still refuses to make love to Grainne – he places a cold stone between her body and his when they sleep together. One day, as they are crossing a stream, muddy water splashes onto Grainne's leg. She taunts Diarmaid that the water is bolder than ever he is. This tart jest shames him and they become lovers. Their story must have had some influence on the Tristan and Isolde legend.

Eventually, after a brief time of escape and perfect communion, the lovers quit their forest hideaway. Tristan goes into exile in Brittany, where he meets another Isolde, her of the White Hands. He falls in love with her, but it is the name which bewitches him. Obsessed with the name Isolde, he adds this refrain to all the songs and airs he composes for the delight of the second Isolde:

> *Isolde my lady*
> *Isolde my lovely*
> *In you my breath*
> *Of life and death.*

Nevertheless, forswearing his undying constancy to Fair Isolde, Tristan marries Isolde of the White Hands. Just as they are going to bed, a ring that the first Isolde gave him slips from his finger and he recalls the full weight of his vow to her; and the second Isolde soon learns that she is to be unlucky:

> In bed, Isolde takes Tristan in her arms, kisses his lips and face; she presses her body against his, aching for the passionate love he will not share with her. Tristan, wanting to make love to her, yet does not want to make love to her. His natural desire draws him on; his mind says no. So, longing for Queen Isolde quenches his lust for this young Isolde.

This is yet another form of martyrdom. If the Church found Tristan's first passion acceptable only because it was the result of a love philtre, his denial of the second passion must have met with wholehearted approval.

Tristan falls ill. Near death he begs that a message be sent to Fair Isolde. If she agrees to come and salve his pain, let the ship hoist white sails to signal her coming. If she refuses, let the sails be black. The white-sailed ship heaves into view of the Brittany coast. Isolde of the White Hands brings the news to Tristan: the sails are black, she says. He dies.

Moralisers applaud: the final chaos in the shambles love causes – white made black, reason and order subverted, Truth and Purity undermined.

Isolde finds Tristan and her heart, at last, gives out. But let us leave them when their love is alive, urgent, inventive. In the late twelfth-century *Tristan's Madness*, Tristan seeks to win Isolde for himself from the King. Like Edgar in *King Lear*, he feigns madness:

'And what says the Wonder of the World?' said the king, laughing.

'I will swap you my sister for Iseut. You're tired of her – try another woman, a foreign woman. Give Iseut to me. I'll do it as a favour.'

The king laughed again. He said to the fool: 'And what would you do with her if I *did* give you the Queen? Where would you take her?'

'King,' said the fool, 'up there in the sky I've got a chamber all made of glass, wide and full of light. I live there. The sunshine teems in. Look, up there, it hangs from the clouds. Completely stable in any wind – it doesn't even rock. Next door is a chamber made of crystal panels. The dawn sun streams in . . . that's where I will take her.'

And, in a manner of speaking, that *is* where he takes her.

The tragedy of Tristan and Isolde undoubtedly inspired other stories in the romances such as those of Cligès and Fenice, Yvain and Laudine, Erec and Enide, in versions following Chrétien de Troyes: in the *Mabinogion*, for instance, where Erec and Enide reappear as Gereint and Enid. The story is not essentially changed; though here is evidence that while the mediaeval Welsh anthology celebrates the old oral tradition, it has also imitated a much later romantic literature. No comparable love stories exist in primitive Celtic lore.

Above all, the point to be emphasised is that Chrétien first and others following him, assert that *fin' amors* had its proper home at the court of Arthur the King. Even the French poets who boosted the rival claim to magnificence of Charlemagne acceded to Arthur the true sponsorship of courtesy.

. . . there be within this land but four lovers, that is Sir Lancelot du Lake and Queen Guenever, and Sir Tristram de Liones and Queen Isoud

Malory Book VIII chapter 31

In these stories are to be found the principal themes which informed all the romances and they demonstrate early tentative steps towards a first recognisable exploration in literature of the subconscious.

LOVE AT FIRST SIGHT

No love affair in the romances ever runs smoothly. The rules of Courtly Love are no match for the vicissitudes of real life and, for all their seeming artificiality, the romances are firmly rooted in actual experience.

In *Cligès*, the lovers Cligès and Fenice fall in love and then endure a familiar torment: Fenice has to marry someone else, Cligès' uncle. She, unlike Tristan's Isolde, refuses to enjoy sex with two men and satisfies her scruple casuistically, by administering a sleeping draught to her husband so that:

When he's asleep he thinks he is awake, holding me in his arms, taking whatever pleasure of me he wants. But I have kept him at arm's length.

Chrétien de Troyes, *Cligès* lines 5184–9

How ineffably cruel.

The subterfuge is allowable, though, for the love of Fenice and Cligès has been destined, prefigured in their stars. As soon as they meet they pledge hearts one to the other. He, 'more handsome than

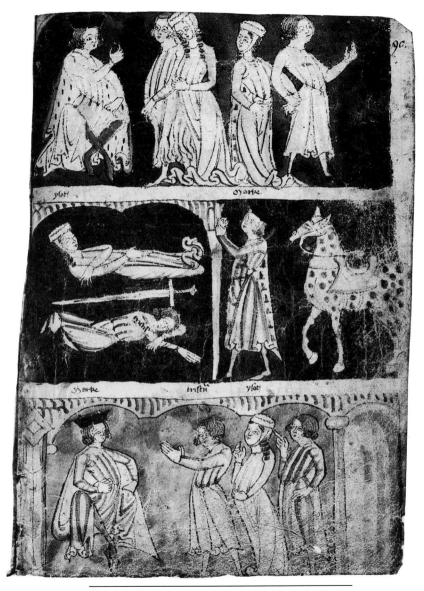

*Scenes from the romance of Tristan and Isolde: Fair Isolde of
Ireland is presented at King Mark's court in Cornwall; Isolde and
Tristan sleep in their forest hideaway; Mark peers in; Tristan is
banished.*

Narcissus . . . hair of fine gold, face like a freshly-opened rose'. Her beauty 'more radiant than four carbuncles lights up the entire hall'.

A mediaeval audience knew that physical beauty indicated noble character; and things haven't changed so much, here, either. Where else does so-called star quality come from? It certainly did not surprise Chrétien's listeners that the pair fell hopelessly in love. It would have amazed them if they hadn't. The fairy-tale marriage of prince and princess has ever been popular.

Arthur had fallen in love with the noble Guenever for her matchless beauty and later takes a fancy to Tristram's Isoud:

> 'Sir,' said Launcelot, 'yonder rideth the fairest
> lady of the world except your Queen'.
> 'Who is that?' said Arthur.
> 'It is Queen Isoud.'
> 'I will see her,' said the king.
> [Launcelot warns him of danger if they stray into
> the forest but the king will not be dissuaded.]
> Right so anon the king rode even to her, and
> saluted her and said, 'God you save'.
> 'Sir,' said she 'you are welcome.'
> Then the king beheld her and liked her wonderly
> well.
>
> Malory Book X chapter 73

LOVE-IN-IDLENESS

Having fallen in love, the lady and the knight were often overwhelmed by mutual self-absorption to such a degree that they slipped into total languor. Doing nothing; going nowhere; being always together, being only in love; thinking of naught but love. Disastrous, of course, for a knight whose reputation depends on feats of arms to go soppy: Chrétien's Erec

was so filled with love for Enide that he took no interest in fighting, went to no tournaments, had no enthusiasm for jousting. His days he spent in courtship of his wife, as if she were his beloved, his lover. He thought only of embracing her, kissing her, that was occupation enough. His fellow knights didn't think much of it; grumbled amongst themselves that this love-obsession of Erec's went too far.

> lines 2430–41

His men friends react badly; their bold lord has turned to womanly pursuits. As the fifteenth-century master huntsman Gaston Phebus warned:

> All sin springs from idleness; when a man is idle
> and stays in bed or chamber, he is drawn to
> fantasies of fleshly pleasure. Man's imaginings
> lean more readily to evil than good because of
> his three enemies: the world, the flesh and the
> devil.

A woman represented all three rolled into one.

Enide realises that her young husband's inaction brings shame on him and blames herself for it. Here is that moment recorded in the *Mabinogion* version of the same story; a stunning piece of writing:

> And one morning in the summer-time they were
> in bed, and he on the outer edge. And Enid was
> without sleep in a chamber of glass; and the sun
> shining on the bed; and the clothes had slipped
> from his breast and arms, and he was asleep. She
> looked upon the great beauty and majesty of the
> sight she saw in him, and said: 'Woe is me,' said
> she, 'if it is through me that these arms and this
> breast are losing fame and prowess as great as
> was theirs.'

Mabinogion, 'Gereint, Son of Erbin' (Everyman
p. 250)

Lovingly, Enide wakes her husband to confide her qualms. He at once rounds on her, scolding and rebuking her presumption. Then leaps out of bed and, abandoning love-drugged trance, hurls himself into the frantic stir of a fame-greedy knight. He spurns her, treats her as a servant, to be seen but not heard. Eventually, mild love pierces his self-righteous monomania and the couple are blissfully reconciled.

Love Spurned

Another hero, Yvain, does things the other way round. He is so utterly preoccupied with the relentless pursuit of glory and renown that he fails to register the love which is blossoming right under his nose, in the shape of the fair Laudine (who, incidentally, shows a much more sprightly reluctance to be toyed with and pushed around than the forbearing Enide).

After many adventures of knightly prowess, tests of manhood (always vis-à-vis other men), ardour, rebuff and misunderstanding, Yvain confesses his folly and beseeches love of the beauteous Laudine. She, having so far played a pretty cool hand, bestows it with all her heart.

> Now my lord Yvain finds contentment after all the anguish he has suffered. A perfect ending for him: to love and be loved, to cherish and be cherished by his lady.
>
> Chrétien de Troyes, **Yvain** lines 6789–95

Meditation on Love

At all times the lover must concentrate his mind on his beloved. This no more than reflects the intensity of love in its first heat when that's all you *can* think of. Indeed, so profound is Lancelot's musing upon

Guenever at one juncture, that he is attacked by enemies and buffeted for some time before he even offers resistance. In Chrétien's Grail story, *Perceval*, the hero sees a wild goose knocked out of the sky by a falcon one snowy winter's morning. It lays awhile on the ground and, from a wound in its neck, ooze three drops of blood. For Perceval:

> . . . the mingled blood and snow recalled the flush on his beloved's cheek. He lost himself in contemplation, rapt at the sight of those three crimson drops of blood on the white snow.
>
> lines 4199–206

In the *Mabinogion* version of the story, the wounded bird is a raven, thus adding the black of his lover's hair to Peredur's trancing.

Love Out Of Control

Love drives men to neglect their feudal obligations, women to forgo ease and contentment. The mediaeval context does not alter the timeless verity: love turns everything upside down, for good, for ill, perhaps for both. The Arthurian romances may seem, to modern taste, hopelessly fanciful, overwrought in every sense, incredible. Yet these tales of romantic bewitchment, emotional frenzy, painful excess, bewilderment, naïve credulity, above all reckless passion, no more than convey, in metaphor, the onslaught of love on men and women better inured to dumb restraint.

Men might know plenty about bloodlust, martial fury, the legacy of a centuries-old warrior tradition. The *chansons de geste* fed deep on that. Of the hot urges of their loins, the churning of their stomach, the tweak of their gonads, they acknowledged less. Women, for long accustomed to being lusted after, dumped, despised, accused of wiles and witchery and worse, now claimed a role closer to the crucial romantic exchange. In practical terms that meant love's duty seen as an extension of feudal obligation. Lord and vassal become lord (or lady) and lover.

However, when love got completely out of hand, as it most often did, the sexual equivalent of fighting madness, anything might and often did happen. To the hectic glory and pain of battle, therefore, is now matched the heartstopping glory and pain of love's rapture. That rapture defeats or overmasters sense. In Béroul's telling, Tristan is cornered but, in a desperate bid, manages to escape by making a crazy leap from a high ledge on a cliff to the jagged rocks dizzyingly far below at the sea's edge. The wind billows into his clothes as he plummets down and wafts him to safe landing. Love out of control, the perilous leap into the unknown, supreme risk . . . but Love Conquers All. And, is not the entire romance of Tristan and Isolde the story of love overcoming the safe control of reason and moderation?

Cynicism

In general, and probably by the encouragement of women and their poet mouthpieces, love was reckoned to exert an ennobling power on heart and soul. In some harder heads, though, love prompted a misogynistic cynicism. Sir Dinadan, a man of honour but a scoffer and a japer, rejects love altogether: 'Marry! [i.e. 'by St Mary!'] fie on that craft'. When Isoud reproves him, he replies:

'I marvel of Sir Tristram and more other lovers what aileth them to be so mad and so sotted upon women.'
'Why,' said La Beale Isoud, 'are ye a knight and be no lover? It is shame to you: wherefore ye may not be called a good knight but if ye make a quarrel for a lady.'

'God defend me,' said Dinadan, 'for the joy of love is too short, and the sorrow thereof, and what cometh thereof, dureth over long.'

Malory Book X chapter 56

There, I should guess, speaks a rueful Malory, languishing in gaol, his narrow bed empty.

The cynical view claimed unarguable proof to hand: the appalling damage love caused. From that view, given solemn authority by a celibate Church, came the impulse to convert the idolatry of Courtly Love into a cult of religious worship centred on the Blessed Virgin Mary, with pronounced emphasis on *Virgin*. As we have seen, the romances record the devotion of both Arthur and Charlemagne to her.

Passion

Sex was to blame for the tragic life and death of Tristan and Isolde; indeed, in the eyes of the Church, for almost everything else, too. And if sex was the crime, who could fail to point the accusing finger at the true culprit?

And when the woman saw that the tree was good for food, and that it was pleasant to the eyes, and a tree to be desired to make one wise, she took of the fruit thereof, and did eat, and gave also unto her husband with her; and he did eat.

Genesis 3 v. 6

That more or less sums up the case against women: voracious appetite (by inference sexual and therefore sinful); vanity − the fruit *looks* good; over-curious, malcontent, wilful; and, worst of all, seductive. Eve was a dangerous creature, quite as risky a prospect as the Queen of Elfinland who appears in disguise to trick and seduce the Good

Knight on the road. Amazing that so little bodily substance, one of Adam's ribs, could generate so much evil.

The immediate and lasting conclusion, however, came in the pithy Bible account. ' "Unto the woman" God said "I will greatly multiply thy sorrow and thy conception; in sorrow thou shalt bring forth children; and thy desire shall be to thy husband, and he shall rule over thee" '. There was the added fizz of enmity between the man and the woman and their seed forever; plus bruising of heads and heels.

In the *Quest of the Holy Grail* (early thirteenth century), ultimate spiritual triumph is denied those knights who have experienced – to couch the description of warm, connubial joy in chilly ecclesiastical language – carnal knowledge of woman. Only chaste Galahad, whose heart seems to pump holy water not blood, wings his ethereal way from Grail communion to celestial paradise. There were even troubadours who extolled the sexless virtue – it can hardly be called pleasure – of unfleshly adoration, the systematic killing of lust in *fin' amors*, pure, true love:

> *Ah, true love, font of goodness,*
> *Light of the whole world.*
> *Mercy! Give me no torment*
> *Of love-in-idleness.*
> *I am your prisoner for life*
> *And you my lasting consolation,*
> *In you my hope of guidance.*

> Marcabru (writing 1130–50)

Woman as whore rehabilitated as woman on a pedestal. So Robert Graves, in *Goodbye to All That*, records how he decided that only by staying a virgin before marriage would he survive the First World War massacre. Chastity: the perfect shield and talisman against death. Death, in Biblical terms, is Satan's province; Life, God's.

The great Cistercian reformer, St Bernard, will have approved. All monks were celibate and the Cistercians were more celibate than most. They preached mystic union with pure principle. The *Quest* shows marked Cistercian influence. St Bernard (1090–1153), supporter of the Crusades, had rounded on the wayward peoples of Provence, hotbed of Satanic ideas about love and lust, and the loose morality purveyed by the odious Infidel and celebrated – celebrated! – by supposedly *Christian* poets:

> The Churches are empty, the people are without priests; the priests do not have the respect due to them, Christians deny Christ and their Churches are like synagogues.

> St Bernard, ***Epistles*** (quoted Topsfield p. 266)

Sexual passion entailed loss of will and diminished control; and such moral irresponsibility exposed the Christian soul to the machinations of the Devil. For, what ensued when Lancelot and Guenever declared and acted on their mutual love? The destruction of Arthur's kingdom, no less.

What could be done? In response to the gratuitous titillation of libido by troubadours and their ilk, the Courtly Love crowd, the Cistercian White Monks pulled a masterstroke. They revived and promoted, with brilliant success, the Cult of the Blessed Virgin Mary. She, by her Immaculate (that is, asexual) Conception of Christ, offered redemption to womankind, eternally spotted with evil. Arthur, you will recall, bears the Virgin's image on his armour to shield him from injury.

Courtly Love offended Church tenets because of its promotion of adulterous attachments, even unfulfilled; and later romances show signs that pure love had become purged love. Worship of mortal woman, with all its snags and entanglements, its unbridled passions and avowals, was foreign to a pious contemplation of Holy redemption; Godhead *not* Maidenhead. Hitherto, romantic poetry had glowed with a quasi-religious ecstasy as in this description of Erec and Enide's wedding night:

> The thirsty hart does not so pant for the spring, nor hawk fly home to the wrist when it is hungry, as these two came greedily naked into each other's arms. That night they repaid themselves the hours they had lost. Alone in the bedchamber, each claimed, by right of love, every intimacy owed them. So much in love were they, the girl abandoned herself to passion; the pain of ecstasy made her cry out. In the morning, no longer virgin, she had become a woman.

Chrétien de Troyes, *Erec and Enide*
lines 2027–36

This quotes Psalm 42: 'As the hart panteth after the water brooks, so panteth my soul after thee, O God.' Now love poetry gave way to poetry of religious devotion which vibrated with subliminal passion. The Blessed Virgin, alone of women, had no smirch of bodily corruption (sex); she, alone of women, could inspire devotion, *fin' amors*. The knight abases himself before his lady . . . the pilgrim kneels at the Virgin's altar. This ruffled no clerical feathers and diverted man's unmentionable urges into proper service. No matter that to our eyes the erotic pulse remains strong. Religious verse had, on occasion, been frankly sensual, often composed by fanatics light-headed with hunger and in subliminal response to giddy torments of sexual frustration. Even writing of the purest devotion has a tender, wooing quality:

> *When I see on the cross*
> *Jesus my sweetheart*
> *Standing beside him*
> *Mary and John*
> *And his back torn*
> *And his side pierced*
> *For the love of man*
> *Well ought I weep*
> *And sin forsake*
> *If I of love can,*
> *If I of love can,*
> *If I of love can.*

On Rode Ihesu My Lemman (thirteenth century)

Chrétien de Troyes' telling of the Lancelot and Guenever story has a happy ending (the tragic upheaval seems to be a British/Welsh colour). His description of their lovemaking groans with religious imagery:

> Lancelot knew such joy, such pleasure the night long, that he could hardly bear the coming of day when he had to leave his lover's bed. Wrenching himself away was crucifixion. Torn with misery he bowed to her bed as if it were an altar, and left the room.

Chrétien de Troyes, *Lancelot* lines 4685–91

The enseamed bed as altar, Crusaders as pilgrims, lovers as martyrs. The insidious St Bernard had done a good job.

CHAPTER SIX

THE CELTIC WILDS

Sliabh gCua, haunt of wolves,
rugged and dark, the wind wails
about its glens, wolves howl round
its chasms; the fierce brown deer
bells in autumn around it, the crane
screams over its crags.

Irish **Anon.** (9th century?)

The historical Arthur had died just as the Roman Empire collapsed in fragments. The long stable world disintegrated. Germanic, barbarian tribes roared across the frontiers into Europe and replaced the city culture, or 'civilisation', of Rome with a Teutonic village and settlement culture: tribal kings in their great halls, sole dispensers of wealth, power, justice; an élite warrior class seated at their chief's board; a subject peasantry toiling in the lord's fields. Law regained a human dimension, with murder being punished by the fine of *wergild*, the price of a man, straight swap, in place of the abstract sophistication of Roman legal theory.

However, one part of Europe, a purely Celtic enclave, Ireland, never yielded to barbarian invasion. Indeed, it never suffered Roman invasion, either. Not armed invasion, that is. Priests and missionaries of the Roman church had come and been welcomed. They had set up churches and shrines, monasteries, libraries and religious colleges, *scriptoria* for the copying and illuminating of vast numbers of texts, sacred and profane. And when Rome fell and the Empire reverted to paganism, this one stronghold of faith and learning, art and culture, survived the onslaught of the unlettered, uncouth barbarian nomads in their land caravans, or sea-keels. Christian Europe owes much, in culture and spiritual influence, to Ireland, home of Finn mac Cumaill and Cuchulainn; to the primitive Celtic Church whose worshippers thought of Christ as a hero Messiah, not a hazy Pauline godhead tricked out in Greek theologico-philosophic enigma.

Celtic Ireland, together with other outposts of the old culture, Wales, Cornwall, the Strathclyde and Galloway region of Scotland, Brittany (Lesser Britain), clung on to vestiges of the Celtic world that had yielded to the Teutonic invaders. But it is Arthur of Britain (Greater Britain) before Guigomar of Brittany, Welsh Pwyll of Pryderi, or Fergus

The monk Gildas emphasises a point, lamenting the partition of Celtic Britain by the pagan barbarians and the burying of the old world under godless invasion.

macRoich, tutor to Cuchulainn, whom we recall most vividly. This is the Arthur of obscure beginnings mentioned in a north British heroic poem, the *Gododdin* (dated variously A.D. 600 or 900), about a hero who 'though he was not Arthur, glutted black ravens on the city's ramparts'. In other words, he slew a lot of men and left them corpses, raven food below the ramparts. There is, too, the earliest Arthurian romance in Welsh *Culhwch and Olwen*. Professor Jones, co-translator of the peerless Everyman *Mabinogion*, dates this to about 1100. Was this one of the tales which Geoffrey of Monmouth heard, either from a professional storyteller or the antiquarian cleric Walter Map? Very likely. In his chronicle of 99 kings of Britain, Geoffrey allots

between one fifth and one quarter of his narrative to Arthur, so the move towards the explosion of the Arthurian legend was under way. There were, I believe, two driving forces behind the awakening of Arthur's *European* as opposed to *British* fame, his transformation from Celtic warlord fighting barbarians of Teutonic blood to mediaeval king.

First, the self-publicising majesty of the Frank and Norman monarchs ruling in Europe from the twelfth century on. Second, the sheer compulsive brilliance of the old Celtic hero stories which provided the romancers with the framework of the newly shaped legend. The Celts themselves possessed qualities which the uncouth, arriviste Teutons admired and envied: glamour, panache, bigness, pre-eminent *style*, all of which added up to *Glory*. And if Arthur, in the tales, embodied one thing it was *Glory*.

So, once a locally known Celt, he re-awoke in the Crusading era as a mediaeval king in a mediaeval world, a Christian warrior prince taking on the forces of evil, irreligion and disorder. It is a commonplace of mediaeval art that all historical figures, no matter what their vintage – pre-Christian, ancient, contemporary – are depicted in current dress, current setting: Alexander the Great as a mediaeval knight, St Paul tramping the missionary road using a mediaeval hand-and-a-half sword as a walking stick, the mail-clad Greek army attacking Troy with mantlets, arbalests and mangonels, under pennons and gonfalons emblazoned with heraldic devices and colours. Mediaeval historical perspective stretched no further than the visible horizon.

So much is evident from the change Arthur himself undergoes: from Geoffrey's homespun, simple-hearted peer of Godfrey of Bouillon, first king of Jerusalem, to the highly cultivated, late mediaeval monarch who dominates the pages of Malory's *Morte d'Arthur*. He is the same king, undeniably, but one who has grown ever more sophisticated in the times' refinement.

The Middle Ages were interested in him primarily as an inspiration to the kings and princes who ruled and quarrelled over France and England. As his descendants, Arthur's supposed European empire boosted their own claims to greatness and leadership over the vast territories of dead Rome. In Arthur's spectacular triumphs and independence they saw reflected their own. Of his Celtic immortality they cared not a jot, except for the glamour it imparted to the story, the bloom it put on their own regality, the potency it lent their power.

Geoffrey's *Historia* achieved instant popularity, whether in French or the original Latin. The Matter of Britain rapidly outstripped the other two Matters, of France, of Troy, favoured by mediaeval writers. We may suppose that while most of them had read Geoffrey's book, few had met *Culhwch and Olwen,* except by hearsay.

Thus, Arthur's romance grew to immense popularity in the Crusading era and it has been the focal story of a nostalgic crusade ever since. Its appeal persists unchanged with men and women alike. The need for heroes does not tail off with the advent of democracy. Popular love of royalty and pageantry seems not to diminish. Nostalgia for a lost but promised-again glorious age lingers as deep in the human heart as ever. Love may go wrong, be inconstant, be less than what it might be, yet romance does not die. Arthur's legend supplies each of these needs and supplies them richly.

Saxon hero sagas and French *chansons de geste,* have, unluckily but, I think, inevitably, dwindled to become the fare of academic seminars, being too one-sided, too one-paced to attract a large, mixed audience today. But the same demerits ousted them in the twelfth century leaving the way clear for Arthurian romance. They were all war and clash of arms, noble death and unrelievedly male sodality.

The noted French historian Léon Gautier actually regrets the corrupt influence of the effeminate and effeminising Arthurian romance. I am convinced that the added dimension secured its survival by broadening scope, dramatic possibility and psychological subtlety.

The essential charm of the romance is what underlies all the best storytelling: enchantment, mystery, escapism. The Celts did not invent mystery but they certainly knew how to manipulate it along with the exploits of the immortal hero, the inspiration of love and honour. *There* is Arthur's Celtic origin, not the tracing back of incidents in his legend as told by Chrétien, Wolfram, Béroul, Gottfried and the anonymous others to details in the stories of the oral tradition, stock-in-trade from the Welsh and Breton *conteurs'* rattlebag. Arthur's sword Excalibur avouches a Celtic origin, being Welsh *Caledfwlch* (or *Caledbwlch*) to Latin *Caliburnus* to French *Excalibor*. Lancelot's name starts Celtic and ends up Breton; so, too, Guenever from Welsh *Gwenhwyfar*. Most of the names of Arthurian romance declare Celtic roots, but they may well have been chosen to give an exotic feel to the story. There is nothing like a sprinkling of esoteric nomenclature to lend a tale antiquity. The modern romancers, not always with much subtlety, are playing exactly the same literary game as their mediaeval forerunners. Besides, plenty of the more familiar episodes in Arthur's story can as easily be traced to Greek myth, to Hebrew prophecy, to Stone Age ritual, to early Christian mysticism.

What concerns us is storytelling, the 'once-upon-a-time' opening, narrative peppered with 'all of a sudden'. Giants and enchantresses and Castles Perilous, and magic.

STORYTELLING

All primitive societies esteemed their storytellers as

the purveyors and memorisers of tribal myths which explained human existence, natural phenomena, the character of the gods, their interference, benign or malign, in mortal affairs and so on. From the central myths radiated a huge and colourful assortment of lesser myths, what we call folklore; these lesser myths chart the development of society through change and growth and decay. Into these variations on the main themes – Life, Birth, Death – poets and bards poured their inventive power in successive generations. As their stories show, the Celtic inventive power was as rich as any. Their poets knew how to woo and tease the audience (*never* readers, note); to entrance them with fabulous detail and a welter of imaginative decoration, to excite their curiosity with magic and mystery, to keep them on tenterhooks, to delight them with a cleverly pitched interplay of tense action and lull. In sum, they told marvellous stories marvellously well. The survival of the stories proves it.

For example, in *Culhwch and Olwen*, the hero Culhwch is brought up humbly by a swineherd. His mother has lost her wits; but recovers them to give him warning that he will never marry ('thy side will never strike against woman') unless he wins Olwen, the beauteous daughter of the Chief Giant Ysbadadden. Culhwch goes to the court of Arthur, whom he discovers to be his first cousin, to beseech the king to grant him pursuit of Olwen as a boon. At court we hear of Arthur's warriors: of Cei and Bedwyr (Kay and Bedivere) and a galaxy of others, every one given individual stamp by name or title or attribute. So we learn of Morfran, of whom it is said 'no one placed his spear in him at Camlann, so exceedingly ugly was he; all thought he was a devil helping. There was hair on him like the hair of a stag' (*Mabinogion*, Everyman p. 102). Arthur grants Culhwch the quest and his adventures follow. At the heart of the story Ysbadadden unfurls a list of some forty tasks to which Culhwch must be equal if

he is to win Olwen. The list runs to such length partly because every time the Giant names a task, always the getting of some impossible object, Culhwch openly scoffs:

'It is easy for me to get that, though thou think it is not easy'.

The Giant thinks again and tops the previous imposition with a harder one: 'Though thou get that, there is that thou wilt not get'. And so it goes on. For the dressing of his beard the Giant requires the blood of the Black Witch from the uplands of Hell and the bottles of Gwyddolwyn the Dwarf to keep it warm. To shave his cheeks and chin he needs the sharp tusk of Ysgithyrwyn the Chief Boar. To groom his hair, the comb and scissors set between the ears of Twrch Trwyth, a king metamorphosed into a swine by God. And so on and so on. But Culhwch must also find a number of specialist hunters to aid him, including Mabon, the whereabouts of whose abode none knows but the oldest animal alive. Culhwch asks, in turn, an Ouzel, a Stag, an Owl, an Eagle. The Eagle does not know but says that the Salmon of Llyn Llyw does and explains:

> I went to seek my meat as far as Llyn Llyw, and
> when I came there I sank my claws into a salmon
> thinking he was meat for me many a long day,
> and he drew me down into the depths, so that it
> was with difficulty I got away from him.

The Eagle returns with all his kindred to kill the Salmon, but the fish offers parley. Now the Eagle will take Culhwch to his pool. So the story unfolds till, at last, Culhwch returns to marry Olwen. Of her the writer says:

> Neither the eye of the mewed hawk, nor the eye
> of the thrice-mewed falcon, not an eye was
> fairer than hers. Whiter were her breasts than

the breast of the white swan, redder were her cheeks than the reddest foxgloves. Whoso beheld her would be filled with love of her. Four white trefoils sprang up behind her wherever she went; and for that reason she was called Olwen.

Assigning a root for names in the Welsh stories is a common trick to fill out the mythic importance of the tale. Apparently the meaning 'White Track' for Olwen is 'charming but fanciful'.

The development of the French Arthurian romance is plainly enough signposted in *Culhwch and Olwen*. However, the crucial difference is that the Welsh story almost bursts at the seams with Druidic complexity and richness of mythical allusion. The rollcall of Arthur's warriors runs to several pages. The Chief Giant sets an unwieldy prolix memory-test of impossible tasks, only a few of which Culhwch fulfils. The reason for this may be that the tale need not always have been told in its entirety and the version we have amounts to a standard narrative aide mémoire from which the storyteller could pick and choose his detail. Nonetheless, the principle at work seems to be: never make do with one splash of colour where ten or twenty come to hand. The lyric descriptions might ring too fulsome to some ears, though not mine: of Culhwch setting out on a 'steed with light grey head, four winters old, with well-built fork, sheel-hoofed, and a gold tubular bridle bit in his mouth'. And of Olwen herself.

The French romancers wrote more sparingly, used the paintpot less extravagantly. They honed Celtic exorbitance to a narrower point, added deliberation on the mental state of hero and heroine, pared away the ebullient verbosity. The resulting stories are more focused, less headstrong, different. Remember, they had to compete with a large corpus of mythic stories currently purveyed by a powerful lobby, namely the Church. The romances needed a steadier pace than the Celtic hero adventure allowed for. The Celts loved a long hunt with false scents and trails, countless blind alleys, fabulous creatures popping out of the thickets, as it were, a brief second or two and then vanishing again. The complex riddling of their tales was not to twelfth-century north European taste. It may once have captivated listeners attuned to the solving of the riddles, the spotting of well-concealed allusions, but the riddles and allusions were lost.

It was the genius of the late twelfth-century French writers to sift through the crammed jewel-box of Celtic myth and lore, select the best stones and set them as brilliants against plainer narrative cloth of their own weaving, where the colours would stand out unmistakably. Marie de France's Breton *Lais* probably demonstrate this process best. Her language is terse, spare of excess, gemlike in clarity, yet it lacks no emotional bite for all its austerity.

Li reis Mark esteit coroucié,
Vers Tristran son neveu irié;
De sa terre le congëa
Pour la reine qu'il ama.
En sa countree en est alés;
En Suhtwales, où il fu nés,
Un an demoura tout entier,
Ne pot ariere repairier;
Mais puis se mist en abandon
De mort et de destruction.
Ne vous esmervelliez neant:
Car qui aime moult lealment,
Moult est dolent et trespensés
Quant il nen a ses volentés.

Le Lai de Chevrefeuil

King Mark was furious,
Enraged with his nephew Tristran
And exiled him from his land
Because he loved the Queen.
He returned to his own country,
South Wales where he'd been born,
And lived there a whole year,
Nor could he return.
But then he put himself at risk
Of death, of loss of everything.
Don't marvel at that. A true lover,
Robbed of what he loves best,
Endures grief and a leaden heart.

Honeysuckle lines 11 ff

Marie's short line, the same as that employed by virtually all her contemporaries, has a musical lilt, a hypnotic pulse. It discourages overlong sentences, enjoins swift narrative pace, lends itself ideally to the shrewd pitching of dramatic and psychological tension. The advent of pen and paper did not obviate the need of storytellers to keep their listeners on the edge of their seat. The writers of the twelfth century on still composed for an *audience*, but, unlike their Celtic predecessors, they wrote down the stories in a fixed version. Marie herself, in *Honeysuckle,* says that she has seen the story written down but, more significantly, has *heard* several versions of it. Thus, Chrétien's Arthurian romances were widely known and performed in *his* original telling by other poets and entertainers across Europe. *And* they were read in manuscript by other writers. Authorial celebrity swept aside the anonymity of the oral tradition.

The old Celtic tales had fulfilled two functions. They served the universal Celtic hero myth; they also served local variations of those myths by puffing the self-esteem and majesty of clan chiefs and kings. The storytellers could, and did, tailor their renderings to suit whichever of the countless circles of warriors they addressed. Imagine a teller of *Culhwch and Olwen* pointing the reference to ugly Morfran at a fighter in the fireside ring with pug nose, lumpish brow and coarse straggly hair. To elicit roars of sympathetic laughter from the others? (Ugly he may be but saved he will be.)

The Arthur story, by contrast, only remotely served the universal myth, now restricted dogmatically to Christian doctrine, by promoting Arthur as the Christian king *par excellence*. The local hero myth, pagan in origin, still clung fast but it had to be disguised. Myth, Classical Greek for 'word, fact', once had meant *truth*. The warriors who listened to hero stories listened to them as truth and claimed direct descent from the heroes named by storytellers whose names did not matter. When the Christian myth, in the form of the one God's truth, bundled pagan myth off into a penumbral world of fiction and folklore, authors achieved fame while they drew their heroes' names from a common pool of pseudonyms.

CELTIC HEROES

Celtic heroes owed their existence to the poets who talked or bribed their way past leery porters into the king's hall, there to regale the company with tales of grand exploit, the derring-do of champions.

Celtic heroes encounter giants and enchantresses and survive on their wits and physical strength, their charisma and energy. They love display and largesse. Once again, an example from a later epoch which might well apply to Celtic ethos – to demonstrate that the Celts do not have a monopoly on Arthurian manners. Here Charlemagne receives a peace offering from the Saracen King Marsilus. (See page 74 for another example of this Moor's open-handed generosity.)

There sits the king who holds sweet France.
White his beard, and all garlanded his head.
Handsome his body, his countenance proud.
No one seeking him need ask which is the king.
The messengers dismount and approach on foot
To greet him in love and goodwill . . .
'King Marsilus sends you this message.
He has studied deeply the laws of truce.
Of his having he wishes to give you
Bears and lions and coupled hounds,
Six hundred camels, a thousand hawks past moulting,
Four hundred pack mules laden with gold and silver . . .

La Chanson de Roland lines 116 ff

The Celts would have recognised at once that unmistakeably Moorish ostentation, that spanking generosity of a race which despised meanness in any shape or form. Lavish expenditure of wealth stemmed from rich-heartedness. It mimicked the gods, spendthrift in power and authority. As Arthur says, in *Culhwch and Olwen,* a romance which spans the strait between ancient Celtic lore and mediaeval legend:

We are noble men so long as we are resorted to. The greater the bounty we show, all the greater will be our nobility and our fame and our glory.

Mabinogion (Everyman p. 99)

The Celtic hero rejoices, too, in uncommon feats of acrobatic skill, dexterity, strength, agility. For him, life was for living to the draining-dry of the cup, and physical death a mere stepping-stone to immortal adventure in the Otherworld. Fear did not exist.

All of this sat very comfortably in the new teaching from even older sources than the tales of early saints.

Yea though I walk through the valley of the Shadow of Death I shall fear no evil, for thou art with me, thy rod and thy staff they comfort me.

Psalm 23 v. 4

I do not, by any means, discount the Celtic elements in the story: they enrich the enchantment with fascinating clues, subtle and false, with ambiguities and sidetracks, with trails that dwindle into nothing or open into wide forest clearings dappled with gold and green light. Put crudely: Christian allegory, more or less identifiable, is wrapped in several layers of vary-coloured Celtic tissue.

Chrétien de Troyes' audience were familiar with the Celtic tissue from the stories told by Breton storytellers: the chevalier werewolf of the Breton forests; the foundling twin girl who eventually marries her noble love; the swan, carrier of secret messages between two lovers; the knight who visits his imprisoned lady in the guise of a hawk, recalling the hero of Welsh legend, 'swift in battle, sharp-thoughted as a falcon'. But when they heard *these* words, from Chrétien's *Perceval*, they will not have cast it in any context but Christian. For the mediaeval era suffered blights of famine, plague and the like, all of which the suffering populace imputed to the wrath of the Christian God:

Perceval's mother tells him: 'Malice, ignobility, fecklessness can never be uprooted from the world, but goodness can wither away. Your father, unbeknownst to you, was maimed by a wound in his thigh. Once a nobleman, he fell into abject poverty. His great estates, his vast wealth were lost and destroyed. After the death of good King Arthur's father, Uther Pendragon, men of rank were unjustly impoverished, robbed of their inheritance, made destitute. Their estates went to ruin, their poor vassals reduced to beggary. Those who could fly the country did so.'

lines 432–49

So, then, a brief sketch of certain key elements in Celtic myth which feature most prominently in Arthurian romance and in the central Arthurian mystery, the quest for the Holy Grail.

THE HERO

All legend begins with the hero and he must be comely and godlike in stature. Here Deirdre laments the death of her lover Noísiu, one of ancient Ulster's heroes, treacherously murdered by his fellow Ulsterman Eoghan. Like Perceval's lady in Chrétien's telling, Noísiu's hair is raven black, his cheeks red as blood, his body white as snow:

A wave the sound of Noísiu's voice —
his singing was ever sweet . . .
Noísiu's grave has now been made
and the accompaniment was mournful.

For him I poured out — hero of heroes,
the deadly drink that killed him.

Dear his short shining hair
a handsome man, even very beautiful;

Dear the grey eyes that women loved;
fierce they were to foes.

The Exile of the Sons of Uisliu, quoted in early
Irish Myths & Sagas (p. 264)

The Celtic warrior lived for a glorious death. That destiny impelled the Gauls fearlessly and hopelessly onto the sharp, stabbing swordpoints of the tightly disciplined Roman armies in bloody droves. Death

Culhwch's battle-axe 'would draw blood from the wind'. Here, two Irishmen fight with the Celtic axe whose shape is reminiscent of the executioner's axe in the Tower of London.

marked a passage between this world and the next, where life would continue, but in the unbroken company of other heroes. The time would pass, without the going-down of suns, in eating, drinking, song and carousal – a post-battle feasting to end all such banquets.

THE CROSSING OF WATER

Life's journey had its several metaphors; perhaps the most obvious being that of the hero stepping aboard a rudderless ship, ready to embark across wild seas of untold peril, incalculable reward and magical experience to the island shores of the Land of Joy:

. . . an island far away, round which the sea-
horses glisten, flowing on their white course

120

against its shining shore; four pillars support it.
It is a delight to the eye, the plain which the
hosts frequent in triumphant ranks; coracle races
against chariot in the plain south of Findargad.

Irish, 7th or 8th century

The crossing of water figured large in the legends of
the island Celts. They were, by and large, *not*
seafaring folk. The ocean didn't tempt them: better
the perils you half knew than the perils you didn't
know at all. They were horsemen, forest hunters,
mountain rangers. They fished the inland freshwater streams rather than pursuing squamous,
brine-swilling, finny creatures. It was as much a
matter of their own temperament as that of the
vile-mooded, flint-backed seas which thundered in
relentlessly on their beaches – Irish Sea, North Sea,
Channel each one notoriously unpredictable and
cold. At least the Mediterranean is warm.

The Celts took to long-distance boats comparatively late, and then with no great enthusiasm,
preferring short hops, inlet to inlet, across to
islands and back. Their Roman masters had learnt
the nautical skill recently, too, and then only as a
necessary aid to conquest. Fighting was properly
done on land. The invading Saxons, master seamen,
confirmed the Celts in their hydrophobia: the
watery domain for low-caste, barbarous pirates *not*
warriors of honour. The Saxons yielded to that
opinion as they assimilated with the native Britons
and settled to farming and combat on *terra firma*. So,
when a new seaborne menace threatened, in the
shape of the terrible Norsemen, the landlubbers of
Britain, Celt and Saxon alike, had to relearn
forgotten seacraft to carry the fight against the
latest marauders in the watery element.

However, to no more than a perverse few of the
original Britons, the salt tang of the sea occasioned
dread. And the rivers which wound like ribbons of
molten silver into the heart of their green land were
to them as moats, cutting off smaller islands within
the bigger island. Some of the rivers, Severn, for
instance, were even broad enough at the estuary to
be called seas, debouching into the greater sea.
Lakes were landlocked seas.

Water was an enchanted element. When the
Welsh Celts did at last see Norway, home of the
sea-wolves, they called it Llychlyn, 'the land
beneath the Waves', its rocky mass drenched in
tumbling streams and snow. All places of enchantment were circled by water; all places circled by
water were enchanted. A bridge was a rare thing –
only the godless Romans could build bridges. You
had to rely for a bridge on the company of one such
as Osla Big-knife:

> . . . who bore Bronllafn Short-broad. When
> Arthur and his hosts came to a torrent's edge, a
> narrow place on the water would be sought and
> Osla's knife in its sheath laid across the torrent.
> That would be bridge enough for the hosts of
> the Island of Britain and its three adjacent
> islands with their spoil.

Mabinogion (Everyman p. 104)

Giants threw chunks of mountain into the flood to
make a causeway of stepping stones. The best a
mortal could hope for is a ford, where the river
water thins out over rocks and pebbles.

Even here, danger haunts the crossing: Cuchulainn sees a young woman of noble figure wrapped
in garments of many colours coming towards him.
She offers him help. He, knowing who she is,
rebuffs her: 'It wasn't for a woman's backside I took
on this ordeal.' (He is defending Ulster against the
men of Connaught, whose aim it is to carry off the
great brown bull of Cooley.) The young woman
snaps back:

'Then I'll hinder. When you are busiest in the fight I'll come against you. I'll get under your feet in the shape of an eel and trip you in the ford.'

'That is easier to believe,' says Cuchulainn. 'You are no king's daughter; but I'll catch and crack your eel's ribs with my toes and you'll carry that mark for ever unless I lift it from you with a blessing.'

'The Cattle Raid of Cooley' trans. Thomas
Kinsella (*The Tain* p. 133)

The woman is none other than the Morrigan, the Irish goddess of Death, 'big-mouthed, swarthy, swift, sooty, lame, with a cast in her left eye'. Also, one should add, adept at disguising herself from all but the most percipient mortals. She often assumed the form of a croaking raven. Her Welsh counterpart, Morgan, came from water, too, as her name suggests: Welsh *Mor-gen* means 'Sea-born'. And of water, in any shape or form, beware, as King Ruadh of Munster knew to his cost:

His fleet became stuck fast from below in the midst of the ocean, and there was no wealth nor treasure thrown into the sea which would set it free.

Irish, Anonymous 8th – 9th century

They consult what to do, and it is decided that one of them must go under the waves to find out the obstruction. The lot falls on King Ruadh who, for the saving of his people:

. . . leaped into the sea and was covered by the waters immediately. He arrived in a great plain, and there he came upon nine lovely women. They confessed it was they who had held up his ships, so that he should come to them. And they offered him nine golden vessels in return for sleeping with them, each one a night. He did so!

In the same way, the matchlessly brave warriors of Connaught plunge below the lake waters to help Fiachna, one of the faery folk, rescue his wife from the evil King Goll and his armies. Beowulf, the Saxon hero, dives down to a submarine cave to fight Grendel and Grendel's mother.

It should be noted that these terrors and the heroic front needed to face and overcome them were the preserve of an aristocratic élite. Only the blood of Irish noblemen chilled at the eldritch wail of the banshee: lowly men did not even hear her. This hideous creature, with a single nostril, one protruding front tooth, long straggly hair and webbed feet, stands in the river washing the clothes of a man fated to die. Constant weeping rims her eyes fiery red. If a mortal man captures her she must divulge the name of the doomed man and grant three wishes besides. In Scotland, however, she was not so fussy about rank or status, but raised her unholy siren under every roof eave, rich and poor alike. She was, like the antichristian Satan, wholly democratic.

The perilous crossing of water features large in Arthurian romance, from the Sword Bridges negotiated by Perceval and Lancelot to the ford where Sir Gareth (alias Sir Beaumains) faces an early trial of his knighthood:

. . . [they] rode on their way until they came to a great forest. And there was a great river and but one passage, and there were ready two knights on the farther side to let [forbid] them the passage.

'What sayest thou,' said the damsel, 'wilt thou match yonder knights or turn again?'

'Nay,' said Sir Beaumains [Gareth], 'I will not turn again and they were six more'.

And therewithal he rushed into the water, and in midst of the water either brake their spears upon other to their hands, and then they drew their swords, and smote eagerly at other. And at the last Sir Beaumains smote the other upon the helm that his head stonied, and therewithal he fell down in the water, and there was he drowned.

Malory Book VII chapter 6

The dangerous passage need not always be of water itself but of what looks like water: an open green dell or glade in the dark forest, what Malory's English calls a *laund*. Gareth/Beaumains again:

And they came to a black laund; and there was a black hawthorn, and thereon hung a black banner, and on the other side there hung a black shield, and by it stood a black spear great and long, and a great black horse covered with silk, and a black stone fast by.

Malory Book VII chapter 6

The Celts knew all about such obstacles and their real and mythical import. Their storytellers are very matter of fact about physical danger because it was no more than a preliminary to heroic endeavour and blissful reward. The knights of Arthurian legend ride out into a less certain world. The evil Giants and Otherworld enchantresses have become minions of one sole master: the Devil. He is as imaginative, as sly and as chameleon-like as the priests and Christian apologists in the ferment of their fear and hostility could make him. But this dark and threatening Evil One lurked *everywhere*,

---

A Celtic horseman before the advent of stirrups. The simple elegance of the drawing emphasises the relaxed nobility of rider, the grace and mettle of his leanly muscled steed.

not only in passages of water. The romance story-tellers reflect that permanent menace with the now familiar narrative trick, the cliffhanger. Knight rides into heavily silent glade; black armour hanging on black thorn tree and . . . end of chapter, to be continued.

THE SEA-GOD'S PALACE

He rode until he saw a strong, well-sited fortress with nothing outside its walls but sea and stretches of water and wasteland.

Chrétien de Troyes, *Perceval* lines 1706–9

The Arthurian romance fills out the rather bare portrait of the sea-girt fortress given in the Welsh tale:

Bendigeidfran, son of Llŷr, was crowned king over this island and exalted with the crown of London. And one afternoon he was at Harddlech in Ardudwy, at a court of his. And they were seated upon the rock of Harddlech overlooking the sea.

Mabinogion (Everyman p. 25)

Harddlech is Harlech, site of a very ancient fortress half a mile from the sea. It was rebuilt in the tenth century and used, finally, by Edward I after his subjugation of Wales (1284–5) for the site of the present castle. The first Prince of Wales assumed power in 1301.

Brân's own fortress loomed high over the river Dee at the northern end of the Vale of Llangollen. He may also have had a palace on a steep-sided mound at the end of a sea-lapped causeway, like St Michael's Mount off the coast of Cornwall or Mont St Michel off the Normandy coast. Or else sub-

merged below the waves, an Atlantis, a Llychlyn, a Caer Siddi 'Castle of Glass'. But, when Dinas Brân poked up out of an encircling swirl of mist or, on a winter's morning, its sides white with hoar frost, twinkling like crystal in the sunshine, it did indeed appear to be heaving up from under the god's liquid element.

At the sea's edge, the Celtic hero might stand when the sea god rides abroad in his *currach*, the Wave-Sweeper:

It is not peaceful, but a wild troubled sleep, with feverish triumph, with furious strife; the swan's hue covers the waves, the plain full of sea-beasts and its denizens; the hair of the wife of Manannán, the sea god, is tossed about.

Irish 11th century

FISH

Brân the Blessed (which is a Christian title tacked onto a pagan name) started life as a sea god. Later – probably because the Celts learned to hate the sea more than ever before as giving roads to the murdering, rapacious Saxons and their ilk in the wooden-keeled Wave-Cutters – Brân shifted quarters to the rivers and became a fisherman.

Fish exercised a peculiar fascination long before eating them from religious duty helped spin out supplies of meat, especially during the lean forty days of Lent at winter's end. Fish had no obvious means of propulsion; they could breathe underwater and live where no other creature could; they seemed to be made of something akin to silver; above all they inhabited the enchanted element. The peerless salmon attracted the Celts most. Against all the rules it leaps upstream to its spawning ground – remember Cuchulainn's Salmon Leap? It was a strong creature, handsome, audacious and cunning: the very image of a Celtic warrior. And one salmon in particular led the rest: the Salmon of Knowledge, lurking in the dark pool beside which grew a hazel, tree of poetic wisdom. The salmon eats the nuts – tight-packed fruit, symbolic of understanding – as they fall into the water. They give him the blemishes on his silver back and endow him with superior wisdom and cunning to evade capture in the shadowy, underwater pockets. The story goes that Finn MaCumail was apprenticed to a teacher who had tried to catch the salmon on many occasions over seven years. At last he succeeded and put the fish to cook. He left Finn in charge. Not to beat about the bush, or as they say with telling wisdom, 'to put it in a nutshell', the boy turned the fish in the pan. As he did so, he burned his thumb on the hot flesh of the salmon and quickly, to cool it, sucked the place and instantly knew everything there was to be known. The poetic wisdom of the fish had gone into him.

THE MAIMED KING

The laming of blacksmiths has already been noted (see chapter 4). A recently discovered corpse in a Cheshire peat bog, dated to between A.D.. 50 and 100, seems to prove that the Celts also carried out ritual murder of high-born members of the tribe to propitiate the gods. The illustrious gold neck torc of this victim marks him out as an aristocrat, along with other rich votive offerings found alongside his body, which has, apparently, endured a triple dealing of blows before being pole-axed, and then garotted; the jugular vein has been neatly cut open, to catch the blood in a cauldron. Finally, the dead body was ceremonially drowned in the lake.

The Roman poet Lucan records (in *Pharsalia*) that the Celts performed a sacrificial drowning, in honour of the god Teutates, by plunging the victim headlong into a cauldron filled with liquid – possibly with the Celts' favourite tipple, ale.

Teutates, God of the People, may well have originally been one of the legendary conquerors of Ireland, Tuatha Techmar. In any event, the noble Celt dredged out of Lindow Moss near Wilmslow departed early on his journey to the Celtic Otherworld, there to placate the high trinity: Taranis, god of Thunder, Esus, Lord of All, and Teutates, in an effort to remove the scourge of the Roman conquerors from Britain.

There runs an obvious parallel between the sacrificial killing or wounding of princes in Celtic rite and Jesus' stigmata and Crucifixion which lie at the very core of Christian myth. Washed in the blood of the Lamb . . . I am the Lamb of God slain for thee . . . He died that all might be saved . . . and so on. Jesus may well have been of aristocratic, even princely, Jewish birth, of similar rank to the noble Celt murdered to appease malign gods. However, St Paul applied the abstractions of Greek philosophical thought to the original myth and Christ emerged in Christian theology as a hero for *all* ranks of men *and* women. He promises salvation on no proviso of exalted birth, but only on belief in his divine power and the ultimate sacrifice of universal love. His Crucifixion is the sacrificial murder to end all sacrificial murder, though it *does* encourage, even demand, sacrifice of one sort or another in imitation.

The early Celtic Church contrarily preferred Christ's heroic, noble aspect, in keeping with popular taste which has rarely ever been for philosophical abstractions, Greek or otherwise. The mediaeval romances celebrate heroic endeavour and noble sacrifice, too, both the preserve of the high-born. The Code of Chivalry may invoke comparison with the heroic love of Christ for mankind, but it is *not* wholly philanthropic. When the Crusaders made what came to be known as the supreme sacrifice, they did it for glory of one kind or another; dying in the sign of the Cross reflected well on them before it saved anyone else.

Galahad approached the Grail and looked into it. As he beheld the mysteries revealed, he trembled violently from head to foot. Lifting his arms to heaven he said: 'Lord God, I worship you and give thanks that you have fulfilled my great desire to see what none could speak of, none imagine. The Grail is the source of fearless courage, of all our striving; it is the miracle surpassing all other miracles. By your power I have laid eyes on it and achieved the crown of my earthly wishes. I pray that you take me now from this life to life eternal.'

   . . . In the very instant of Galahad's death, Bors and Perceval witnessed a great wonder. They saw a disembodied hand come down from the sky and take the vessel and the lance up into heaven. Since that time, no man has ever dared say he saw the Holy Grail.

Quest of the Holy Grail, chapter 15

The lance, so vital a relic to the Crusaders of the First Crusade, recalls the many heroic weapons celebrated in Celtic myth. The sword and lance of the Grail Quest may well be phallic, symbolising male potency. Equally, they signify the main strength of pagan kings and chiefs whose earthly power depended on victory in battle, just as, for Christian knights, the securing of Christ's kingdom on earth rested on the taking of his Holy City, Jerusalem.

The Celtic hero Brân is also connected with a lance and a city. In the *Mabinogion* tale of *Branwen* daughter of Llŷr, Brân leads an army to fight in England. The victory cost them cruel, though, and Brân himself is wounded in the foot by a poisoned spear. He orders his men to cut off his head, carry it to London and there bury it on the White Mount with its face towards France. He promises them that 'the head will be as pleasant company to you as when it was at best when it was on me'. They bury it as he commanded, on the site chosen by William the Conqueror for his great Tower.

Brân means raven, hence the tradition about the ravens at the Tower of London: if they fly away England is doomed. The Celts took the skulls of beaten enemies – only the leaders', probably, and decorated them with gold or silver for use as cups for libation to the gods. This grisly practice had to do with draining out and imbibing the virtue of their foes. Brân's severed head retains his living virtue; and in that sense is like any holy relic. Except that his followers bury it, they do not worship it.

Elements of Brân's story resurface in Arthur's. For instance, the wounding in the foot with a poisoned spear. Several accounts of Arthur's last battle state that the fighting begins when an adder bites one of the knights in the foot. He draws his sword to kill it, the blade flashes in the sun and both sides, taking it for a signal, attack. And, as to the burying of the head, an old Welsh poem records that Arthur discloses the hiding place of Brân's head because he will have no one save the kingdom but himself, therefore better it be destroyed with him. But Arthur here also stands for the new king declaring the power of the old king defunct, just as the mediaeval romance pushes the old Celtic myth back into the primitive, pagan shade.

PLAGUE LEAVES THE LAND WASTE

After the burying of Brân's head, 'In Ireland no person was left alive save five pregnant women in the Irish wilderness'. Primitive fears of crop failure, stalking hunger, barren soil, ruinous wind, storm and flood, dogged a society wholly dependent on

To modern eyes, mediaeval illustration often has a nursery book aspect. But these two baby dragons fighting in the margin of a devotional book were reckoned to be the very embodiment of evil power.

the caprices of Nature for survival. The long, sterile winter months emptied provision stores; nor could the harvest be hurried along – a late season could prove calamitous. Infertility would fill the people's mouths and stomachs with dust. The seed quickening in womb or earth drew on a vital magic which fused green into the blackened shoots, irrigated the Waste Land. For this Waste Land was no poetic fiction but a dreaded possibility, a visitation of angry god and goddess: the Morrigan croaking death at them all from the withered branches.

The Welsh story of Lludd, legendary founder of London (Caer Ludd, then, by false etymology, Caer Lundein), records the fate which befell the land after his death:

1. The first plague: an invasion by the Coranieid against whom no plan could be laid because any whisper that met the wind blew into their ears.
2. The second plague: a scream raised over every hearth in Britain at May-eve. Men lost their hue and strength by it, and women miscarried, and young men and maidens went mad, and all animals and trees and the earth and the waters were left barren.
3. The third plague: however much food and drink was laid up in the king's court, even provision for a whole year, after the first night's feasting none would be left.

This should not be written off as exorbitant show of grief for the loss of a great king. His health was intimately bound up with that of his folk; in his power lay theirs.

Stories of dragons, those visitants from the subterranean, dark caverns, devastating the land of the upper world, scorching it black with fire, and blanking out its sun, are familiar. The dragon (see chapter 8), 'red in tooth and claw', embodies every most violent and cruel aspect of Nature. Familiar, too, is the offering of a virgin girl, her womb a fruit unpeeled, to propitiate the monster, and her rescue, at the stroke of doom, by a young hero. The origin lies in primal fear of famine; and fructification rituals, where men and women copulated in furrowed fields to stimulate, and simulate, fertility in the earth. And who, roving the green land in spring or summer could mistake the voluptuous form of her mounds and valleys, the thick-forested clefts and hollows, as any but that of a sprawling woman, her womb the dark cave where life grumbles awake?

In winter she is an ugly hag, of bleak and wretched aspect. But when she couples with the sungod, the hero of Celtic myth, in springtime, she is transformed into the lovely maiden celebrated as Eriu in Irish legend:

> . . .her fragrance like an odorous herb garden,
> her countenance blooming in hue like the
> crimson lichen of Leinster crags, her locks like
> Bregon's buttercups; a mantle of matchless green
> about her.

The Hero Promises Life

The hero, or sun, is the being who ensures the continuation of life by his vanquishing of Death. Put another way, by his union with winter. For the Celtic hero, life stretched into immortality; his glory did not perish but, like the sun he imitates in his splendour of courage, rose day after day into eternity. Christ made similar promises to *all* who followed His way, not just the heroes. The Celtic promise of deathlessness explains the story, in *Branwen Daughter of Llŷr*, of Brân's cauldron of rebirth and recalls the ritual drowning in Teutates' cauldron.

The Irish warriors in the tale cast their dead into the cauldron; they arise next day 'as good fighting men as before', except that they cannot speak. In fact, they have passed on to commence the second part of their life beyond death; this explains their silence.

According to an early Welsh writing, one of the Thirteen Treasures of the Island of Britain is the Horn of Brân: it gave whatever food and drink the owner asked for. Other similar miraculous vessels 'would not serve a coward'. The cauldron of Diwrnach the Irishman, which Culhwch is set to find by Ysbaddaden, will never boil the meat of a coward though it will boil a hero's meat quickly enough. And Diwrnach says of it, in terms similar to those used by Galahad of the Holy Grail, 'God knows, though he [Arthur] should be the better for one glimpse of it, he should not have it' (*Mabinogion* p. 130). Other myths talk of miraculous vessels. Greek myth, for instance, has the horn of the Cretan goat-nymph Amaltheia, which becomes the Cornucopia, or Horn of Plenty. The goats of Crete sprout very large horns.

Death As Initiation

The rewarded Celtic hero crosses the watery strait dividing life's mortal phase to immortality. He traverses the Bridge of Dread no broader than a thread. This marks an initiation into timeless memory, a metaphor that was soon Christianised.

The Irish monk Brendan, roughly contemporaneous with Arthur and whose name sounds an intriguing echo with that of Brân, writes of a voyage to an island where there is no need of food or drink, nor of clothing, nor even sleep for it is daylight perpetually, dusk and darkness being unknown. (A yearly occurrence in Orkney, Hebrides and Shetland, in high summer, of course.) A river divides this island in two. There is but one season – autumn. The fruit is ever-ripe, the crops full-eared.

The Welsh Celts called their Paradise *Annwn* or *Annwfn*, Otherworld. The journey to it across mountain top, into misty valley, through ferny wood, might entail an encounter with the Lord of the Otherworld, Arawn, whose name means Eloquence. Pwyll, Prince of Dyffed, meets him one day, out hunting a stag; the stag is Pwyll's soul. Arawn is mounted on his big, dapple-grey steed (Death's pale horse?) with his distinctive pack of hounds:

> the colour that was on them was a shining white and their ears red; and as the exceeding whiteness of the dogs glittered, so glittered the exceeding redness of their ears.

(Whenever an animal in the romances has red ears, it comes from the Underworld.) Arawn invites Pwyll to take his place in Arawn for a year while he takes Pwyll's own place in Dyffed. The bargain is struck. At the end of the year, Pwyll returns to his domain and asks the gentles of the land how his rule had been over them during the past year, compared with what it had been before that.

> 'Lord,' said they, 'never was thy discernment so marked; never wast thou so lovable a man thyself; never wast thou so free in spending thy goods; never was thy rule better than during this year.'

Mabinogion (Everyman p. 8)

Death, it seemed, liberated a man from *all* meanness of spirit as well as from the travails of daily existence.

The mediaeval romances gathered in handfuls of loose threads from earlier myth and wove them into the synthesis on which modern European literature is based. The Church supervised that process closely. Its principal concern was to dilute the claims of the old tribal myths on the new religion. For example, the Christian Crusader knights began to claim a rank and status on a par with the hero status of the old Celtic warrior aristocracy. The Templar knights certainly thought of themselves as reincarnations of the nobility from which the Merovingian priest kings had sprung. As we have seen, the Teutonic Merovingians cast their eyes enviously backwards to the Celtic fighting élite for similar reasons: pedigree, heroic stature.

Christian theologians, like St Bernard and St Thomas Aquinas, employed philosophical abstraction to win the intellectual *and* historical argument in favour of a Church with supreme authority over *everyone*, kings included. In such a scheme there was no room for a separate élite, except one given Church blessing. Hence *all* the romances labour the point that the Knights of the Round Table fight in the name of Christ, first and foremost, their allegiance to Arthur the King merely an extension of that pious duty. The Crusader, then, looked forward to life after death but it would be in Paradise open freely to all ranks of the faithful army. The military élite of the old myth had insisted on hero status. The new, Church-dominated, order could not accommodate heroes except as officially canonised saints.

Nonetheless, the old dream of glory persisted and with it the notion that somehow courage, as well as pure faith in Christ, transcended Death. Galahad embodied a subtle combination of faith *and* courage, but the story, here, begins to drift into mysticism. The short but glorious life of the Celtic hero, the Greek Achilles, the young Crusader knight, commended itself to many of the Christian knights who swore Death before Dishonour. So, inevitably, we are drawn back to the ideal of the hero, that demigod, fêted by the Immortal gods. Is not Christ's triumphant glory a version of that? The Celtic hero personified the superhuman quality requisite for the ultimate initiation, the achieving of legendary glory. Christian knights had their own ceremonies: the ritual dubbing, the mystery of entry into the order of Templars (the so-called Little Death), and the veneration of holy relics, lance and True Cross.

The gods of the early Irish pantheon, as of any primitive society, were gods of vegetation and increase; 'Lords and Masters of Life' as they were called. They warmed the earth back to life each year at Springtide; they had power to restore slain warriors to life through the magical properties of their treasures: cup (or drinking horn), lance, sword, stone (or blacksmith's anvil). These items appear in Christian symbolism, too: as chalice of Communion, Crusader's sword, Holy Lance and altar.

The Christian Church could not so easily spiritualise the old initiation myth where Death marked an ordeal to be undergone, eyes open, mind alert to the terrors of the passage between Life and Immortality. St Paul's Greek abstraction separated body from soul, an idea stolen from Pythagoras. At death, Paul insisted, the pure Christian soul flies clear of the body's corrupt matter. The Celts would have found such a proposition inimical, hateful. Their heroes, like the princes of old Egypt and the Etruscan aristocrats, made their journey from Life to Death body and soul intact.

For a while the Church fudged the issue and dressed up the pagan narrative in its own lendings. One early legend, derived from eastern source material, recounts the adventures of a hero, Fortunatus (Lucky). He makes the descent into a mysterious cave in Lough Derg in Ireland known as St Patrick's Purgatory, the Celtic Otherworld by any other name. A late twelfth-century Benedictine monk, one Henry of Saltrey, wrote a story of another visit which gained wide enough currency within a very short time to be translated by the Breton poet, Marie de France. One element is changed in these late versions. Instead of a horn of plenty to aid him in his travels, Fortunatus has an inexhaustible purse and a cap which grants wishes.

After the initiation into Death's mystery came acceptance as a hero, the truest assay of prowess under the eye of the gods. Now would follow the eternity of carousal and celebration in the halls of the Otherworld.

An Irish tale, dating from the middle of the twelfth century, tells how one of the ancient Irish heroes Caílte leads the Fenians, or Fianna, great Finn's band of warriors, on a journey during which they come by chance on a faery palace in Connaught; the Otherworld, of course.

They are invited to enter by Fergus Fairhair, son of the great god Dagda. Caílte sits in a crystal chair and gazes round. He sees twenty-eight warriors on one side of the house with a lovely, fairheaded woman beside everyman of them, and six gentle, youthful yellow-haired girls on the other side of the house. Fergus asks Caílte to repair a broken sword which the Tuath Dé Danaan, the chief Irish gods, had refused to mend. Caílte takes a day at the task (here we have the sword-furbishing skill in action again), and also mends a spear and a javelin. Then Caílte hears that these are weapons fated to slay, each one, an enemy of the Irish gods; and declares that it is *his* destiny to perform some deed to make those very gods and their people grateful. Caílte and his companions proceed to another faery palace where they are entertained by beautiful women. The Tuath Dé Danaan's enemies attack (summoned by the beautiful women, no doubt) and Caílte slays the King of Norway in the ensuing battle with the mended spear. The weapon becomes an emblem of the warrior's valour; break the sword, break the man, as in the ceremonial breaking of a sword in the act of surrender, and the disgracing of an army officer, Dreyfus, for example. In the *Quest*, Galahad mends the Broken Sword which wounded Joseph of Arimathea.

Another hero of Ireland, Lugh of the Long Arm, sends the three sons of Turenn, Brian, Iuchar and Iucharba, to fetch the talismanic spear of Pisear. (Some scholars reckon Pisear to be the same as Pecheoir, that is Fisherman.) They fight their way into King Pisear's palace and find the spear 'with its head deep down in a cauldron of water, which hissed and bubbled round it. Brian, seizing it boldly in his hand, drew it forth and departed' (quoted R.S. Loomis *Arthurian Tradition* p. 380). It becomes Lugh's spear and thereafter, 'when battle was near . . . it roared and struggled against its thongs; fire flashed from it; and once slipped from its leash it tore through and through the ranks of the enemy'. Lugh was a sun god: the flashing of his spear is the darting of his brilliant rays. Men become heroes and heroes become gods.

When Lugh visits the court of Nuada, he picks up and hurls a stone which it took no fewer than 80 oxen to shift. By this feat of strength he proves himself to be not only the long-awaited *Samildanach* or Master of Many Arts, but the chosen warrior who will rid Ireland of their oppressors, the mysterious Formosians who invaded Ireland from their mythical home Lochlann, beneath the sea.

The heroes have godlike qualities; oddly, perhaps to us, they have technical skills, too; and they are young, no respecters of older authority. Christ was such a one. And the lateness of these stories suggests cross-fertilisation between Celtic and Christian myth. For here, almost contemporaneous with the earliest Arthurian romances, are written versions of what must have been much older tales. Caílte's visit to the faery palace cannot have seemed so far distant, either, from the First Crusaders' arrival in Palestine and their first, breathtaking glimpse of the Holy City. In his *Art of Loving*, Andreas Capellanus described Camelot as a rectangular palace, the roof and outer walls of gold, silver, the interior of gold studded with precious stones.

Did he steal that from Celtic legend or from St John's description of the New Jerusalem in his Book of Revelation? We shall, perhaps, see in the next chapter.

MERLIN

I am aware that Merlin, Samuel to King Arthur's David, who straddles the gulf between Celtic and Christian world, gets short commons in this book, as he does in Malory. In the *Quest* he is said to have designed the Round Table. He makes no appearance in Chrétien de Troyes and his role in Malory seems to be that of unofficial, plenipotentiary advisor to the Church. At his suggestion the Archbishop of Canterbury calls the kings of Britain together to settle the matter of kingship. The bishop in Geoffrey of Monmouth is Dubricius, the Welsh Archbishop churchman who resigns his primacy in favour of St David. And Merlin's essential Celtic character emerges in Geoffrey: that of the archetypal wizard capable of stunning insight and prescience as well as remarkable feats of magic.

In a Celtic version of the Immaculate Conception, Merlin, born without a father to a daughter of a king of Demetia (Dyffed), confounds the royal magicians even though a stripling boy. King Vortigern's tower will not stand firm; the magi have no solution. Merlin explains that the foundations are rocking because two dragons – the red dragon of Britain and the white dragon of the Saxons invited to the island by Vortigern – are fighting together under the earth. He even has the temerity to predict that the red dragon is destined to lose; Britain's mountains and valleys will be levelled and the streams will run with blood. Merlin expands sonorously on the approaching cataclysm in a manner which hints that, for all his Druidic origins, the Christian Church accommodated him as a sort of Old Testament prophet: another Isaiah, tongue fired with the sacred coal; or Elijah conjuring flame out of the teeming heavens onto the drenched altar (Elijah who had been brought food by the ravens when he languished in the wilderness); even Samson smiting the Philistines hip and thigh with the jawbone of an ass.

A lot of nonsense has been talked about Druids, largely prompted by sensationalist accounts in Latin authors, with propaganda points to score against a barbarian priesthood they knew little about. The Druids were, evidently, priests of high learning; their secret lore they wrote down in Greek; to their book-craft they added medicinal skills always viewed with suspicion by officialdom and the ignorant. In the land of the uneducated the man who can read a book is king; the man who can read two books at once is a magician. Druids could certainly talk, too, with very Welsh silver tongues – persuasion was not the least of the shots in their locker.

Merlin, besotted of Morgan le Fay's helper Nimuë, winds up immured by the tricky maiden under the earth; like a dragon with its fire extinguished. That happens quite early on in the Arthurian romances where, in fact, he plays little part. He has caught later fancy, though; indeed, had already fathered his own pre-Arthurian literature as Myrddin the Welsh prophet. Geoffrey of Monmouth, seduced, perhaps, as Julius Caesar had been, by the chance of adding a fair-sized helping of Celtic spice to his history, introduces Merlin's dual role and nature: the Druid who has spawned a vast web of fiction in the Celtic twilight, ancient and modern; the quasi-priest who works alongside bishops and archbishops, much in the way that the great monastic abbots like Bernard did. Merlin's Druistic presence must have done more than raise eyebrows among the mediaeval Church authorities. Certainly, Geoffrey of Monmouth's *Prophecies of Merlin* didn't catch on; they may even have stalled Geoffrey's hopes of preferment. Merlin was allowed to stay

only as half shadowy presence, half irregular priest – akin to the holy hermit, in fact.

THE CHRISTIAN VERSION

Celtic elements survive, and prominently, in Arthurian romance, precisely because the Celtic tradition of storytelling is *the* tradition. The intrinsic appeal of magic, heroic exploit, mystery, worked in as narrative devices to create atmosphere, heighten tension, spin the enchanted web about the listener, was not lost on the mediaeval writers. The Celtic brew was heady stuff and the Christian myth pretty bland without it. By degrees, though, the Christian mythmakers extended the scope of the basic myth, hero against evil, saviour of the people, to embrace all mankind by establishing Christ as *the* universal hero, founthead of inspiration to poor and rich, high and baseborn alike. The Christian myth went further: uniquely, Christianity offered divine largesse *with preference* to the poor and underprivileged. Wealthy masters had short commons for once. 'Gold and silver is cankered,' says the Apostle James; and Christ himself promised: 'I have refined thee, but not with silver; I have chosen thee in the furnace of affliction'. The wealthy did have a lien on poverty, too: the spiritual poverty of a contrite heart, the inner heroism of humility, wholly inimical to a warrior caste. As the worthy man advises King Arthur in the prose *Lancelot:*

> Whenever you meet a poor knight bachelor humbled by poverty, yet still fit and strong, taking his meal with the paupers below the salt, do not despise him because he lacks wealth or rank. Underneath material poverty may be found great richness of spirit; while a mean spirit is often plated over with vast riches and lands.

Section 287

But the unctuous voice of the monks is all too apparent there. No self-respecting Crusader knight, brimful of haughty pride in his own fighting strength and deeming himself the heir of the Round Table Knights, would be glad to hear himself urged to mix it with the down-at-heel, no matter what great heart beat under the scruffy tunic. Indeed, this late romance is disappointingly larded with sententious homilising in such vein. It presents a sickly, casuistical excuse for the adultery of Lancelot and Guenever, and a saccharine happy ending.

Gradually the Christian myth settled into a coherent unity. The Gospel accounts might vary; the central story must not be allowed to. Pagan stories were adapted rather than suppressed: they were only myths from a universal pool, after all.

The transition of old Celtic pagan myth and initiation ritual to the Christian version was relatively easy and untroubled, it seems. So many elements in both were similar: Maimed King/Crucified Lord; Heroic sacrifice and the passage to the Otherworld: the dead Christ harrowing Hell; The cauldron of rebirth: Christ's Resurrection. Waste Land: the Wilderness – Moses and the children of Israel, and Christ during his period of temptation. And so on.

The Christian Celtic church provided a new social cohesion to replace the old, especially in Ireland, against the destructive impact of the barbarian invasions. This naturally encouraged the retention of the old hero stories, now in a Christian setting. And it was these stories which the new warrior élite, Frankish and Norman mailed knights, seized on. They thought of themselves as heirs to the Celtic tradition of fighting aristocracy, even if they had no Celtic blood as title of their own pedigree. What is more, the priests of *their* society gave them new rituals of rebirth and initiation: Baptism, Eucharist, *In hoc signo vinces.* Their authority had, now, to be established from generation to generation by descent. The days of warrior chiefs fighting for power had been too disruptive for the growing order in Europe, the Church-guided equilibrium. Instead of a fresh leader at each succession, majesty was conveyed through royal birth. But Celtic warrior or mailed knight, both had pride to buck with praise. The need for self-belief had not changed. That need the romances, in large measure, supplied, like the Celtic hero stories before them.

As a result, the Christian story received the full boost of the mediaeval romances. The rich, highly coloured form of the fiction lends a great appeal to the Christian myth which it certainly did not have before. Especially in the development of the Grail legend, there is a steady refinement from its first, apparently secular, airing by Chrétien de Troyes, where the *graal*, not yet 'holy', is described as a superior serving dish – 'of pure, refined gold set with precious stones; incomparable', to its startling potency as the holiest of holy relics in the *Quest of the Holy Grail* written by an ecclesiastic half a century later.

The Grail story is characterised, at first, by a homely folkloric mixture of hero adventure, magic and enchantment; the intrepid passage through the twilight zone. No diabolism to speak of; simply an allegory of untutored and callow youth achieving self-knowledge. There is also, I suggest, a veiled allusion to the new Crusader reaching the Holy Land and slowly opening his eyes wider and wider and wider. There is no more nor less strict Christianity in the story than frank paganism in a nursery rhyme.

But the popularity of the story galloped away fast. The Church saw a huge potential in it for the promotion of doctrine and the Grail story changed and ripened into a highly charged visionary epic – rumbling with Satanic thunder, brilliantly lit with celestial refulgence, altogether as apocalyptic as St John's *Revelation.*

It is my own firm belief that the Grail legend, before it *did* vanish, played a vital part in the long process whereby all Europe was brought to acknowledge Roman Christianity in the authorised, doctrinal, scholastic form it still presents today. But that edifice of official Catholicism was built only centuries after the first, less sophisticated, conversion of the heathen invaders had been effected. The missionaries had come back into the Europe once Christian by virtue of being Roman, and the pagans took baptism, when baptism had the force of a passport to the new social order where barbarian invaders became accepted as settlers. Parvenu envy of old power, even after it has supplanted that old power, is no quirk of the modern world.

The pagans instinctively worshipped Christ in various idiosyncratic ways, drawing on the myths and stories of their former beliefs. As Papal Rome grew stronger in its leadership of western Christianity, the need for dogma (fixed opinion) became more urgent. Dogma had to be protected against countervailing ideas – everything from local variation in worship to full-blown heresy.

The Grail legend started as a local variation, little more than an intriguing story; it became a full-blown ritualistic myth of Christian endeavour and sanctity; and then, for reasons we can only guess at, outgrew its welcome, being, perhaps, too exotic a guest in a Roman Church dedicated to rigid, and oddly puritanical, orthodoxy, a necessary order after centuries of ferment and change. The exterior threat from Islam gave way, after the loss of Jerusalem, to a threat which the Church's hottest apologists described, luridly, as much worse: a threat *from within*, the irregularity of heretical ideas, an invisible, more insidious enemy than the hideous Moors whom you could at least see and kill.

Celtic charm and enchantment was out, precisely because it wasn't *Christian* charm and enchantment. The Celtic elements in the story pervade it as being part of the shared culture of the men (and women) who told it over a period of some 150 years. This is only to say that myth, in spite of regional difference, tends to be universal.

Indeed, the world was beginning to open out. The Crusades acquainted thousands of Europeans, noble and humble alike, with the staggering reality of oriental opulence. The Celtic stories may have expatiated in vivid terms on the marvels of an enchanted world. In the Holy Land, the knights of Christ met a similar enchantment head on. It was *real*. The men of Provence knew the radiance of hot sunlight well; but nothing can have prepared any Crusader, especially one from the grey north, for the startling white brilliance of Palestine.

Not enough weight, in my view, has been given to that climactic experience of the European soldiers, of mixed Teuton, Celt and Norse blood, who arrived in the pure Semitic Holy Land having already traversed eastern Europe and Greek Asia. Niches in the Templar church in London's Inner Temple are adorned with all manner of exotic carvings – heraldic devices, heads, fruits, flowers, pharmacopoeic herbs . . . cullings, as it were, from the casbah of foreign travel. Tokens, no less, of the astonishment, say, of dour English arriving in Syria and Palestine, to that sensual assault of wholesale otherness. Think of the amazement evoked by Marco Polo's memoirs in his stay-at-home neighbours; of Sir John Mandeville's fantastic accounts of his voyages . . . 'Here be Monsters'. Yes, monsters, and much else besides: the romances drew, and drew richly on the world of old Celtic lore *and* the world of the Arabian nights.

It is probably no exaggeration to say that the Crusaders simply did not believe what they saw in the mysterious east. They returned home with such tales of things unimaginable but true, true, true. What could the stay-at-home storytellers do to keep up, but dip into the old Celtic pedlar's pack?

CHAPTER SEVEN

QUEST FOR THE HOLY GRAIL

And when our bottles and all we
Are fild with immortalitie
Then the holy paths weele travell

Strewde with Rubies thicke as gravell,
Seelings of Diamonds, Saphire floores,
High walles of Corall and Pearl Bowres.

Walter Raleigh, **'The Passionate Man's**
Pilgrimage' lines 29 ff

A.D. 1227: London. Henry III, the king they said had a heart of wax, ascends the throne. Hawthorn buds are splitting open to announce May.

A bowshot from the river Thames stands the round Church of the Knights Templar, where the king will ask to be buried. Outside the English Temple, dawn breaks. The sun's bright shafts fly in low swift raid from the east across the Kent and Essex marshes where the glass river, wide at the mouth, fuses with the glass sea. The glittering solar battalions, dipping under the ramparts of low cloud, reclaim the shadowy river marches from Night's dark lordship. The fleet course of light broadens at the point into a bludgeon, prodding London awake. Birds asleep in trees along the water's margin stir and cry daytime alarm, 'Somer is y-comen in, lude sing cuccu! cuccu!' at the thieving cuckoo stealing into the nest.

Inside the cave-like crypt under the floor of the Temple Church kneel three men: each one of knight and lady born. They have been asked and tested each one as to their birth and family, their vocation and purpose in coming here to ask the secret. In the Church, high above their heads, symbol of Earth to the underworld of the Crypt, yellow sunlight warms its flame at the circular lantern in the roof; the glass of the panes thick and watery like ice; light swims in it. Morning tips its own several noises out of the silence, like crystal beads trilling onto slate. No light and only vague muffled sound way off penetrate into the crypt.

The three men remain kneeling as they have done a long, long time: backs, legs, arms, in attitude of prayer, stiff and their knees aching; the cold stone flags an anvil from the continual hammer stroke at body, mind and spirit. The 'little death' they call it, this long vigil between their old worldly life and the new spiritual life as warrior monks in the service of Christ. They have seen the candles lit, burn down to the holder and gutter out, this night alone in the eerily silent church. They have witnessed mysterious processions of people and things: the holy ritual of mass, sacred chalices and dishes glinting in the candleglow; the feast of the Eucharist at Christ's table, sacring bread and wine as flesh and blood of the Crucified Saviour, the holy vessels on shining white linen. They have heard murmur and incantation; dismay whispering in one ear, joy in the other; have felt a clammy chill like Death and the hot fevers of exultation; been brought to the margin of endurance, physical and spiritual; the strings of their understanding pulled taut and cut through. Simple, downright men, not given to lurid imaginings, they have been initiated into the close-guarded, secret ways of the Temple.

This is the secret of their hearts: 'To all who disdain to follow after their own wills and desire with purity of mind to fight for the high and true king, be here in membership of this Order of the Poor Knights of Christ and the Temple of Solomon.'

Amen.

Sealed in the holy benison of the Eucharist: *Hoc est corpus meum . . .* This is My body. Amen.

Silence. The initiation process has begun.

The Grand Master beckons the three postulants forward. Candle flames burn molten amber at the rich beeswax. The fumes mingle with the aromatic plumes of incense.

'Kneel, in the name of God and His Son.'

They kneel. The Grand Master begins the litany of their vows and undertakings – spacious to their heart, narrow to their mind: own no wealth or possessions (Amen) . . . eat thy bread in silence (Amen) . . . devote all strength of mind, body and spirit to the service of God and the keeping of His Holy Places (Amen) . . . clad in armour of obedience (Amen) . . . in St Paul's helmet of salvation and breastplate of righteousness and sword of the spirit (Amen) . . . and they will wear the Templar's white robe to single them out from other knights, dove white of chastity. For St John in Revelation says the four and twenty elders sit round the throne, clothed in white raiment. And the throne is of green jasper and golden sard, and round the throne a rainbow, in sight like unto a crystal.

The Templars' white robe is gashed with a blood-red cross, splayed at the tips so it resembles a bloodstain. For the robe of Him in Revelation who is called the Word of God, is 'cleansed in the blood of the Lamb'.

At last the Master leaves them to the night and solitude.

They think on. Of their chastity. They are enjoined to shun feminine kisses . . . Amen. For see where the Devil comes dressed as a woman, drunk with the blood of the saints, his lips are scarlet with it, the blood of the Martyrs of Jesus, like Salome who danced for the head of John the Baptist . . . The darkness wears on. They grow numb, sunk in their trance-like contemplation.

Suddenly, the door opens. A glimmer of light tumbles in down the stairwell. Fuzzily, the three of them hear a heavy stride, slap of mail coat at metal-bound scabbard. The Grand Master, his white, crimson-splashed mantle catching the spillage of early sun, returns. They blink, eyes glazed and half shut.

'Rise and be received.'

One of them slumps forward and struggles to his feet, ungainly as a horse. The other two heave themselves upright, like King Arthur waking at the sound of the trumpet, centuries asleep in a mimicry of death, but the spirit surging in him, hot as the day it was forged together from two parts.

FROM QUEST TO ENLIGHTENMENT

The Quest for the Holy Grail, that most potent of all themes in Arthurian literature, is bound up with

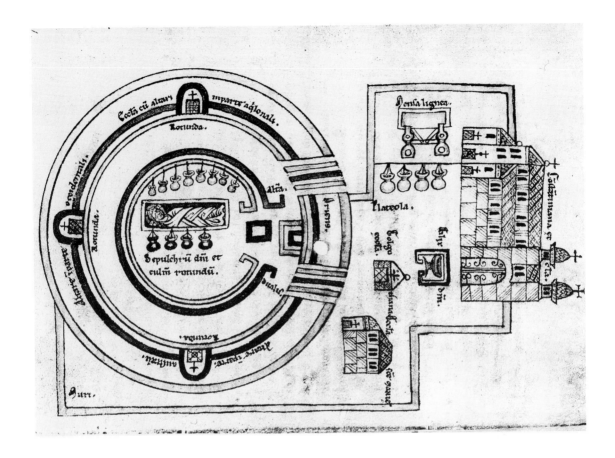

Plan of the Church of the Holy Sepulchre, Templar Headquarters in Jerusalem. At the centre of the mystic labyrinth of circles lies Christ's entombed body, his feet pointing east towards the sun rising over the Holy Land.

religious mystery and ceremonial, with spiritual initiation, with the secret rituals of knighthood, but especially, I believe, those required by the Order of Templars. The Templars led the rest of the Crusaders in prestige and fighting commitment, even if their sense of élitism was entirely self-cultivated. For the most part they not only saw themselves as the Round Table come to life; they behaved as if it had. Their mission, equally with the Grail Quest, might be summed up as a divine blessing on the profession of arms. Their famous warcry in the Holy Land was 'The Holy Sepulchre!' Thus:

The sword is the key of heaven and of hell; a drop of blood shed in the cause of God, a night spent in arms, is of more avail than two months of fasting and of prayer. Whosoever falls in battle, his sins are forgiven him at the day of judgement. His wounds will be resplendent as vermilion and odoriferous as musk, and the loss

137

of limbs shall be supplied by the wings of angels and cherubim.

I have played a trick on you, though. That comes not from a Christian writer but from the sayings of the prophet Mohammed. Did the Moors teach it to the Christians or *vice versa*?

In seeking to win the Holy City of Jerusalem by feat of arms, the Crusaders pursued a real goal: God's kingdom on earth. The Church, based in Rome, acceded in this for a while, but it was distracted by internal squabbles: the Pope in Rome faced challenge by another Pope in France, and for some years the papal government even shifted to Avignon. But while the Crusades lasted, the triumph of the armed quest would be real, the spiritual dividend calculable in terms of land and cities won from God's foes, the infidel usurpers. The glory which accrued would be almost tangible. As the impetus of the Crusades wavered and failed, however, first Jerusalem and then the Holy Land entire slipped from the grasp of the Christian knights. The real journey to God's kingdom on earth had, perforce, to become a spiritual quest, a search for spiritual enlightenment through moral perfection, penitence, chivalric code and so on, all under terms of religious obligation derived from Church teaching and theology. The visible Jerusalem becomes a transcendent mystery, a New Sion the Golden, revealed in John's apocalyptic vision.

A similar refinement, from adventure story to religious allegory, can be observed in the development of the Grail romance.

The early Grail stories match the old heroic yarns of adventure beloved of the fighting tribes. The very word *adventure* means going out and finding something. The models were the *Odyssey*, the *Aeneid*, the Celtic raid stories. A more recent literary impulse came from hagiography, saints' lives, written in torrents by monks and priests (the literate few) during the so-called Dark Ages; and very popular, too, if only because nothing else much got written to challenge the monopoly and the Church had a pretty firm hold on the ear of the listening public. Like his heroic predecessors, the typical saint confronts devilish hardship and evil machination, treading the stony path to perfection. The Grail Quest story combined heroic endeavour with saintly striving.

The first of the Quest knights in literature appears in Chrétien's unfinished *Perceval* (c.1181). Perceval rides a long, arduous road: from callow youth, garrulous, over-eager, bursting with vitality to a midway stage of bafflement. Tutored out of his irrepressible Welsh chatterboxing by an older knight whom he meets on the way, Perceval arrives at the mysterious Castle of the Fisher King. There he sees the Grail carried before him in procession. His Quest seems to be over: he set out to discover something and here, surely, it is. But, like a Crusader in the mirage-shifting sands of the Syrian and Palestinian deserts, does he really know what he is looking for? A simple mistake means that his journey is far from over. He learns that when he saw the Grail the required clue to learning its secret was to ask: 'Whom does the Grail serve?' This he would certainly have done if he had seen it when he was still a red-cheeked country boy. But he had lost some of his naïvety and been schooled in discretion, holding back his thoughts and emotions. He would have done better to heed the advice of the scriptures: asking he would have received. Instead, he bridles his curiosity from a newly acquired sense of politeness, thoroughly chivalric and unCeltic. Next morning he awakes to find the castle deserted and himself abandoned: the first wearing disappointment of his life's journey, strewn with obstacles as it will be. Perceval loses heart and his faith in God; he wanders through a spiritual desolation, a Waste Land of the soul, until he re-emerges to new belief in Christ *and* in himself.

Only then does he resume the proper quest for enlightenment through self-knowledge. A hermit in the forest (who turns out to be his uncle) explains the reason for his earlier failure of heart: when Perceval set out to be a knight, it caused his mother such grief that she died. Ignorant of that, Perceval nonetheless endured many trials because of it. This is more than a metaphor of how complex a process knowing oneself is; it also reflects the actual circumstances in which true wisdom matures.

Other knights of the Round Table, notably Gawain, appear on the fringes of the Grail Quest, but thanks to Malory the knight most indelibly linked, in English minds at least, to the Quest is Galahad, Lancelot's son by Elaine. Malory's source book for this section of his romance was the *Quest of the Holy Grail*. In the *Morte d'Arthur*, Lancelot, who, we learn in the prose *Launcelot du Lac*, had originally been christened Galahad, also seeks the Grail. He fails as he knows he is doomed to fail having endured a madness induced by sin (nervous collapse from adulterous guilt), so he renounces the Quest in favour of his chaste and immaculate son.

Galahad, who appears in only the *Quest* and Malory's adaptation, probably derives his name from the mount where Jacob and his father-in-law swear a covenant and mark it with a stone pillar (in Hebrew, Galeed or 'heap of testimony').

And Laban said, This heap is a witness between me and thee this day. Therefore was the name of it called Galeed.

Genesis 31 v. 48

Perceval, Gawain, Lancelot, and others have too much worldly flaw in them to be accorded the full sainthood of Galahad. Their path is the strait and narrow path of real adversity; *he* walks unstoppably along a golden pavement. He possesses a sort of angelic intelligence which knows all there is to be known without learning it by the usual route of experience. *They* witness the Grail but do not achieve it: that is to say they fail its obscure test, much as the man who does not know the correct form or password is refused admission into the secret society. On a broader level, their journey to self-knowledge takes their whole life. The purpose of the Grail in these stories seems to be an elaborate way of saying: Search out your own heart, know thyself. No specially religious abracadabra in that.

Galahad is not prey to introspective qualm. He is, as Berlioz' Dido calls Aeneas, a monster of piety. With his appearance on the grail trail, the highly coloured Arthurian romance slips back into the plodding predictability of the dullest tales of saints' lives. Is that monochrome or garish technicolour? Perhaps a muddle of both. A very manufactured sanctity, nevertheless, which anticipates, by many centuries, the gooiest pap dished up by the celluloid sentimentalists. Gone the unsteady progress; now it is Life, Triumph, Death and Transfiguration – a very inhuman process which can never eclipse, for verity or punch, the toils and lost turnings of the flesh-and-blood heroes who precede Galahad.

With Galahad, the Quest of the Holy Grail has become the trite abstraction of an allegorical spiritual journey. The hypocritical, sentimentalising Victorians loved that because it confirmed them in their own smug view of a divinely ordered world with *them* in control. The attitude of thirteenth-century churchmen was not so far removed. Such sanctimonious lack of self-doubt permeates Galahad's story. He foretells his death, speaks of witnessing the disclosure of the hidden mysteries hidden from common, that is uninitiated, view:

If I had died at the very moment when I saw the Grail's mysteries, I know no other man would die in such a state of perfect bliss. So great a company of angels stood before me, such a multitude of celestial beings, I was borne in that instant from earth to heaven, to share the joy of the glorious martyrs and Our Lord's beloved. Pray God, by his blessing I shall depart this life gazing upon the glories of the Holy Grail.

Quest chapter 15

Glossy evangelism has replaced the muscular, Christian heroism of the romances.

We find a curious throwback to the flesh-and-blood questing knight in the marvellous fourteenth-century Lancashire dialect poem *Sir Gawain and the Green Knight*. Gawain is given an irreproachable character, as the markings of his shield tell us:

> *Therefore it goes with Sir Gawain and his gleaming*
> *armour*
> *For, ever faithful in five things, each in fivefold manner*
> *Gawain was reputed good and, like gold well refined,*
> *He was devoid of all villainy, every virtue displaying*
>   *In the field.*
>   *Thus this Pentangle new*
>   *He carried on coat and shield,*
>   *As a man of troth most true*
>   *And knightly name annealed.*
>
> *Canto 27*

Faultless in his five wits – senses; and strong in his five-fingered hand, all his trust on earth was in Christ's five wounds, the holy stigmata. His prowess depended on the five joys of Christ and his Mother: Annunciation, Nativity, Resurrection, Ascension, Assumption. Finally, the five virtues: liberality, loving kindness, continence, courtesy, piety.

It all sounds very Galahad so far. However, Gawain has to weather a pretty torrid chapter of temptations *and* he faces the ultimate proof of courage: the beheading test at the hands of the mysterious Green Knight. And this poem is no religious tract. Gawain's human frailty is exposed; he tells a lie to protect himself and is redeemed from plaster sainthood to attractive manhood. I urge you to read the story. When the *graal,* French for Grail, first appears in Chrétien's unfinished *Perceval* (*c.*1181), it is neither holy nor precisely described. It could be a magical dish from Celtic legend. Within a few years, however, Robert de Boron's *Joseph d'Arimathie* (*c.*1200) identifies the Grail as the Chalice of the Last Supper, filled with the Blood shed on the Cross, without actually naming its sanctity. The *Perlesvaus* or 'High History of the Most Holy Grail' appeared in about 1212 to be followed by the *Quest of the Holy Grail* in which the saintly knight Galahad, a warrior monk like the Templars, makes his entrance. Both the *Perlesvaus* and the *Quest* reveal plain Cistercian influence (see page 164).

Some commentators refer to the *Quest* as a spiritual fable, not a romance. Certainly Church, and particularly White Monk, thinking has, to the great detriment of storytelling power, settled leadenly on the narrative. In fact, the all-pervasive pious argument turns this mystical, otherworldly exposition of the Grail Quest into more or less the last word on the subject. By shifting the earthly struggle with physical and psychological demons onto the spiritual plane, the beguiling romance, a fanciful version of real life, peters out into allegory and symbol, stiff with theological abstraction. The prose *Lancelot*, written about the same time, has a similar moralising crust.

The latest Grail text would seem to be a continuation of Chrétien's story by one Manessier, possibly as late as 1244. That date, as we shall we, has great significance in the history of Europe, the Church and the Crusades. All three are bound together.

The allegory of the Christian soul making a journey through life's adversities and, at the end, proceeding to the celestial bourne in God's mansions, is one of the most enduring in religious metaphor. The semantic change in the word *progress* – from movement, plain and simple, to enrichment, ennoblement through experience – encapsulates the restless drive in humankind equated with thirst for knowledge, novelty, intellectual and spiritual illumination. The nomadic Arab races play a large part in this story of Arthur; not only as the reviled and hated paynim, the armies of the aliens, bugbears of the Christian chevaliers but as disseminators of ideas throughout a world whose princes sought to destroy and discredit them at the behest of a dogmatising Church. Destroying and discrediting, needless to say, did not include having to repudiate the benefits reaped from copying.

The Church had eagerly promoted *actual* Christian journey through life to the various pilgrim shrines; especially to those of the Holy Land. With the failure of the Crusades, the Church shifted emphasis. Pilgrimages went on, but there were new doctrines relating to stability and order. Europe had had enough shifting about, territories changing hands, invaders of one stripe and another trooping backwards and forwards across the ever-realigned frontiers. Kings grew stronger and more insistent on the loyalty of their vassals. National kingdoms began to emerge; travellers, vagrants by another name, did not pass so freely from one territory to the next. The Church, having outstripped many of the temporal kingdoms in brilliance of riches and pomp, sought its own Empire of spiritual unity which recognised *no* temporal or geographic frontiers. The Franks lost the Holy Land; Jerusalem reverted to being a symbol, an abstraction. In keeping with that, the Christian journey had better become spiritual, allegorical, as Galahad's in the *Quest*. In the official view of Church, and state, that was safer. The Crusader armies had always behaved very much as a law unto themselves.

Pilgrims still made their parlous long treks, to Santiago, Rome, even Jerusalem itself if they yearned for real, old-fashioned adventure; but they went in smaller numbers. For they could now view all life, in John Bunyan's words, as a spiritual pilgrimage through the wilderness of this world. The conduct of that pilgrimage was dictated by an ascendant Church. The great Pope Innocent III (1198–1216) described temporal power of kings as the light of the moon in relation to the sun of spiritual power, the exclusive right of the Church.

One important commodity with which the armed pilgrimage to the Holy Land had supplied Europe, to the great advantage of the Church, was holy relics: an abundance of sundry bits of metal and wood, scraps of material and bones complete or in fragment, all venerated for their sanctity. Cults of objects and shrines revered for their association with holy men originated in the Middle East, became a fundamental practice of Islam and, later, an avid enthusiasm of the Christian Church. The Crusades had been fired to a passionate heat by the cult of relics. The holy lumber carried by the priests of the Crusader armies inspired phenomenal, outlandish courage, self-assurance and undaunted faith in the victorious power of God the Father, Son and Holy Ghost.

For example, in 1102, Raymond IV, Count of Toulouse (the leader of the Provençals who had discovered what they took to be the authentic Holy Lance in Antioch cathedral), found himself caught outside Tripoli by a Moslem army which outnumbered his 300 knights by twenty to one:

> Raymond placed a hundred of his men to oppose
> the Damascenes a hundred to oppose the Banu
> Ammar, fifty to oppose the men of Homs and
> the remaining fifty to be his own bodyguard. The

Homs men began the attack; but when it failed they suddenly panicked; and the panic spread among the troops of Damascus. The Tripolitans were enjoying greater success when Raymond, finding his other foes in flight, swung his whole army against them. The shock was too much and they turned and fled.

S. Runciman, *History of the Crusades*
(vol. 2 p. 58)

Raymond had once more proved, and dramatically, the truth of the Crusaders' motto *In hoc signo vinces.* We may, from this twentieth-century height of rationalism, pooh-pooh the naïvety of the mediaeval soldiers, fortified in their belief that the billet of timber hauled up and down their lines by ardent churchmen actually came from the Cross to which Christ had been nailed. The fact remains that they often fought with irresistible boldness and apparent vulnerability. *And* they endured privations with a fortitude which left the Turks, no soft men themselves, open-mouthed in amazement. That proves some virtue, not spurious either, in the cult of relics.

The Grail Quest, particularly in the later romances, stands as the supreme literary exposition of that cult. The adventure story became, in a very short time, a lofty, spiritual odyssey. We know that the Arthurian romances made popular listening among the Crusaders engaged on their own journey to the winning of an earthly kingdom, and the *Quest* fuses armed pilgrimage with the desire to worship at the Holy Sepulchre on the site of Christ's tomb. The one insuperable difficulty posed by making the Holy Grail a cipher for the holiest of sacred relics was that, despite the plethora of other holy bits and pieces, it quite plainly did not exist. No one could actually produce it. The Holy Grail, being secret, invisible, mysterious, smacked of nasty oriental idolatry. In the *Perlesvaus* it is recorded that none may pass into the Castle of Endeavour on the Grail Quest, save only he that goes to vanquish the knight there and thus win the Golden Circlet and the Grail and do away with the false law with its horns of copper. Thoroughly Baal and Moloch-sounding, that, and not something the orthodox Church, once the rule of theology had been established, could tolerate.

Christ's injunction was: 'Seek and ye shall find; knock and it shall be opened unto you' (Matthew 7 v. 7). The Crusaders did that and, for a time, found the door opened to them. When the Crusades eventually failed, their ideal tarnished and discredited, that door was firmly shut in their face. The seeking had to become interior, spiritual. In spite of their deliberate Christian context and symbolism, the adventure stories of the Grail Quest begun by Perceval began to smell of paganism at worst, unorthodoxy at best. Perhaps the romance hero was painted too close to the saint for church comfort. Perhaps Galahad seemed too Christlike. Was the *Quest of the Holy Grail* fiction or what? Either way it had the odour of unorthodoxy. The Church alone had the power to dispense the glories Galahad describes as emanating from the Grail.

The holy war shifted onto a higher plane, with the Church taking refuge in theological abstraction. Galahad achieves the Grail and is translated to heaven. There is nowhere else he can go: God's City on earth was no more. If the Kingdom of God could *not* be found on this earth, it would have to be discovered in the spirit of the Faithful. The kings of the earth might have their temporal power. The Church would go one better and share celestial power with God. So, at the conclusion of Malory's retelling, the Church takes possession of Arthur's body and memory:

Then Sir Bedivere came into the chapel and saw where lay an hermit grovelling on all four, there fast by a tomb was new graven. When the hermit saw Sir Bedivere he knew him well, for he was but little tofore Bishop of Canterbury, that Sir Mordred flemed [banished].

'Sir,' said Bedivere, 'what man is there interred that ye pray so fast for?'

'Fair son,' said the hermit, 'I wot not verily, but by deeming [guessing]. But this night, at midnight, here came a number of ladies, and brought hither a dead corpse, and prayed me to bury him; and here they offered an hundred tapers, and they gave me an hundred bezants.'

'Alas,' said Sir Bedivere, 'that was my lord King Arthur, that here lieth buried in this chapel . . . from hence will I never go, by my will, but all the days of my life here to pray for my lord Arthur.'

Book XXI chapter 6

How does Christian symbolism overlay the original Grail romances? This is a large question to which I can no more than sketch an answer in a short book. The exploits of the Christian Crusaders undoubtedly seemed, at the time, to match the old Celtic hero stories reproduced by French poets. The chivalric pursuit of glory accorded neatly with a quest for the ultimate holy relic, the summit of earthly desire. The Bible, too, provides clues as to why the Grail Quest struck resonant chords of recognition in a Christian audience, such that it almost inevitably became the *Holy* Grail. The Church, remember, sought, and achieved, domination of every aspect of human existence, from dogmatic strictures on morality to the governing of what was permissible in books. Scriptural references would be adduced to prove or disprove any point of Church ruling. The Grail romances are no exception.

THE FISHER KING

On his first quest as a knight, Perceval comes to a river but can see no way across. Surely, he thinks, he will find his mother on the other side, if only she is still alive? He spies a boat drifting towards him, two men aboard. They anchor in midstream. The man in the bows fishes with rod and line, his hook baited with small fry. Perceval hails the men; asks if there is a bridge. No, they reply, no ferry, bridge or ford within twenty leagues up or down the river. Their boat is too small to ferry him over. Perceval is stranded. But, the angler offers him overnight lodging in his house. If the knight will climb up through a narrow defile in the cliff to the top, he will see the house, close to woods and river, in a valley stretching out below him. Perceval ascends the crag but from the summit can see nothing but sky and earth. He reviles the fisherman, now out of sight, for so misleading him – pure malice. Then, to Perceval's amazement, the top of a tower swims up out of the valley into view 'none so splendid' [writes Chrétien] 'or well-situated this side of Beirut,' the rich, fortified seaport captured by the Frankish Crusaders in 1110. It is square, built of dark grey stone, flanked by two smaller towers. Perceval rides down to it, loud, now, in his praise of the fisherman. Next day, after the curious adventure of the *graal* and the empty castle, Perceval encounters a damsel in the forest who explains that the young knight has lodged with the Fisher King.

The connections between Christianity and fishing are many: the first disciples were fishermen; Christ himself, after his resurrection, helped them one long night of empty nets to land a miraculous draught of fishes; admonishing them to preach the

Perceval looks on as Galahad prays for the mystery of the Grail to be revealed. The heavenly kingdom stands atop a hill far in the distance.

Gospel, he said, 'I will make you fishers of men'. The early Christians used the fish (two curved lines kissing at the mouth, crossing over at the tail) as a secret symbol; the Greek word *ichthus* ('fish') forms an acronym for Christ's name and title: I (Iesous) CH (Christos) TH (of God) U (the Son) S (and Saviour).

The fish was also a universal life symbol, coming out of the Flood which covered the earth; it lived where no other creature could. Babylonian myth speaks of Adapa, the Wise Fisher, and Buddha is called the Fisherman. Aphrodite (Venus in Roman mythology), the goddess of Love, comes out of the sea; her name means Foamchild, and the creatures of her domain inspire passion. (Some truth, there: shellfish contain large quantities of zinc, a major constituent of semen.) In fact, Classical myth reports her as being carried ashore after her birth in a scallop shell (as in Botticelli's 'Birth of Venus'). The scallop shell, symbol of St James, Christ's brother whose famous shrine in Compostela was, and still is, the goal of many pilgrims, became adopted as the pilgrim's badge from early days. That spelt trouble, of course: holy symbol *and* aphrodisiac. In fact pilgrimages gained a bad reputation as offering cover for more than rendezvous with saints' bones. They were, very often, the mediaeval equivalent of the so-called business trip.

Another coincidence impresses itself, here. The Roman Emperor Hadrian built a temple to Aphrodite on the same site as the Dome of the Rock, where the Templars had their headquarters in a wing of the old Temple of Solomon (hence their name). Below the Rock lay the Holy Sepulchre, Christ's tomb. The Dome of the Rock itself was a goldfoil Mosque, built in the seventh century, whence Mahomet the Prophet ascended to heaven. Inside the Dome, at the very centre, stood the rock itself. Over this rock, says the prophet Samuel, the exterminating angel stretched out his hand upon Jerusalem to destroy it. But God, repenting of his curse on the city, had stayed the angel's hand from the evil, and David came. David, first king of the city, David the Psalmist who danced for the Lord; David, who, like Perceval, had feet swifter than hind's feet; David, whose hands, like Launcelot's, were taught to war, so that a bow of steel is broken by his arm. David, whose men took Jerusalem by surprise attack, climbing up the well-shaft piercing the rock through its centre, as it were a scabbard in shape, a long sheath cut through the stone.

The link between Aphrodite and the Dome of the Rock may well be fortuitous, but the mediaeval mind had an unquenchable thirst for coincidence and symbolic parallel. Even the planets had their influence. Aphrodite/Venus' planetary day is Friday, named after her Norse cousin Freya (French retains Venus in *vendredi*), and on Friday sea voyages are to be discouraged. This became the principal fish day of the Catholic Church: a practical measure, as it had ever been, to help conserve stocks of meat, though strong mythic symbolism helped. And there was the implicit encouragement of Christ:

Jesus [risen from the dead] saith unto them, Come and dine. And none of the disciples durst ask him, Who art thou? knowing that it was the Lord. Jesus then cometh and taketh bread and giveth them, and fish likewise.

John 21 vv. 12–13

The primitive Church observed a Messianic fish meal, prompted by the miracle of the loaves and fishes, and characterised by this acrostic litany to Christ:

ICHTHUS	Divine race of the heavenly fish
CHI	Among all the mortal ones take and taste the one immortal spring of the god-given waters
THETA	Refresh, O friend, thy soul with the everflowing flood of blissful wisdom
UPSILON	Take the Saviour's honey-like food, the meat of the saints
SIGMA	Eat, O starving one, holding the fish in thy hands

Quoted in **Quest, a journal of mediaeval studies**
(volume IV)

Jewish custom dating from the time immediately after the Babylonian exile, when protein was in short supply, called for a fish meal on Friday (the eve of the Sabbath) but Mosaic law does not mention the practice.

Thus pagan sea-god and fisherman have a counterpart in Christian myth: sacred fisherman and fish as symbol of life, rather than wisdom. As if on cue, two days before I wrote these words, a medical journal published research that proves the benefit of oily fish: a thrice weekly consumption of mackerel, herring, kipper, for example, reduces mortality from heart disease by 29 per cent. The first Elizabethans had to eat three fish meals a week *by law*. In the year of Shakespeare's birth, Wednesday became a fish day, along with the Church-instituted fish day, Friday, and the lately reintroduced statutory fish day, Saturday (on the eve of the Christian Sabbath).

The Celtic Salmon of Wisdom is remembered in the old tradition that fish stimulates mental powers – Jeeves always trots down to the fishmongers for a herring whenever the young master lands in the mulligatawny, just as I learnt to do on the eve of school exams. Curiously, Classical Greek slang uses ichthus for 'dolt, blockhead'. You can never tell.

WATER

I have discussed the Celtic fascination with water. The Arthurian romances abound with episodes where villainous knights pitch their pavilion on the far side of a river or ford to challenge any knight who comes that way and attempts the crossing. The Black Knight is Death's representative; the river is Death's line in the pavement over which you may not step and hope to come back again.

Classical mythology tells of four rivers which encircle Hades, the Greek Underworld and a metaphor for death. On the banks of one, the Styx

(Hateful), waits the ferryman Charon, to carry the departed soul to the far side. It is important to remember that the romances drew on many different fonts of inspiration, not Celtic alone. One element that *is* uniquely Celtic is the Sword Bridge, translated into an ordeal for the Christian (that is Crusader) knight.

In his story of Lancelot, Chrétien de Troyes uses the approach to this dreaded obstacle with a brilliant flourish of dramatic skill. He conceals the awesome terror of it just out of sight; what is hidden scares us most. Then, finally, the Sword Bridge startles us, like a shaft of hot light slicing through shadow:

> The bridge was like no other bridge: a rigid sword of polished white steel, the length of two lances.

> line 3030

The water thundering through the chasm below is black and turbid, as fearsome as the Devil's own river. As if that weren't enough, two lions (or leopards) guard the far end. Lancelot strips off and crosses, with considerable pain and distress; except that 'Love guides him, keeps him going, relieves and eases his pain and makes his suffering sweet.' The original Celtic Sword Bridge was a sort of bailey bridge like the one laid down by Osla Big-Knife (see page 121). The blade spanning the torrent is a gesture of defiance – warriors brandishing steel against the inhospitable element. It also hints at contrary magic: the silvery metal calming the bright water, while the fighters traverse in safety.

The romances preferred the grim aspects of water crossings, though. The prose *Lancelot* reveals a positive obsession with the perils of crossing water, fighting malign guardians of various fords and narrow, evil bridges:

> At the entrance to the castle stood a very narrow bridge of grim aspect over deep, black water . . . Gawain crossed the bridge on foot and on the other side two armed knights confronted him with a challenge to fight.

> section 251

The use of a boat to cross water symbolises death, as I have said. Dead Vikings were burned in their boats until Christian priests forbade cremation. (Fire was a sacred element in eastern mystic religion.) Thereafter they were buried within a container of stones heaped into the shape of a keel. Coffins are still boat-shaped.

Elaine of Astolat (Tennyson's Lady of Shalott), who dies of a hopeless passion for Guenever-obsessed Lancelot, floats down the river Thames; King Arthur and Queen Guenever see the black barge and send knights to investigate what it means. The knights:

> . . . departed and came to the barge and went in; and there they found the fairest corpse lying in a rich bed, and a poor man sitting in the barge's end, and no word would he speak.

He is the ferryman, like Charon, the ferryman of the Styx. Arthur and the Queen come to see and there:

> . . . saw the fairest woman lie in a rich bed, covered unto her middle with many rich clothes, and all was of cloth of gold, and she lay as though she had smiled.

Arthur himself is taken off to his rest in Avalon by water:

> Then Sir Bedevere took the king upon his back, and so went with him to that water side. And when they were at the water side, even fast by the bank hoved a little barge with many fair ladies in it, and among them all was a queen, and all they had black hoods, and all they wept and shrieked when they saw King Arthur.
>
> 'Now put me into the barge,' said the king.
>
> And so then they rowed from the land, and Sir Bedevere beheld all those ladies go from him.
>
> Then Sir Bedevere cried, 'Ah, my lord Arthur, what shall become of me, now ye go from me and leave me here alone among my enemies?'
>
> 'Comfort thyself,' said the king, 'and do as well as thou mayest, for in me is no trust to trust in; for I will into the vale of Avalon to heal me of my grievous wound . . .'

Malory Book XXI chapter 5

The Vale of Avalon draws us on to those vales and valleys familiar in the Bible. The Valley of the Shadow of Death; the Vale of Hinnom, that is Slaughter, where the Jewish hell, Gehenna, is located; the Vale of Baca, Mystery, turned into a pool by the man whose strength is in the Lord; and so on.

Generally the Bible is kind about water, as is to be expected in an arid land where cool streams betokened refreshment, oasis irrigation. Even the names evoke a luxuriance of liquid, somehow: the pool of Shiloam, streams from Lebanon, the pool of Hebron. Certainly those names will have resonated in the ears of the Crusaders visiting the Holy Land. Most of all they must have longed to see the river where John the Baptist christened Jesus: the Jordan, which, like the Red Sea, God had once dried up to allow the Israelites to elude their enemies.

Alas for romance, the Jordan was, from early times, a rather murky river, full of marl deposits and industrial effluent sluiced into it from the bankside brick factories and the brass foundry established by Solomon. The Hebrew poets reserved their encomiums for the pellucid streams of Damascus. Still, the Jordan kept the fields moist and, for the Jews captive in Babylon, the river symbolised the barrier separating them from their homeland.

The idea that crossing over Jordan marked a Christian's passage from the wilderness of this world into the Promised Land harks back to the Old Testament story in Deuteronomy where Moses, having led the Israelites out of Egypt, asks God to be allowed to go over the river to see the good land which lay beyond – namely the paradisal Canaan flowing with milk and honey. Jordan as heaven's river is a later, Christian invention stemming from that. Crusaders and pilgrims both brought home water from the river in what came to be called Jordan bottles.

In general, the idea of a water barrier separating this world from the next, heaven from hell, is more obviously European, particularly north European. It is rooted in the damp, wintry view of water prevalent among the peoples who saw not much sunshine and a thin version of it when they did. Water was a chilly, black, treacherous moat dividing dry land from quite what you could never be sure. It might be the dreaded whirlpool where nine contrary tides meet in a rush between Norway and Orkney, the Maelstrom, which 'maketh such a terrible noise, that is shaketh the rings in the doores of the inhabitants houses on Orkney ten miles off'. The Bible, though, confirmed the Celtic mistrust of the sea in the stories of Jonah, and of the shipwrecks of St Paul. He it was who spoke of his 'journeyings often, in perils of water' (Corinthians

11 v. 26). Revelation speaks, too, of seas of glass, and rivers of crystal, imagery well known to those who knew the stories of the Celtic tradition.

But there is one episode in the romances which points to a more equivocal symbolism of water. It seems to echo the words of Jesus in John's Gospel:

> Verily, verily, I say unto thee, Except a man be born of water and of the Spirit, he cannot enter into the kingdom of God.

In the prose *Lancelot of the Lake*, King Arthur has a nightmare; the interpreter warns him that it portends:

> that you must lose all earthly honour, and those you most rely on will fail you in spite of themselves, for that is how it must be.

Section 285

He does add a word of comfort, though: 'unless you are saved by the Lion in Water and the Doctor without Medicine and the counsel of the flower'.

Arthur has to wait for a full explanation of this cryptic message until he meets a worthy man (perhaps another of the Arthurian hermits) who solves the enigma: the Doctor without Medicine is God; the flower is the 'fruit which satisfied the five thousand in the meadows ... and by which the people of Israel were sustained for fifteen years in the desert [manna]'. And:

> The Lion, so different in nature to other beasts, signifies God. But the Lion seen in water has special significance. For the water is taken to mean the world. And, just as a fish cannot live but in water, so we cannot live without the human world and all that is created in it.

'The things of this world' represent flesh and blood – water's living streams used in Christian baptism. Here water, then, represents the world of human failing but of human life, too.

THE CASTLE

We are used to the Gothic chill of castles silhouetted against storm-torn skies; vampires, Frankenstein, Zenda. But even in the days when most of the European castles were being constructed they had a similar aspect. Built as defensive strongholds their secondary purpose was to cow and terrorise by their imposing bulk, by their forbidding walls that offered no ready access. Castles embodied martial strength and force, just as cathedrals symbolised man's spiritual ascent heavenwards. And castles were dungeons, too. Arthur, Count of Brittany, grandson of Henry II and Eleanor of Aquitaine, opposed his uncle, King John, and met defeat on Lammastide in 1202 at the battle of Mirebeau. He was taken prisoner, incarcerated in Falaise Castle and never seen in public again.

The Grail Castle holds terrors and enchantments – either from diabolic powers or the awful ('awe-inspiring') majesty of God. One of the most frightening is in the prose *Lancelot of the Lake*, a fair blueprint for a blood-tingling house of horrors, the like of which a mediaeval torturer might dream up for unsuspecting travellers who knock at the door on a wild night and ask for lodging.

Fouke Fitz-Warin, a romance composed by a Shropshire author between 1256 and 1264, centres on the hilltop site of Brân's ancient fortress, Dinas Brân; a castle which occupies an important place in the Grail legend, so it is thought. Breton storytellers at William the Conqueror's court told how Brân kept a buried treasure in Dinas Brân. The castle was burnt and the country round about laid waste. Many came to see the wonders of the place, the blackened teeth of its ruined walls gnawing at the bloody dusk sky, but only one knight survived the ordeal. One of the Grail storytellers was a famous Welsh *fabulator* who, according to the writer Thomas in his *Tristan*, 'knew the deeds and histories of every king and every story ever told in Brittany'. His name: Bleheris, or Bledhericus, or Bledri ap Cadivor; he may have written the *Perlesvaus.*

Dinas Brân reputedly inspired the gaunt Castle of Inquest belonging to the rich Fisher King in *Perlesvaus*, where the service of the most Holy Graal is conducted. A chained lion guards the gateway, flanked on either side by two beaten copper sergeants holding crossbows from which 'shot forth quarrels [short, heavy, square-headed bolts] with great force and great wrath'. Each crenellation of the wall contains a tiny chapel and a cross just like the plastered wall niches in the round Temple Church in London. Inside the castle live priests and knights, bald (and bearded?) and clad in white mantles. Templars.

A short distance from Dinas Brân, at the foot of Brân's hill, stood a Cistercian abbey – the Valle Crucis (Valley of the Cross), founded in about 1200 by Madoc ap Gruffydd, lord of Dinas Brân; the Cistercians probably had an interest there before then. Templars, Cistercians and a Grail Castle – of course. St Bernard, the great Cistercian abbot reformer, had drawn up a monastic rule for the Templars, those warrior monks, knights of Christ whose religious houses doubled as castles.

The coalition of Cistercians and Templars has bearing on the Grail romance as part of the Arthurian story. Both Orders were powerful, in wealth and influence, throughout Europe; especially so in England.

In the Templar Church in London, there are nine tombs of knights – not Templars but members of Templar fraternities. Four belong to the Welsh Pembroke family, Earls of Shrewsbury. Three of them lie, half-turned, left leg crossed over right, right hand drawing the sword out of its sheath. The attitude may well symbolise guarding the Templar's secret and mark a degree of Templar initiation. The fourth Pembroke drives his fully naked sword, alongside which he lies (or, originally, stands?), clean through the head of a devilish-visaged imp – cousin, by its look, to a Chinese dragon. Another Pembroke stands on a winged dragon which gnaws at the strap of his right spur.

Do these knights mimic the once and future king Arthur of romance, frozen in attitude of death yet ready, when the last trumpet sounds the call for battle and the graves open, to draw their swords and ride out with him from under the dark hill? Arthur sleeps there with the main body of his faithful knights according to legend. The Templars cherished the frank opinion that, in spirit at least, they belonged to that company and would return in the hour of need.

The Cistercian Order of White Monks and the Order of Templars owned vast estates throughout Europe, almost all Yorkshire in England, for example, secured by patronage and a prodigious accumulation of wealth. The Cistercians, leading sheepfarmers of the day, paid a large proportion of the 35 tons of silver demanded in ransom for Richard the Lionheart. Templar barns still dot the English landscape, vestiges of their once-extensive landholdings.

The political and spiritual influence attendant on such a forward status in mediaeval society was always considerable. At a time when even a small body of heavily armed cavalry posed a substantial threat, the Templars stabled many such companies of knights all over Europe. The intimate bond between Cistercians and Crusades has already been noted. So, the white mantle which belonged, originally, to all Crusaders became the jealous monopoly of Cistercian monks and their warrior brothers the Templars; *they* lurk behind all reference to white robes in romance. Their abbeys and fortified priories, too, enclosed from the rest of the world, hushed in secrecy, swathed in what the religious called 'the great silence', undoubtedly coloured descriptions of the Grail Castle.

The nomad Celts and the Teuton invaders after them, tended to build earthwork forts, palisaded with wood. The stone fortress arrived in Europe in about the eleventh century, for the most part a crude blockhouse. The masons who travelled with the Crusaders had much to learn (and *did* learn) from the far-advanced skills of the Byzantine Greeks. They had for long been used to girdling their cities round with cunningly engineered, formidable buttressed stone walls and ramparts. The Europeans learnt, too, from the sophisticated Moorish engineers responsible for the walled cities and castles which throng Spain.

As castles proliferated in Europe, so Christian theologians began to describe the heavenly mansions in terms of a fortified dwelling place guarded from evil forces rampant in the unprotected open country; like the writers of romance they, too, used common metaphor to blend reality and fiction.

Joachim de Fiore (1145–1202), a Cistercian abbot and mystic theologian, wrote: 'The Cistercian Order is a city of the sun; it shines forth in Clairvaux.' Clairvaux ('Bright Valleys') was St Bernard's Abbey and, although the Order had been founded at Cîteaux in 1098, Clairvaux had become the great centre of the Order of White Monks. Joachim went further: Rome had become a sink of iniquity, the whore of Babylon herself, apocalyptic symbol of depravity. He declared that the true Church was Jerusalem, but *not* necessarily the Jerusalem of the Holy Land, rather New Jerusalem, the spiritual city of perfection described in Revelation. And, Joachim said, that mystic vision had its reality in the abbey of White Monks at Clairvaux.

There, if you like, was the pure fish of wisdom and holiness swimming in the water of the world, the abbey cut off from earthly corruption. The Order of Templars called its churches and institutions 'temples', in conscious reference to its parent house on the Temple rock in the Holy City. The combination of monastic isolation and military impregnability, Templar and Cistercian together, characterises the castles of the Grail quest in the romances: moated, high-walled forts; silent, monkish houses locked off from the world; forest chapels deep in the forest; temples of mystery with exotic names – Munsalvaesche ('Wild Mountain' in *Parzival*), the Castle of the Black Hermit, the Castle of Inquest, the Castle of King Gurgulain in *Perlesvaus*, Belrepeire, Rock of Chanpguin (probably a disguised form of *sanguin* from *sang*: 'blood') in Chrétien de Troyes. Castle and Cathedral in one.

Cathedrals had made as stunning an impact on the mediaeval landscape as castles: massive ecclesiastical ships (nave is Latin for ship), spire tilted at the clouds like a mast, towering up from domed mound and wide flatland as if from the main. New palaces of glass and crystal, the bleached stone walls perforated with deep-stained and clear windows. In A.D. 442, St Jerome had talked in raptures of the gemmed light flooding St Sophia in Constantinople; glass being another oriental invention. Now the glassmakers of France at last brought the same glories to western Europe.

The Celtic reverence for glass in all likelihood has this prosaic explanation: they could not make it and hardly knew what it was. The Romans imported some glass ware to Britain but they established no industry there. The Venerable Bede, in his *History*, records how in 674 the Abbot Benedict had been obliged to hire glass workers from distant Gaul to install windows in the abbey at Wearmouth. Glass, rare enough when the Romans occupied Britain, had virtually disappeared with them, until the age of cathedral construction reintroduced it. The cathedral stained glass opened dazzling, royal windows on heaven, streaming with jewelled light. This did not revive Celtic awe of glass; why should only the Celts see the view through glass as mysterious? Having no glass they pointed to its natural surrogates: frost, ice, water, mist. The richly endowed builders of the mediaeval cathedrals were able to use the real thing. As the first Grail romances emerged, coincidentally (or perhaps not), the first great cathedrals were being constructed: Nôtre Dame de Paris, Reims, Wells, Chartres, Salisbury, the choir at Lincoln . . . monumental symbols of human faith and exaltation striving heavenwards. The Grail romances are a literary equivalent.

GLASTONBURY: HOLY RELIC CENTRE

At a more basic level, the churches and abbeys dotting the landscape of Europe claimed to be anterooms of the promised heavenly mansions. One such was the Benedictine (Black Monk) abbey at Glastonbury. Founded in A.D. 700, Glastonbury had for a long time enjoyed prominent and largely self-promoted celebrity, attracting scholars and theologians from all over the old Celtic world – Wales, Ireland, Brittany. During the Dark Ages a constant stream of heroic and mythic lore flowed into the abbey from Ireland: Glastonbury, sited near the Bristol Channel in the heart of Arthur's old kingdom, became a proto-university of fringe literature; Old French and British legend met, mingled and fused here.

In 1184 calamity struck: a fire destroyed the abbey, including, we presume, a valuable stock of books. Henry II answered a plea for help. Grants to religious foundations were an established method of expiating guilt and Henry's conscience buckled under the combined weight of his adulterous passion for Fair Rosamond *and* his deadly quarrel with Archbishop Thomas à Becket; he contributed lavishly. Not that the monks, sniffing a comfy alternative to scratching a bare subsistence out of the vegetable garden, were solely dependent on him. The holy places had become highly commercialised tourist centres, the target of pilgrims ready to worship *and* spend at the shrines. The monks of Glastonbury saw their chance. They had been poking around in the ashes of the fire and prodded up a phoenix which laid a massive golden egg. In 1191 they announced to the astonished world that they had exhumed the coffins of King Arthur and Queen Guenever in a foundation trench on the building site. The monastic publicity machine, well-oiled and primed, went into rapid action. This discovery, according to the monks, corroborated emphatically the link between Glastonbury and the old Celtic Otherworld, where Arthur was said to have gone after the last battle. The ancient Britons had called that place Ynys yr Afalon (*Avallonia* in Latin), or else Ynys Vitrin, Glass Island. Both were famous as the Celtic Elysium. *But,* said the monks, Glastonbury (Saxon *Glaestingaburg*) also meant Glass Town. The Romans had called it *Glastonia* meaning 'the town where the woad (*glastum*) comes from'; but there is another Latin word for woad, that all-important source of green-blue dye, namely *vitrum* 'glass'. Roman glass was green-blue, as I said earlier, and this *vitrum* was the word adapted by the Welsh for their *gwydrin*, 'glassy'. If that all sounds rather complicated, it no more than shows to what lengths the Glastonbury monks went to prove that Avalon *was* the Glass Town dominated by their abbey. And here, of course, reposed the mortal remains of Arthur the King and his Queen; most conveniently for the Church, both of them demonstrably stone cold dead and buried with due Christian rite. This talk of lying under the hill asleep had the tiniest reek of sulphur in it . . .

unholy unorthodoxy. The Celtic bit could be taken too far. Besides, relics were business.

The monks warmed gleefully to their theme: a lot more holiness equalled a lot more income. Not far from the uncontroversially mortal remains of King Arthur, the monkish navvies unearthed the scourging post and the scourge used to flog Christ; the garment in which Herod clothed him; the two sponges – the one soaked in wine and myrrh, the other in vinegar – offered to the dying Saviour on the Cross; sundry bits of the Cross itself, needless to say, plus rubble from Mount Calvary and so on and so on; quite a haul. It also emerged – surprise, surprise – that St David (King Arthur's uncle according to Geoffrey of Monmouth) had built a church at Glastonbury; following the lead, presumably, of St Patrick of Ireland who had given the foundation a charter in 400 and something. Also, the renowned pietist and polemicist Gildas had come there when it was 'besieged by the tyrant Arthur with a countless host because his wife Guennuvar had been raped and stolen by the aforesaid evil king [Melvas] and had been carried thither by reason of the refuge afforded by its inviolate site and the reeds rover and marsh which protected it'. (*Life of Gildas* Caradoc of Lancarvan, pre-1136, quoted in Loomis *Arthurian Tradition*.) Never mind Gildas' snub of tyranny: he had a thing about kings. The important point is that Glastonbury held the stage, and any publicity is good publicity.

Now came the biggest find of all, the fruits of painstaking research in the apocryphal *Gospel of Nicodemus,* known in England from the eighth century. Glastonbury, declared the monks, had

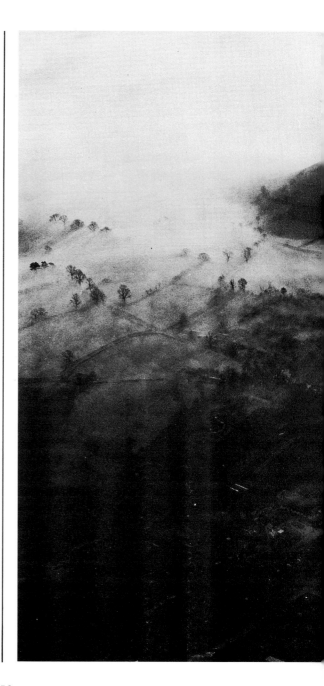

Glastonbury Tor, seemingly an island afloat in a sea of mist, looms up out of the Somerset wetlands.

been founded by none other than Joseph of Arimathea, the rich man who begged Christ's crucified body from the Roman authorities and entombed it in the sepulchre he had prepared for himself in his own garden; the Holy Sepulchre as it was known to the Crusaders. The story went thus: imprisoned after the disappearance of Christ's body from the tomb, Joseph, given neither food nor drink, was sustained by the risen Lord who visited him in his cell and fed and watered him from the cup He had used at the Last Supper. This chalice had passed into Joseph's possession; in fact he had used it to catch drops of blood shed by Christ on the Cross. Somehow Jesus regained possession after his resurrection and for forty years (the same time spent by the Israelites wandering in the wilderness) kept Joseph miraculously alive from its invisible plenty. Released from prison (didn't they ask him how he'd managed?), Joseph, plus chalice, left Judaea in company with his sister Enygeus and her husband Hebron (or Bron for short – Brân to the echo). The Vale of Hebron lies beyond Jordan in Canaan. Eventually the party arrive in Glastonbury where Joseph, signalling journey's end, plants his staff in the ground, as the Apostle Peter had planted his outside Rome. From its stock grew the Christmas- and spring-flowering Glastonbury Thorn. Close by a source of water, rusty red as blood, purled out of the ground – the Chalice Well. Actually it's a chalybeate (ferrous) spring, rich in iron, and cura- tive of the green sickness or 'vapours' much suffered by eighteenth-century young ladies and the heroines of romantic fiction. On the whereabouts of the Chalice, also known as the Holy Grail, the Black Monks kept silent.

However, across the Channel at Fescamps Abbey, sister house to Glastonbury, the Black Monks had for some time revered a phial of the Saviour's blood, brought from the newly conquered Holy Land (unless, perhaps, Joseph of Arimathea had dropped it off on his way through?). A Cult of Holy Blood had been inaugurated there by the end of the eleventh century. Fescamps also had a guild of minstrels attached to its foundation from the early 1000s and, as one of the Grail romancers, Wauchier (who may have been the Welshman Bleheris) claims: 'The whole story [of the Grail] is written down at Fescamps'.

So: the White Monks claim the Grail Castle in mountainous Wales; the Black Monks claim, if not the Grail itself then its contents or as near as dammit in Somerset and Normandy. The White Monks, originally renegade Black Monks, had renounced relics. The Black Monks loved nothing better – their foundations burst at the seams with relics; relics brought pilgrims. Within a few years of the momentous exhumations at Glastonbury, a pilgrimage to damp Somerset reaped grander promise of indulgence (forgiveness of sins) than trips to Canterbury, Rome and Jerusalem put together, so laden was the Benedictine house below the mysterious Tor with sacred bric-à-brac.

What sense can we make of it? The solution is fairly straightforward. The White Cistercians, in ascetic revulsion at the opulence of the relic-hungry Order based at Cluny, sought to redefine monastic poverty. Their cells would be bare of treasure in the material sense, but rich in spiritual bounty. The great reformer St Bernard articulated the assault on the slack-moralled, materialistic approach of the Benedictines. To their idolatrous cult of the Holy Blood *he* opposed the devotional cult of the Blessed Virgin Mary. This theological shift is reflected in the change from flesh-and-blood Grail adventure, as written by Chrétien de Troyes, to the spiritualised *Quest*, heavy with religious symbolism and Cister- cian mysticism.

The down-to-earth Black Monks hit back at their airy-fairy White Monk rivals. Popular senti- ment was on their side, too – people *liked* saints' bones, scraps of wood and rust-stained bottles. Was not the Grail Castle in the *Quest* and other romances in fact the Castle of Corbenic, Blessed Body? *Cor* can also mean horn, but if it is *benic* or blessed (Latin *benedictus* as in Benedictine), that would make it the horn of plenty, surely? If, though, it is a Blessed Body (*cor* as in *corpse*) then it would have to be the most blessed body of all, namely Christ's; the body that Joseph of Arimathea had taken such care of. Either way, Corbenic Castle lies at the very centre of the Holy Grail story which, the Black Monks said, was as true as anything in the Bible. And where did the title Corbenic originate? Why, in the Benedictine at Corbie near Amiens, or else the other Benedictine at Corbény, between Laon and Reims. The Abbot of Glastonbury clinched the argument: he produced an item holier than all the rest, brought the long way to Somerset by Joseph of Arimathea; the tip of the Holy Lance driven into Jesus' side, making him the Maimed King. This was the third authentic Holy Lance in Christendom.

THE MAIMED KING

But when they came to Jesus and saw that he was dead already, they brake not his legs. But one of the soldiers with a spear pierced his side and forthwith came there out blood and water.

John 19 vv. 33–4

The breaking of a crucified felon's legs was a small act of mercy, hastening death by suffocation as the body, sagging without the legs' support, compressed the lungs. That the soldier, traditionally Longinus, saw fit to stab Christ with a spear indicates that ritual wounding or maiming, whether by spear or hammer, formed part of crucifixion.

In *The White Goddess*, Robert Graves postulates that crucifixion originated in Carthage where the annual sacred king suffered death for the good of the tribe, much as the royal scapegoat of the Aztecs. His feet were pinioned to a cross of elderwood, ill-omened ever since, though its worthlessness as wood for carpentry or firemaking may have a lot to do with that. A nail was driven between his ankle bone and Achilles tendon, that spot in the wren's foot split through by dead-eye Llew Llaw Gyffes. The identity of the wren, the smallest bird in the British Isles? None other than Bendigeidfran, Brân the Blessed, to whom, as well as the raven, the bird was sacred. In fact in Devon the wren used to be called 'Brân's sparrow'. The wren is the spirit of the Old Year killed at the Winter Solstice. The New Year rises up like an eagle, just as Llew Llaw Gyffes' soul becomes an eagle, and the wren rides up on the eagle's back just as one year runs into the next. The ancient Irish, commemorating this, hunted the wren on the feast of the martyr St Stephen (December 26), and killed the bird, just as St Stephen himself was killed, with stones. So, in the English romance *Merlin* (1450) we hear:

> Thus shull the knyghtes of the rounde table go
> to avenge the deth of the wrenne.

Stoning, torture, in all its macabre and grisly forms, first maimed, then despatched the King of Kings.

The flux of water mingled with blood from Christ's wounded side proves, say many commentators, that Christ did *not* die on the Cross, since dead men don't bleed. Howsoever that may be, the spear thrust is commemorated in Arthurian romance as the Dolorous Stroke. Thus, Balin, the worshipful knight, fights King Pellam (who appears elsewhere as Pelles, the Fisher King) on a matter of vengeance. Balin's sword breaks and he runs from chamber to chamber searching for a replacement. Finally, in a richly furnished bed chamber in Pellam's palace, the bed draped with gold cloth, Balin sees:

a table of clean gold with four silver pillars . . . and upon the table stood a marvellous spear strangely wrought.

And when Balin saw that spear he gat it in his hand and turned him to King Pellam, and smote him passingly sore with that spear, that King Pellam fell down in a swoon and therewith the castle roof and walls brake and fell to the earth, and Balin fell down so that he moght not stir foot or hand. And so the most part of the castle, that was fal down through that Dolorous Stroke lay upon Pellam and Balin three days [the length of Christ's death].

Malory Book II chapter 15

The spear is that of Longinus; King Pellam is related to Joseph of Arimathea.

And King Pellam lay so, many years sore wounded, and might never be whole till Galahad the Haut [high] Prince healed him in the quest of the Sangrail, for in that place was part of the blood of Our Lord Jesus Christ, that Joseph of Arimathea brought into this land, and there himself lay in that rich bed.

So, Arthurian romance documents the finding of a holy relic, the Lance used by Longinus, whether it be the Holy Lance dug up from under the floor of Antioch cathedral, or preserved in Constantinople, or, according to William of Malmesbury, a Benedictine monk (c. 1080–1143), wielded by Charlemagne against the Spanish Saracens; or excavated from the subsoil of Glastonbury.

The Maimed King suffers for his people. In his health lies theirs; in his suffering, their ill. Walter Map, a cleric born in France who spent time at the court of Henry II, and was parson of Westbury in Gloucestershire at some stage, records a Breton story about Alan, King of Brittany being castrated. As a result: 'no animals even today can bring forth young, but, when ripe for bearing, they go outside of the parish to deliver the offspring'. (From *Court Trifles c.* 1181, quoted by R.S. Loomis in his essay *Origin of the Grail Legends*.) Map is also reckoned by some to be the author of both the *Quest of the Holy Grail* and the *Death of Arthur the King*.

The Fisher King whom Perceval meets is maimed; he travels by boat because he cannot walk. Nor is fishing a recreation – he is seeking to recapture the Life spirit, in the shape of a fish, from the enchanted liquid element. (This last detail in the familiar story caused some awkwardness for Wolfram von Eschenbach, high master of the Grail romance. German gentlemen of the Middle Ages considered it beneath their dignity to fish.)

Another version of the maiming wound also appears in several romances. As I pointed out, the dying warrior expects a woman in a boat; the living warrior had better beware of her – she comes from the other side and means him ill. Malory describes how Sir Perceval:

. . . saw a ship came rowing in the sea as all the wind of the world had driven it. And so it drove under that rock. And when Sir Perceval hied him thither he found the ship covered with silk more blacker than any bear, and therein was a gentlewoman of great beauty, and she was clothed richly that none might be better.

She promises him comfort; he accepts:

And anon she was unclothed and laid therein. And then Sir Perceval laid him down by her naked; and by adventure and grace he saw his sword lie on the ground naked, in whose pommel was a red cross and the sign of the crucifix therein, and bethought him on his knighthood and his promise . . .

He makes the sign of the cross in his forehead, and

therewith the pavilion turned up-so-down, and then it changed unto a smoke, and a black cloud and then he was adread and cried aloud . . .

He draws his sword and reproaches himself for this lapse of chastity:

'Sithen my flesh will be my master I shall punish it,' and therewith he rove himself through the thigh that the blood start about him, and said, 'O good Lord, take this in recompensation of that I have done against Thee, my Lord'.

Malory Book XIV chapters 8–10

Perceval's self-inflicted thrust into the thigh chastises his lubricious flesh. This wound is common throughout the romances – Lancelot, Perceval, Tristan and others suffer it, from arrow or lance. The arrows *ought*, by the way, to be made of mistletoe because mistletoe is a phallic emblem. The Druids cut it from the oaks in a ritual emasculation; the glutinous white berries are reminiscent of semen. The origin of the wound, as is plain from Perceval's reason for hurting himself, is phallic: it symbolises emasculation. This is not the place to go into primitive castration phobias; suffice it to say that all phallic symbolism has to do with fertility and the rites of manhood and male initiation into the élite warrior caste. The dubbing stroke of the royal sword on shoulders is a residual form of the rite: beheading stands for removal of the penis, ejaculation a symbolic exsanguination. Womanhood

is seen as interior, recumbent; the female vagina the scabbard (its Latin meaning) for the penetrating and vulnerable shaft. Fertility depended on action, insertion, thrust; hence the symbolism of sword and lance in *all* primitive religions whose influence can be detected in Christianity.

The Maimed King – Brân wounded in the foot, Llew Llaw Gyffes lamed like a smith, Joseph of Arimathea, owner of the Holy Sepulchre – is a surrogate for the Saviour himself, of whom John says, in Revelation: 'For thou wast slain and hast redeemed us to God by thy blood'. The wound, which can be cured by some heroic act or spiritual triumph, holds out the all-important promise that death and disaster is never absolute, that redemption is never wholly unthinkable.

The sumptuous canopies and hangings of the Maimed King's chamber force comparison with mediaeval papal magnificence. The *Perlesvaus* describes him lying on a bed hung with cords and stays of ivory, the mattress covered with sables; on his head a cap of sable; he wears a gown of red (cardinalatial colour) samite, a rich silk stuff; round his neck a golden pectoral cross; his pillow scented with balm. At each of the bed's four corners a stone emits a marvellous effulgence of light; by the bed tapers of wax in four gold candlesticks, and a pillar of copper surmounted by an eagle, holding a gold cross in its beak, and in the gold cross a piece of the True Cross. The chamber is strewn with balm, green herbs and reeds; and in the anteroom a gold and silver chess set. It is a far cry from the prophet Isaiah's description of the apostolic Maimed King, the Messiah:

. . . wounded for our transgressions, he was bruised for our iniquities: the chastisement of our peace was upon him; and with his stripes we are healed.

Isaiah 53 v. 5

And before his coming, 'the fishers also shall mourn, and all they that cast angle into the brooks shall lament' (19 v. 8). For they inhabit the Waste Land.

THE WASTE LAND

The poet Isaiah, mimicking in language the fire and brimstone which the Lord caused to rain down upon the wicked cities of Sodom and Gomorrah, denounces spiritual degeneracy, calling it a desert: blasted land, parched and empty valleys, ragged rocks, briers and thorns, vines unpruned, the houses without occupants, the heads of the daughters of Sion smitten with a scab, instead of sweet odours stink, baldness instead of hair, burning instead of beauty. Still not satisfied with the level of punishment he has meted out, 'the Lord shall hiss for the fly that is in the uppermost part of the rivers of Egypt, and for the bee that is in the land of Assyria'.

> Your country is desolate, your cities are burned with fire: your land, strangers devour it in your presence, and it is desolate, as overthrown by strangers.
>
> *Isaiah 1 v. 7*

Mediaeval churchmen, poring over Holy Scripture for texts to pad out and stiffen the Crusade sermons, almost certainly identified these last two afflictions as 'those sons of whores, the race of Cain', the Saracens of Egypt and Assyria.

The Waste Land of the Grail story is biblical; and only God's miracle of fertility ('behold, a virgin shall conceive') will end it. Galahad is a virgin like the Biblical Christ and, as the religious orders in general but the Cistercians most fervently, preached, the deepest power of spiritual regeneration resided in chastity. Only the purest heart can bring life to a spiritual desolation, in other words.

The Celts knew bleak infertile regions: Dartmoor, the bogs of northern Ireland, the rocky fastnesses of the Welsh mountains, the Pennine ridges, bare as a bone, the wild heathlands round the Wirral. However, the Waste Land contained no spiritual metaphor in Celtic lore: it came from natural disaster and human invaders who drove them into the rocks and moors for ill-supplied refuge. The sacrifice of a nobleman might reverse the catastrophe; heroic death in battle, maybe, but spiritual regeneration, in the theological sense implicit in Isaiah's imagery and in the allegory of the Grail romance, meant nothing to them. That was altogether too mystical an idea. The Celts believed in magic, the active conjuring and wielding of supernatural powers. They did not believe in mysticism, which deals with similar powers but on a contemplative, essentially inactive, level.

Mysticism is Semitic in origin, born of the hot desert: the necessities of life are pared to the bone, and mind, imagination, spirit attenuated by hunger and concentration to a fine clarity of vision. Such was the practice of the mediaeval visionaries who imitated the desert fathers of the early Church; who, in turn, had followed the example of the first, pre-Christian holy men.

One such visionary, St Bernard, implanted this practice of intense spiritual introspection in his rule for both Cistercians and Templars. The Grail legends evince a peculiarly Cistercian character. Their imagery is penetratingly religious, not mythical, in the sense of an elemental struggle; here the combat is, primarily, spiritual; indeed, the Grail knights, finally, lay down their swords. The mystic fervour of St Bernard, dynamic proponent of the Crusades and spiritual patron of the Templars, rings insistently in the Grail legends; and this accords exactly and, I believe, deliberately, with the Messianic urgency of Isaiah's extended prophecy. Herein he foretells the coming of Christ, the Man of Sorrows, the Maimed King who, in his forty days' sojourn in the wilderness, tempted by Satan, recalls the forty years of Israel's penitential wanderings in another wilderness.

The homilies and tirades of St Bernard and other religious leaders, the mystic vision of the Cistercians, the Crusading fervour, the ideal world of Arthurian romance, all at once nostalgic and consciously predictive in nature, must be seen against the prevailing mediaeval opinion that the end of the world was near. The Middle Ages were dominated by what Norman Cohn, in his detailed study of this phenomenon, calls the 'Pursuit of the Millennium'; the millennium being that 1000 years allotted to God's kingdom forecast in John's Revelation. The Cistercian Joachim de Fiore spoke of Three Ages of Man: the final age, prefigured at the new Jerusalem, Clairvaux, would be the Age of Spirit, 'as broad daylight compared with starlight and the dawn, as high summer compared with winter and spring . . . the world would be one vast monastery, in which all men would be contemplative monks, rapt in mystical ecstasy, and united in singing the praises of God'. Adolf Hitler, who saw himself, in a 1936 poster, as a Grail knight, his mind clanging with heavy brass symbolism of Wagnerian Twilight of the Gods and Brunhilde torching the world's pyre, declared that his *Third* Reich was intended to last for a thousand years. Did he have plans for the aftermath, I wonder?

As to the Waste Land of the romances, we might place it on the bleak and hostile plateaux of Anatolia, across which the Crusaders straggled on their arduous way to Palestine. Even the arid *maquis* of the Massif Central and the troubadour stronghold Provence, those thorn brakes and thickets where the French Resistance hid out during the Second World War, might fix the picture of a real Waste Land. But the romances do not come supplied with maps, nor do they require them. By their account, olive trees grow in Wales. Topographical detail is a lure for curiosity, not much more.

Yet we can see how closely the romances drew on fact. For instance, chroniclers record that an exceptionally harsh winter in 1144 led to catastrophic food shortages which drove thousands of people off their land in a desperate hunt for provisions elsewhere; many went overseas. Areas like Brittany, which had never recovered from the depredatory Viking raids, were almost denuded of populace. This may have seemed like a withering judgement of God in retribution for sin. However, the preachers spoke of the Waste Land as a permanent condition, a symbol of imminent evil. The Grail romances echoed them, employing a common metaphor, that of barbarian invasion:

> In the kingdom of Logres [England] total war raged between King Lambar, father of him known as the Maimed King, and King Urlain, a pagan from birth who had just been baptised and was reckoned one of the finest men alive. One day the opposing armies clashed on the beach. Offshore lay a ship at anchor. King Lambar's men had the better of the fight and when Urlain saw himself beaten and his men butchered, he fled to the ship in terror of his life. There he found this sword. He drew it from the scabbard, returned to the fray and made for King Lambar, a man whose faith and trust in Our Lord was stauncher than anyone's. King Urlain confronted Lambar and struck him so hard on the helmet with this sword that he split him and his horse clean in two. Such was the first blow struck by this sword in the kingdom of Logres, and so great a devastation did it bring to both kingdoms that no man had reward of his labour in the fields, no corn or other vegetation grew, no trees yielded fruit, no fish swam in the pond or

stream. And so the two kingdoms were called the Waste Land when they had been laid desolate by the blow of this sword.

Quest of the Holy Grail , chapter 9

The sword is eventually drawn from the blood-red stone by Galahad. He is the one knight foretold who 'can outdo and outdare every other'.

The Waste Land might be crossed, and the Promised Land entered, by seeking the Holy Grail, or spiritual oneness with Christ. Then, as Isaiah puts it:

. . . the parched ground shall become a pool, and the thirsty land springs of water: in the habitation of dragons, where each lay, shall be grass with reeds and rushes. And an highway shall be there, and a way, and it shall be called The way of holiness; the unclean shall not pass over it.

Isaiah 35 vv. 7–8

THE GRAIL

And he took the cup and gave thanks, and gave it to them saying, Drink ye all of it. For this is my blood of the new testament, which is shed for many for the remission of sins.

Matthew 26 vv. 27–8

How did the *graal* become the *san graal*?

Writing some fifty years after Chrétien de Troyes, the Chronicler Helinandus described the Grail in his account of a vision revealed to a hermit in Brittany:

The Gallic name of the grail is *gradalis*, a wide, fairly deep dish, the sort used for delicacies at a rich man's table; from it, every guest, irrespective of social rank, receives an equal portion.

Quoted R.S. Loomis in *The grail: from Celtic myth to Christian symbol* (p. 29)

Helinandus' Latin makes a play of words on *gradatim*, which can mean 'portion by portion' or 'according to rank'. So Helinandus spells it out: the *graal* gets its name from the *gradalis* dish, carried round a circle of guests, just as the gradual hymn is sung during a liturgical procession, another name for which is 'grail'. Thus *graal* confers an ideal hospitality, no one guest honoured above the others, no lord receiving the hero's portion or lion's share; the host bestows his largesse in equal proportion to everyone. As Christ said: 'Drink it, every one of you'. Does this revive the Celtic fireside circle of warriors, gathered for ale, food and bardic song? Or Christ's Last Supper and inaugural feast of the Holy Eucharist? Unquestionably the latter. What links both is that a Lord presides over a close company of initiates. The equality is not so much of rank as of admission to an élite mystery. A Celtic lord and host would, like Odysseus, have claimed double helpings as a mark of his status, even from Brân's plenteous horn. The Round Table may have its distant origin in the fireside place-setting, but its symbolism is rooted in the mediaeval circle of perfection of all beings and the timeless equality of God's creation. So, too, we observe that symbolism in the circular Temple churches, modelled, as they were, on the round Dome Mosque.

As soon as the *graal* had made its first appearance in literature, at the centre of a plainly liturgically inspired mystery (procession of talismanic objects, flickering candles, reverential atmosphere), it was bound to become holy. The Crusades flooded Europe with holy relics: how could a dish providing miraculous foodstuff remain unconsecrated? Christian teachings groaned with food symbolism as a well-loaded table groans with real food: bread as staff of life; manna in the wilderness; Satan's temptation to turn stones to bread, recalling how Elijah had turned a miserly landowner's melons into stones; the miracle of the loaves and fishes; the miracle of water turned to wine at the wedding in Cana; the grand promise in Luke's Gospel resonantly translated in the Book of Common Prayer:

> He hath filled the hungry with good things, and the rich he hath sent empty away.

The Celts did not invent the provident horn; they shared it with other peoples in other cultures, people who knew about tightened belts and dreams of non-stop plenty. The first *graal* seems to have been a wide salver, used in early mediaeval Wales and, presumably, a familiar object at 'rich men's tables' in many parts of Europe. It soon became a cup, from reference to Christ's Eucharist cup and, perhaps, the cup of his agony which he asked God to take from his lips during the vigil in Gethsemane on the eve of his Crucifixion. As soon as it became *san graal*, mediaeval etymology made another connection, entirely spurious, and produced *sang raal*, or *real*: holy grail . . . blood royal, which added mystique and mystery and majesty to kingship in general but, in particular, to the sacred kingship of Jerusalem, whose streets Jesus, Son of Man and King of Kings, had walked.

So, the mystic process of the Eucharist – transubstantiation of wine and bread into flesh and blood of the Redeemer by the unique, and by any other word, magical power of the priest – became the central enchantment of the romances. By its holy property, the Grail offered that eternal life and

plenty which Isaiah promised would terminate the Waste Land:

> Rejoice thee with Jerusalem, and be glad with her, all ye that love her: rejoice for joy with her, all ye that mourn for her: That ye may suck, and be satisfied with the breasts of her consolation; that ye may milk out and be delighted with the abundance of her glory.

Isaiah 66 vv. 10–11

THE GRAIL PROCESSION

I believe, nor am I the first, that the Grail procession, variously described in the romances but always as exotic, foreign, highly mysterious, probably owes much to the eastern, Byzantine rite of the Mass as it will have been observed by the Crusaders in transit to the Holy Land. The Grail ritual is patently liturgical from the very start; the mysterious world of romance demanded still greater mystification. The Byzantine liturgy had, for centuries before that practised in Rome, referred to the bread and wine as 'king of all things'; and the so-called Great Entrance of the Greek rite (following the elaborate Little Entrance) was a protracted, highly theatrical affair: ceremonial holding up of the sacred vessels (*Prothesis*), gradual procession to the altar and the full celebration of the Eucharist, when transubstantiation takes place; there was a calling down of Christ's spirit and power (*Epiklesis*) to enter the wine and bread – as in the Protestant hymn, 'Spirit of Love come down'. It is perhaps significant to note that the western Church did not introduce elevation of the host (wafer) or chalice until 1208, and then in Paris.

The eastern liturgies, more complex, more elaborate in form and style, more highly developed in symbolism than the western rite, formed the central act of worship in all the churches from Constantinople to Antioch to Jerusalem. It harked back to Jewish ritual feasts, and in particular to that act of blessing a meal on which Christ's Last Supper with the disciples is based – the Quiddush, the breaking of bread and passing round of a wine cup with benediction to all present. The Byzantine church took this simple act, symbolic as it was, and turned it into a performance of at once dark and splendid pomp.

In the procession of the Grail recorded in the romances, we observe lance, sword, cup and blood – the totems of Christ's Crucifixion, preceded by Eucharist, and their redemptive significance: the shining lance, from the point of which oozes a drop of crimson blood to run down the shaft onto the hand of the boy who holds it aloft; the sword of priceless gold (Chrétien) or the lance bleeding into the *graal* (*Perlesvaus*).

If the Roman Mass gave us *hocus pocus* (a derisory gabble of *Hoc est corpus meum*, 'This is my body'), we may say that the Greek Mass gave the Middle Ages a *mumbo-jumbo* which surfaced in the Grail ceremonial; as in the *Perlesvaus*:

> The graal appeared at the sacring of the Mass in five several manners that none ought to tell; for the secret things of the sacrament none ought to tell openly but he to whom God hath given it.

Vol. II (p. 112)

That is a very Templar sort of hugger-mugger with mysterious secrets.

IDENTIFYING THE GRAIL

The *History of the Holy Grail* (written, probably, between 1200 and 1225) refers to Christ administering the sacred wafer from the grail to twelve knights in the Castle of Corbenic. The author claims that 'Corbenic' is a Chaldean word meaning 'holy vessel'. The final 'c' causes misgiving; change it to a more French-looking 't' and it becomes Corbenit, plainly a badly spelled Corbenoit, *benoit* being the Old French for *benedictus* or 'blessed'. Thus Castle of the Blessed Horn (*cor*, Latin *cornu*). However, the author of the *Quest of the Holy Grail* had already staked a claim for a different reading: *cors benoiz* ('t' and 'z' were interchangeable), which means 'sacred body', exactly what the bread of the Eucharist is, the body of the Crucified Lord. In fact the bread, or wafer, is defined elsewhere as 'thrice-blessed body in the form of bread'. That was a symbolic body. Perhaps *cors* (Latin *corpus*) referred to that real body which was in the possession of the Fisher King and surely this recalls the guardian of the most holy and blessed *cors* of all: Joseph of Arimathea who took Christ's body from the Cross? The Grail Castle, then, becomes none other than the temple of the Holy Sepulchre, in the guardianship of the Order of Templar Knights. Such an explanation held more holy water in the Church-sensitive Middle Ages than making the Grail a *cor* of plenty belonging to Celtic Brân, the sparrow and wren hero.

I suppose, irreverently, that the *cor* might well be a trumpet, the Last Trumpet, yet; or else one of those war trumpets amidst the violent braying of which the prophet Isaiah shouted contemptuously: 'Ha! Ha!'

The writer of the first continuation of Chrétien's *Perceval* declares that the Grail contains 'one hundred boar's heads', most pleasing to the Breton compatriots of Asterix and Obelix. Another speaks of a bleeding head on a plate, reminiscent of the grisly trophy presented to Salome. But the Celts dealt in severed heads, too. Which influence first? Call it useful mythological coincidence.

Finally, and against a very strong tide of opinion, Wolfram von Eschenbach in his *Parzival* describes the Grail as a stone; a garnet-hyacinth as long and broad as a table top, cut thin to make it light enough to be carried in procession:

> After them came the Princess; so luminous and radiant her face she made it seem as though dawn were breaking. Her clothes were of Arabian silk; and on a green achmardi she bore the innermost essence of Paradise, a thing beyond all earthly joy called the Gral. Her name was Bringer of Joy, Repanse de Schoy; her nature was of the Gral itself, or pure chastity and perfect honesty.

> Book 5 section 235 line 15 ff

Wolfram draws, here, on the mediaeval symbolism of gemstones: garnet for Constancy, hyacinth the zodiacal jewel of Libra (Balance, Equilibrium, Moderation). The *achmardi*, a bogus Arab-sounding name, is the emerald (Greek *smaragdos*) notedly sovereign against snake venom, as, too, is the 'Emerald Isle' of Ireland. It is also sacred to Venus and, therefore, propitious to love affairs. The Genoese crusaders purloined a cup made of solid emerald from Caesarea Cathedral in 1101 and installed it as the Holy Grail in their own cathedral.

Later, Wolfram lends the *Gral* a cod Latin term: *Lapsit exillis,* which is mumbo-jumbo, like most of the rest of his nomenclature; a deliberate veil. He alludes to the *lapis exilis* ('thin stone'), the Philosopher's Stone of alchemy, by whose virtue the phoenix rises up again out of its own ashes. This stone is also mentioned in the mediaeval romance *Alexander the Great's Journey to Paradise.* Here the pagan Alexander, as susceptible to pride as Parzival, arrives outside the Christian Paradise where a hermit tells him he cannot enter yet; he must first go and practise humility. To illustrate the point, the hermit shows Alexander a stone: placed in one pan of a set of scales, no amount of gold in the other pan can raise it. Substitute a feather for the gold and the stone rises instantly. Heaven's gates swing wide only for the humble of spirit, regardless of earthly rank or majesty. Those weighed down with pride must endure, first, an initiation into self-knowledge akin to the spiritual exile endured by Perceval, as of Christ when he descended into Hell.

THE CHRISTIAN OTHERWORLD

Whether the Quest for the Holy Grail is a real adventure, like the arduous Crusade to the Holy Land, or a pursuit of spiritual enlightenment, both pass through what the Psalmist David called 'the valley of the shadow of death'. But the armour of faith protects the doughty Christian, for God travels with him, comforting the pilgrim with rod and staff.

At the beginning of the *Quest of the Holy Grail*, King Arthur says goodbye to his nephew Gawain and weeps for the danger, perhaps mortal danger, that he will face:

> 'Gawain, Gawain, my heart is weighed down with sorrow, and so it will be until I know how this Quest ends. I am so afraid I will never see these my dear friends again.'
>
> 'My lord king,' said Lancelot, 'what are you saying? You should have no other hope but good hope. Take heart. For, if we die on this Quest, there can be no greater honour in the world.'

> chapter 1

The basic tenets of the Grail theology – spiritual quest, moral refinement, enlightenment or 'rebirth' – loosely match the Celtic warrior's heroic progress over the battlefield. Much more relevant, however, are the mystic teachings of a sect to which Christ had pronounced leanings, if he did not actually count himself a member: the Essenes. The disciples called him Rabbi, since he was steeped in Jewish lore. The teachings of the Essenes may well be apparent in the fundamental simplicity of his gospel. They lived a self-sufficient, monastic existence in communities mostly grouped round the western shore of the Dead Sea. They despised luxury and pleasure and declared this austerity in the wearing of plain white garments foreshadowing the Cistercians. Their belief in the Resurrection (a crucial undercurrent in the Grail romances) was, according to Josephus, a Pharisee turned Roman sympathiser and historian, borrowed by Pythagoras and the Stoics. Their central doctrine held the flesh to be an encumbrance on the pure, interior spirit. ('The body is a tomb', as Pythagoras expressed it.) So, they encouraged mortification of the flesh (Christ in the wilderness, the knight on the Quest) to render the body dead to the world, thus anticipating the glorious release of the spirit at death.

Their rhapsodic teachings were greatly cherished by the mediaeval saints and visionaries. The trials of the spirit on earth are no more than the soul struggling to get out of its bodily charnel house prison. Old-fashioned non-Conformists talked of keeping body and soul together. The mystics, Christ amongst them, preached the exact opposite, in a way. And that separation of body and soul, the ultimate triumph of faith, may be described as walking through the Valley of the Shadow of Death. This is precisely why the Cistercians called their abbey near Llangollen the Valley of The Cross. It's the same thing, as is the Perilous Journey to the Grail Castle, and symbolic of Christ's descent into Hell where he removed Death's sting and trounced the victory of the grave. And, as if to ram home the image of bold knight repeating Christ's victory in the ultimate ordeal of the spirit, the Redeemer will come from the Judgement Seat, at the Last Trumpet, with *drawn sword*, to separate sheep from goats. The 'little death' of knightly vigil and initiation into the Order of Templars mimics Christ's descent into Hell (the church crypt) and his resurrection (ascent from the crypt in the morning).

Cistercian Influence

The *Quest of the Holy Grail* begins with the companions of the Round Table assembled in Camelot at none on the eve of Pentecost:

> After Mass, the tables were set up in the hall for dinner. At three o'clock, a young woman rode into the hall on horseback. She had driven her mount hard; it was lathered with sweat. She dismounted, approached the king and curtsied. He blessed her in the name of God.
>
> 'Sire,' she said, 'tell me if Lancelot du Lac is here.'
>
> 'Indeed he is,' said the king. 'Here in the hall', and he pointed to him. The young woman went up to Lancelot and said: 'I ask you, Sir Lancelot, in the name of King Pelles, to follow me into the forest.'

Shortly after the damsel's departure with Lancelot, the knights discover that the Perilous Siege, the Seat of Danger, which, of all seats at the Round Table remains unoccupied, has been inscribed with these words:

> Four hundred and fifty years have passed since the passion of our Lord Jesus Christ: and on the day of Pentecost this seat shall find its master.

A page enters the hall to report a great wonder – a large stone floating on the surface of the river; fastened into the red marble a magnificent sword with jewel-encrusted scabbard, on which is inscribed the legend:

> None shall take me hence but He at whose side I am to hang. And he shall be the best knight in the world.

The grail adventure has begun.

King Pelles is the Maimed Fisher King; Pentecost, the old Jewish harvest festival, seven weeks after Easter, when the Holy Spirit descended upon the disciples' heads in tongues of fire. None is the canonical hour, 3 p.m., when monks sing the office preceding dinner. Psalm 118, which forms part of that liturgy, celebrates the Lord's strong protection of his servant. The White Monks of the Cistercian Order observed an important vigil at none; thus the *Quest* announces its Cistercian character at the outset.

In the *Perlesvaus*, the Castle of the ogrish Gurgulain houses a sword of similar richness to that in the *Quest*. Each day at noon its blade runs with blood, after which the metal becomes clear and green as an emerald. This, we are told, is the sword used to behead St John the Baptist. But whose sword protrudes from the stone, the sword (surely?) which, on another occasion, Arthur had pulled out of an anvil placed on an altar? I believe it belongs, properly, to the Psalmist David, King of Jerusalem, forefather of Christ and Galahad. I cannot prove it – *nothing* in the story of Arthur can be *proved* – but it does tie in: the curious tale of David's capture of Jerusalem by ascending the slim, sheath-like well-shaft cut through the bedrock; the story of him confronting the exterminating angel, sword in hand, stretched over the Dome of the Rock; the building of a white marble altar (in the *Quest* the white has been raddled with the Saviour's blood) on that very site by the Order of Knights Templar;

Christ's statement that he brings not easeful peace but the sword (of tribulation); and the apostolic imagery of the sword of the spirit.

All sound Biblical authority for literary romance. The story of Arthur and the Round Table Knights is so bound up with the fortunes of the Frankish kingdom of Jerusalem that there must be a link between the theology that justified the Crusades and the religious symbolism of the romances; particularly, of course, those treating of the Holy Grail. Celtic lore offered no pedigree, quite the reverse, possibly – a pagan tar brush. The Franks, moreover, were interlopers in Celtic Europe. Faced with the chance of establishing themselves as the kings and princes of the Holy Land, the Frankish leaders set out to prove that it was to David that their line stretched unbroken, not to Brân, Lugh and Cuchulainn. The storytellers larded their narratives with Celticisms; but I believe that the Churchmen, whose interest in the romances was both doctrinal *and* propagandist, found the story of David's entry into Jerusalem irresistible, as a starting-point for the ultimate proof that the Crusaders were destined to rule in Jerusalem: the Bible said so. Did not the Franks cut their own subterranean passage out of the bedrock under their great fortress Krak des Chevaliers, that 'bone in the Saracen's craw', so that the knights could ride up into the citadel in safety?

The sword in the stone must probably remain a conundrum. Drawing a regal sword from a cleft in rock (phallic blade from earth vagina) formed part of a Bronze Age coronation ritual, apparently. One thing, however, is sure. The romance sword is the sword which the true knight, 'endowed with purity of mind and disdaining to follow after his own will and desire, wields in his fight for the most high and true king', as St Bernard put it in his rules for the Templars. The true King is, of course, God; it could be, and by implication *was* and remains, King Arthur.

THE TEMPLAR CONNECTION

In *Parzival*, Wolfram von Eschenbach calls the white-robed guardians of the Grail *templeis*; but we have seen other examples of his wordplay. It should upset no scruple to come clean and name them: Templars, who wore their red cross on a white mantle. Red cross on white robe appears in the *Perlesvaus* also; Galahad, like Byzantine St George, sports it. So too all the Crusaders, but only in battle: the Templars wore theirs (splayed or flattened at the tips, as distinct from the simple cross) all the time. For, lodged in their monastery-fortress on the Temple Rock in Jerusalem they, more than any other participants in the Holy War, came to embody the Crusading ideal. They both inspired and starred in the quintessential Holy Grail legends; the combination of chivalric principle and Cistercian teaching overwhelmingly supports such a conclusion. Cistercian homilies on chastity and purity, on the salutary power of divine grace over all fleshly intrigue and desire, the concentration on spirit and the spurning of bodily lusts and urges by single-minded devotion and contemplation (almost an interior Crusade against the pernicious, Saracen-like afflictions of sin and temptation) transformed the Grail story from romance to supercharged epic of Christian passage through the wilderness of this world to the heavenly city.

For a while this spiritual, romance version of the bloody, fighting Crusade seems to have enjoyed full Church approval; backing, even. St Bernard, who died in 1153, an orator and writer of extraordinary persuasive eloquence, had the willing ear of popes and bishops throughout western Christendom. His sermons injected tremendous impetus into the Crusading movement; his teachings inspired many successive generations of Cistercian apologists for the journey through the Valley of the Cross. And Bernard's vitriolic denunciation of the wayward Church in Provence instigated a groundswell of self-righteous opposition to the ascetic Cathars which burst out in the Albigensian Crusade.

By the time that that particularly dismal atrocity had come to an end (1244), Europe was becoming sick of and sickened by Crusades, whether against Saracens or against members of their own community. Practical considerations also had bearing: the Saracens had, comprehensively, won the Outremer wars; as for the Albigensians, there weren't any of them left. So, with Jerusalem and Holy Land lost, once more, to the Arabs, the Byzantine Empire now Venetian after the sack of Constantinople; of the pentangle of cities, only Rome and Camelot held their interest. And Rome was beginning to cut itself free into sole eminence.

It is a mistake to imagine that Rome, the Eternal City, assumed leadership of the Catholic Church without challenge. In fact it had to work long and hard, not always successfully, to establish the unbroken line of authority between St Peter, to whom Christ had given the keys of heaven and hell, and the Bishop of Rome, as Christ's own vicar on earth. (Vicar is Latin for 'stand-in', French: *lieutenant*.) Indeed, for some years the popes actually resided in Avignon, rival popes in Italy issuing disclaimers to the popes in France. However, by the mid-thirteenth century, boosted by the consolidating achievements of perhaps the most impressive of mediaeval popes, Innocent III (pope from 1198 to 1216), Rome had asserted its authority as the city of Christ's throne on earth. And St Thomas Aquinas had embarked on his monumental work of theological analysis and synthesis which would form the basis of Roman Catholic dogma from now on, his *Summa Theologica*, shot through with the influence of the pagan thinker Aristotle. *His* works arrived in Europe as Latin versions of Arab translations of the Greek original. After Aquinas, the Greek texts received their first official airing by Church licence.

If Rome was now the holy capital of the terrestrial kingdom, Jerusalem had better resume its place as the heavenly city of John's Revelation. The mystic vision of the White Monks, among others, had to be revised. Even the mention of the golden city of Sion in Outremer awoke painful and, given the new vision at Rome, unnecessary memory. No more new Jerusalem at Clairvaux.

The dream of Clairvaux as the earthly Jerusalem soured; so too, inevitably, the fortunes of its most stalwart champions, the Templars, waned. They had been accused of cowardice when Saladin crushed the Frankish armies at Hattin in 1187. As the frontiers of Outremer shrank, the Christian rulers of the kingdom turned on each other, squabbling fiercely, backbiting, their fighting unity gone to pieces. Partisan rivalry dominated the ineffectual last-ditch resistance. The Templars, untimely proud and isolated from the rest, as they always had been, with their own exaggerated and sanctimonious sense of mission – a rapidly failing mission – had embodied the Crusading vigour at its height. Now they became the scapegoats of its decline. Their comportment was guaranteed to entrench aversion to them: they were immensely rich in property and lands, a law unto themselves, swearing allegiance only to the pope. They had always been difficult members of armies not noted for their tight discipline; now, their very existence linked indissolubly to the Holy Land, they had outlived their purpose.

In 1304, Templar leaders all over Europe – where they had retreated after the final withdrawal from Palestine and Syria – were arrested, tortured over a long period and many of them burned at the stake. Years of trial, investigation and witchhunt followed till, in 1312, by papal decree, the Order of Templars was suppressed. Envy of their wealth and arrogance played a large part and Philip IV of France, who organised the first swoop, had been refused admission to the Order. He almost certainly had an eye on their treasures *and* their secrets. Many claims have since been made as to the exact nature of both: the treasures of Solomon's temple, the shroud in which Christ's body was wrapped, the crown of the kingdom of Jerusalem. Perhaps the Templars had a Holy Grail, too. Nothing was ever recovered. However, it *is* true, that when the Templars vanished so, too, for a long time did Camelot and Arthur.

The last Grail stories were written about the time of the Albigensian Crusade's stuttering to a blood-choked finish, and the emergence of sharply defined doctrinal orthodoxy from Rome. The specific war against the Saracens was in the process of becoming the general war against heresy. Jerusalem had faded out of focus. So too did Camelot. Why? I think because, in some way, Camelot and Jerusalem were one and the same place. A Dominican friar, Bernard Guidonis, was now embarked on the enunciation of a formal theory of the Inquisition against heretical opinion. Rome had ushered in the last phase of her assumption of total, unassailable control of dogma; all heterodox ideas were, gradually, to be extirpated, and the doctors of the Church were busy preparing chapter and verse in justification. Amongst the more difficult weeds in the garden they dug up was (I think) the highly suspect romance of the Holy Grail, smelling rank with oriental, wildly mystic visionary, altogether *unbalanced* ideas. It was a nasty, heterodoxical, hot-climate, mischievous Greek-Byzantine *fiction*.

But the three knights in the crypt do not yet know anything of this. They walk up the steps from the infernal dark crypt into the blazing light of the circular Temple church. They have made a transition, real, not merely symbolic: from their old life, froward and perverse, across the black waters of the river which courses through the Little Death's dark vale, through ordeal of temptation, spiritual and carnal, through a waste land of the soul, into perpetual light. They have been initiated into the solemn, binding, sublime mystery and secret of the Templars, the world of illumination. From now on, dead to bodily desires and personal will, they dedicate themselves to the service of their Maimed King, the Saviour Jesus, broken on the Cross for all mankind, to enable the spirit of His mercy to irrigate the arid deserts of men's hearts. Raising the chalice of the Eucharist, they renew their devotion to the sacrifice of Christ's flesh and blood, knowing that His grace alone makes them worthy of their quest for holy fellowship with Him. Nor, probably, do they know or care that Brân's horn would not serve a coward. Their Grail is in heaven; they will sit at God's high table to be served above the rest. Not even the monks of Glastonbury dared put the Holy Grail on show.

Effigies of knights await the last call to arms at Doomsday in the Templar Church, London. They are lying down; were they originally standing?

CHAPTER EIGHT

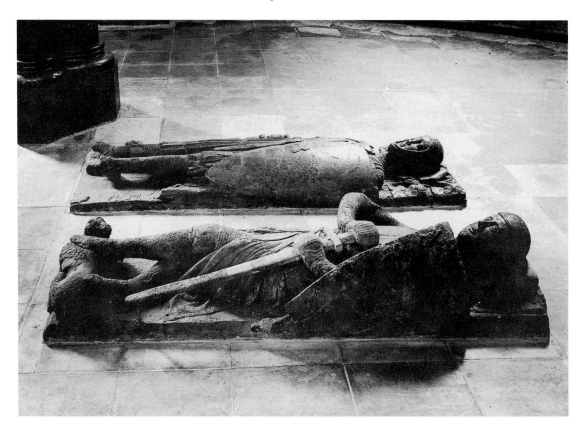

HUNTING AND HERALDRY

'A stag I have seen in the forest, and I never saw the like of it,' said the forester to the king.

'What is there about it,' asked Arthur, 'that thou shouldst never have seen its like?'

'It is pure white, lord, and it goes not with any animal for presumption and pride, so exceeding majestical it is.'

Mabinogion (Everyman p. 230)

One day, Merlin enters the hall of Arthur the King. To the knights assembled at the Round Table he gives notice of a strange and marvellous sight. Even as he speaks, into the hall bounds a white hart pursued by a white brachet, or bitch scent-hound, and thirty couples of running hounds, yelping and barking. As the white hart circles the Table, the brachet snaps at its rump and takes a bite of flesh. The hart kicks out in pain, lurches into one of the knights and knocks him out of his seat. The knight scrambles up, grabs hold of the brachet and leaves the hall, mounts his horse and rides off.

Right so anon came in a lady on a white palfrey, and cried aloud to King Arthur, 'Sir, suffer me not to have this despite, for the bratchet was mine that the knight led away'.

Malory Book III chapter 5

The ensuing hunt draws the knights into the realm of sinister uncertainty and mystery. Thick-gladed trees first mottle then block out altogether the sunlight; the woodland becomes a penumbral night world – the creatures that lurk quiet and unseen, or dart across clearings in a flicker of dun colour, belong, it seems, to another creation. A blur of white through the trees ahead: the scenting hounds have flushed the white hart from its lair. Majestic beast; cunning, strong, elusive.

The horns wail. Hounds drunk with adrenalin – greyhound and alaunt, fast and muscular – thump into the chase to bring the hart down; it may well take all day till they corner him. But the sunlight wears thin, the day's power wanes; huntsmen are separated in the pillared labyrinth of beech, oak, elm and chestnut. Sucked into the depths of the forest they lose their way; night crowds in alongside trees and brakes; the thickets crack and rustle with odd sounds. A bird startles from cover with a dry flutter of wings. And silence.

In the forests of the romances, the quest for knighthood's prize – the testing of valour, saving of fair lady, facing out of perils, venture into the Otherworld's fringes and confrontation with things unknown – meets the known and familiar world of the hunt. The very word 'quest', so familiar to Arthurian romance, is first used of dogs pursuing their quarry.

A mediaeval nobleman knew one overriding priority which put all other considerations in the shade: to win glory in tests of his mettle. To his skill at arms and devotion to the chivalric ideal, a nobleman added necessary prowess in the chase; notably for the royal hart and the savage boar. They embodied brute nature which it was his duty to vanquish. As Chastelain de Coucy put it before he died in 1203 on the Fourth Crusade:

De maintes choses ont parlé
D'armes, d'amours, de chiens, d'oiseaux
De tournoiments et de combiaus.

They talked of many things,
Of war, of love, of hounds, of hawks,
Of tournaments and personal combat.

Amorous dalliance had its place only because it stoked up passion for combat or the chase and kept the adrenalin pumping. Besides, it was hunting too.

Noble rank demanded skill and aptitude in two kinds of hunting: falconry and venery (the chase), and both were exact sciences requiring extensive knowledge and training. A knight had to be adept in the four principal lessons of the management of hawks: their flight, feeding, calling and holding. The training of a hawk exacted long hours of patience and meticulous attention. In venery, he had to learn the entire repertoire of hunting calls which directed the conduct of the hunt from start to finish, and

woe betide anyone who mistook the horn signal and got himself out of position, especially if he impeded a huntsman of senior rank, even the king himself. He must learn the employment of the various breeds of hound, though managing them would be left to inferior social classes. He must learn, by experience and close observation in the field, to match his wits to the cunning wiles of the hunted animals, especially the swift-thinking, swift-footed hart. Above all, he must learn the complicated and precise etiquette which governed the unmaking (that is, the butchering) of the captured quarry. The craft of hunting apart, in the frantic mounted chase through dense forest and open field, by thicket and overhanging bough and concealed ditch, he needed a calm nerve, a clear head and tenacity; for the duel with the cornered boar, all his every fibre of courage. To flinch was unthinkable, ignoble. Huon de Bordeaux sums it up:

I know how to mew the hawk and I can hunt wild board and stag. I know how to wind the horn when I have slain the animal, and I know how to give meat portions from the quarry to the hounds.

To mew was to cage the hawk at moulting time, a very delicate business.

The hunt, by its mimicry of battle, combined the élan of pace, action, triumph, horsemanship, weaponry skill with the parade of rank and status so vital to the self-esteem of the nobleman. They were the heroes of real life as well as of romance. While hunting might not deliver the high glory of war it attuned the noble huntsman to an eager and confident expectation of it. Most of all the kings.

The mediaeval kings made hunting their preserve not only because they owned the land and the creatures that lived on it and had the time and money requisite for hunting, but also because hunting symbolised regal heroism, a vital ingredient in the maintaining of prestige. The Spanish bullfight preserves and typifies this mettlesome view of the lone swordsman duelling with brute evil incarnated in the black *toro*. To this day, a herd of *white* wild bulls roam a field in Chillingham, Northumberland, on the Cheviot Hills. They have their own herd law and a king bull who wins his leadership by fighting off rivals and only surrenders it when he succumbs to a stronger challenge. About fifteen miles away from this famous herd, probably introduced by the late Romans and kept, by them, for sacrifice to the legionaries' favourite god, the Persian Mithras, stands Bamburgh Castle. Malory identified this magnificent fort on a headland overlooking the North Sea with Lancelot's castle Joyous Gard. His grounds may seem shaky, although the Saxon Chronicle states that King Ida of Northumberland built a fort at Bamburgh in around 560, not long after the death of the historic Arthur.

One of the last hunts of the Chillingham king bull, for long an established local custom, took place in 1872 when the young Prince of Wales, later Edward VII, shot him with a rifle. Times had changed. No monarch would formerly have used so rascally a weapon. The only true way to wrest an animal's strength and virtue out of him into the hunter was at the end of honed steel. And that went for ogres, too:

But the king drew his sword and, shield held out
across his body, charged full tilt at the giant
before he could land a blow with his club . . .
Then, the king, inflamed with fighting rage,
hacked with his sword full into the giant's face,
and drove the blade with main strength up to
the hilt through his monstrous neck.

Geoffrey of Monmouth x. 3

The glory of the mediaeval king was polished and exalted in the hurly-burly of war and tournament and chase. The Arthurian romances dwell lavishly on and reflect the dedicated pursuit of all three.

WHITE HART, ROYAL HART

If the King or Queen doe hunt or chase him, and
he escape away alive, then . . . he is called a Hart
Royall

Manwood, *Lawes Forest*, 1598

The hunt for the white hart sets in train more than one adventure for the Round Table knights. In the *Erec* story, told by both Chrétien and Hartmann, the knight who kills the white hart — whose ghostly pallor announce it to have been, originally, a beast from the Otherworld — must pick out and kiss the most beautiful maiden in King Arthur's court, no matter what the consequence. Such is the hunting prize — itself a hunting term meaning 'kill', from French *prise*, 'the take'. The kiss invariably leads to trouble: with five hundred high-born, attractive and intelligent damsels at court, each with a knight for a lover, the choice is invidious. It rolls a golden apple of strife down the hall, as happened when Paris, prince of Troy, faced a similar judgement of the rival charms of three goddesses: Aphrodite, Hera and Athene. The outcome? The Trojan War.

King Arthur's pursuit of the white hart leads him, too, into calamity; having ridden so hard that his horse founders, dead, under him, Arthur and the others:

. . . were ware of the hart that lay on a great
water bank, and a bratchet biting on his throat,
and more other hounds came after. Then King
Arthur blew the prize and dight [slew] the hart.

Then the king looked about the world, and saw afore him in a great water a little ship, all apparelled with silk down to the water, and the ship came right unto them and landed on the sands. Then Arthur went to the bank and looked in and saw none earthly creature therein.

Malory Book IV chapter 6

They go on board. Night descends; a hundred torches flare out. Twelve damsels arrive. The company feasts and goes to sleep. Next morning the other knights wake in Camelot; but 'when King Arthur awoke he found himself in a dark prison, hearing about him many complaints of woeful knights'.

This docile white hart appears to be close kin to that other creature of ghostly hide and fabulous origin, the unicorn, of whom gloomy Job wrote:

Canst thou bind the unicorn with this band in the furrow? or will he harrow the valleys after thee?

Job 39 v. 10

The third-century Roman writer Solinus, who plagiarised Pliny and Mela and invented the description 'Mediterranean Sea', portrays the unicorn as the cruellest animal alive, 'a Monster that belloweth horriblie, bodyed like a horse, footed like an Elephant, tayled like a swine and headed like a Stagge. His horne sticketh out of the middle of his forehead of a wonderful brightness aboute foure foot long, so sharp that whatsoever he pusheth at he striketh it through easily. He is never caught alive; kylled he may be, but taken he cannot bee' (translated Golding).

His strength is also recorded in Numbers (xxii v. 22) and the Early English Psalter of 1300 offers a plea:

Sauf me fra mouth of liounes
And fra hornes of unicornes mi mekenes.

Alas, the Unicorn is beyond our scope, here; suffice it to say that legendarily the fierce and uncontrollable unicorn, the very embodiment of Lust, is quelled only by a pure virgin in the woodland groves and comes to her and lays his head meekly in her lap. He seems to have something, at least, in common with the hart of strange appearance who, by devious ways, leads King Mark to Tristan and Isolde's refuge in the forest:

They let slip the hounds which, immediately, flush out a white hart unlike any other, being much larger and stronger, with horse's mane and tiny horns.

Gottfried von Strassburg **Tristan** chapter 27

The horn of the unicorn dipped in a poisoned pool removes all venom from it; but the beast, however strong, always takes second best to the lion, chosen as their emblem early on by the English kings. As Wace said:

The Britons ranged like lions amongst their enemies. They were as lions anhungered for their prey . . .

During the quest for the Holy Grail, Sir Galahad, Sir Bors and Sir Percival chase a white hart guarded by four lions. They lead the knights to a forest hermitage. The hermit begins Mass.

And at the secrets of the Mass they three saw the hart become a man, the which marvelled them, and set him upon the altar in a rich siege; and saw the four lions were changed, the one to the form of a man, the other to the form of a

The fierce unicorn, emblem of sexual lust, lays its head meekly in the lap of a pure virgin. Only she can tame him. The watching knight's approach is less subtle.

lion, and the third to an eagle, and the fourth was changed to an ox.

Malory Book XVII chapter 9

Malory's hermit proceeds to identify the hart as Christ, white in purity, the royal beast pursued through the dark tangles of the wild wood as the human soul hunts after perfection and oneness with God.

The hart symbolises immortality, too, and figures in the legend of St Eustace, supposedly a general in the Emperor Trajan's army, who experienced a vision, while out hunting, of a stag with a radiant crucifix between its antlers. The story offers no more, perhaps, than a reworking of the story of Paul's conversion on the road to Damascus when the voice of Jesus rebuked him from a blinding light: 'Saul, Saul, why persecutest [pursue, hunt] thou me?'

Hubert, the eighth-century bishop of Maestricht, had a vision identical to Eustace's, and was regarded as their patron by hunters and trappers in the Ardennes region. Here the symbolism identifies Christ as the hart pursued by evil, in other words the failure of the soul to confess faith in Him; like St Augustine resisting the call of God.

The Welsh Celts thought of the stag as the man's soul – in the story of Pwyll and Arawn, Prince of Annwn, for example – and the Psalmist David had supplied this metaphor over two thousand years before the Arthurian romances were written:

> As the hart panteth after the water brooks, so panteth my soul after thee.

> *Psalm 42 v.1*

This, curiously, formed the basis of an explanation of the hart's immortality. The *Physiologus,* a bestiary originating from the fourth century A.D. and augmented, expanded, embroidered upon by successive mediaeval writers, supplied a reason for the hart's driving thirst, as if living in a desert region with scant few pools and fountains were not sufficient cause. Reaching the age of fifty (and Malory had heard of this), a hart scours the hills for a snake's hole. When it has found one it places a nostril over the hole and sucks the snake out. If, within three hours, it can find water to drink it will shed and renew its antlers and live another fifty years. If not, it dies. The snake, which wriggles out of the old, sloughed skin, had long seduced men into a hope for rebirth and immortality. In Shakespeare's day, eating snakes was believed to renew youth and vigour. (Inhaling them remained a peculiarity of the hart.)

The hart's fabled thirst provided mediaeval writers with another metaphor: the sexual hunger of lovers, as between the newly married Erec and Enide (see chapter 5). And a jealous lover might dream of his treacherous mistress harried to her death by avenging knights and pack of hounds who rip her faithless body to pieces, to be rewarded with her heart. The reward is *curée* in French, English 'quarry'. In more loving, though sombre mood still, an early French lyric records how a dying knight beseeches his friends to remove his heart and carry it to his beloved as a token of his undying love.

'THE BOAR'S HEAD IN HAND I BRING . . .' *(Mediaeval Song)*

Uther Pendragon, says Merlin in Layamon's *Brut* (dedicated to Eleanor of Aquitaine):

> shall have a son, out of Cornwall shall he come,
> that shall be a wild boar, bristled with steel . . .
> he shall be a man most brave and noble in thought.

He was, of course, Arthur, warlord, puissant king, conceived one blustery night in Tintagel.

The boar was the most terrifying, most savage of the hunted beasts and the hardest to kill. He *looked* mean – wicked tusks, foaming jaws, hell-black bristles – and he *was* mean. His unmitigated ferocity was a byword. In the *Mabinogion* tale 'Culhwch and Olwen', the Giant Ysbadadden sets the Round Table knights a number of difficult and hazardous tasks, one of which he sets out thus:

> I must needs wash my head and shave my beard.
> The tusk of Ysgithyrwyn ('Tusker') Chief Boar I must have, wherewith to shave myself. I shall be none the better for that unless it be plucked from his head while alive.

That would demand the rawest courage, as the description of the hunt for the wild boar in *Gawain and the Green Knight* shows:

> *He got the bank at his back and began to abrade the ground.*
> *The froth was foaming foully at his mouth,*
> *And he whetted his white tusks; a weary time it was*
> *For the bold men about, who were bound to harass him*
> *From a distance, for none dared to draw near him*
> *For dread . . .*

Till the castellan himself came, encouraging his horse,
And saw the boar at bay with his band of men around.
He alighted in lively fashion, left his courser,
Drew and brandished his bright sword and boldly strode
forward
Striding at speed through the stream to where the
savage beast was.

Multiplying the hazard, the boar's thick skin and bristles make him virtually impervious, like the Spanish *toro*, to all but the *coup de grâce*:

Then men shoved forward, shaped to shoot at him,
Loosed arrows at him, hitting him often,
But the points, for all their power, could not pierce his
flanks
Nor would the barbs bite on his bristling brow.

When the lord plunges into the stream to do battle with the boar, the knightly quest becomes a dark duel of champions from different worlds − one from the world of light, the other from the world of base earth and nether darkness. The boar in Arthurian romance stands for warrior fury but also man's bestial nature, crude lust. In Gottfried von Strassburg's *Tristan*, Marjodoc, the steward, tormented by thoughts of Tristan wallowing adulterously in bed with Isolde, dreams of him as a rampaging boar, 'foaming at the mouth and whetting his tusks and charging everything in his path'. In the Gawain story this allegory is apposite. Knee-deep in the stream the lord marks the boar's chest:

Put the sword point precisely at the pit of his
chest
And drove it in to the hilt so that the heart was
shattered.

As his host braces himself on the stout shaft of his sword against the fearsome boar, Gawain, idling in the castle as he waits the time for the beheading test, dallies with the hostess who comes, unbidden, to his bedroom:

. . . that stately lady tempted him and tried him with
questions
To win him to wickedness, whatever else she thought.
But he defended himself so firmly that no fault
appeared
Nor was there any evil apparent on either side,
  But bliss.

This is the second day of her visiting. The previous day, in the faint light before dawn, the lord and his huntsmen had stirred and galloped out to the hunting field, horns blaring the various signals to muster the different hounds, place the huntsmen at their appointed stations, called *trysts*, and then raise the hunt for the brave buck in the coverts, the noble hart.

THE SIXTH YEAR AN HART OF TEN TINES AND THEN IS HE CHASEABLE

Now when the hart had been killed, the Huntsman-in-Chief laid it out on the grass all four legs stretched out like a boar.
'What do you think you are doing?' interposed Tristan, a man of courtly breeding. 'In God's name stop! Whoever saw a hart broken in this fashion −'

Gottfried von Strassburg, ***Tristan*** chapter 4

Tristan is the most celebrated huntsman in the Arthurian romances being an acknowledged expert in the precise form to be observed in unmaking the hart; that is to say the ritual flaying and dismemberment of the slain animal. Malory records his fame:

> . . . he began good measures of blowing [horn calls] of beasts of venery and beasts of chase and all manner of vermins, and all these terms we have yet of hawking and hunting. And therefore the book of venery, of hawking and hunting is called the book of Sir Tristram.

> Malory Book VIII chapter 3

In Gottfried we have a detailed account of how the well-bred huntsman honoured his quarry by neat butchery and portioning. The ancient Greek altar priests had to be deft hands with the butcher's knife, too. This art, as so many others in royal procedure and punctilio, came to its great refinement in France.

A mediaeval English writer scoffed at the niminy-piminy rigmarole of the French hunters, but most observed the courtly practice in unmaking the hart. The skin cut and stripped back, the meat pared neatly; titbits – liver, numbles, pizzle – removed and set in the tines of a special fork stuck in the ground; the quartered heart, milt, lungs, paunch cut into small colpons and tossed onto the flayed hide as a present for the dogs – çâ! çâ! çâ! . . . 'here boy, take it!'. In mediaeval southwestern France, Albigensian country, a man who killed a boar unaided with his sword received what the Normans called the numbles (kidneys with their packing of suet) as a reward. These made the ingredients of the so-called numbles or humble pie, regarded with such contempt in seventeenth-century England. The point was that the Puritans, who made the unsmiling St Benedict, formulator of the monastic rule, look jolly, decided that if a man was eating numbles he must have been hunting,

which meant that he had been gratuitously enjoying himself which was the work of the Devil and entirely indefensible. Worse: humiliating for the soul which should dwell on higher things.

In *Gawain* the hounds receive morsels of 'bread well imbrued with blood', often crisped over the fire. Meanwhile, in his first encounter with the winsome lady of the castle, 'seated softly on the side of his bed', Gawain's emotions begin to churn just like the hart when it hears the shrill horn . . . that sudden catch at the pluck which triggers uncertainty and worse. For the pluck – heart, liver and lungs tossed to the unleashed hounds to reward them after the chase – make the core of Gawain's manhood. Not only does he await a severe test of courage (the beheading ordeal); but here he is wooed by fair lady, his host's wife, as rare in beauty as fair Isolt, perhaps, 'erect as a sparrowhawk'.

HAWKS

The eagle, the vulture, and the merloun for an emperor, the goshawk for a yeoman, and the sparrowhawk for a priest

Sparrowhawks, as the name implies, came low in the ranks of hunting birds: they were less susceptible of training than the top-flight birds – peregrine, gyrfalcon, saker, lanner, alphanet, merlin. Only the female worked with any efficiency and then for small prey – nothing bigger than a blackbird, thrush, occasional lark, though a good sparrowhawk might just down a lumbering partridge. In fact, henbirds of all species, the *falcons*, generally commanded higher prices than male birds, or *tercels*, being more biddable, swifter in flight and keener in the kill. The sparrowhawk, a lady's or priest's bird, cost a sixth the price of a peregrine. The number of yearly moultings determined age: six moultings would indicate a full-fledged bird, at its prime.

Falconry was introduced to Europe by the Moors, who taught management and training of the sleek raptor, soaring arrowlike into the sunstream and, from the rolling level of the high air currents, stooping with the main force and speed of a crossbow quarrel at her victim – birds as large as heron, crane, stork, bustard, wild goose, animals as dainty-footed as the jinking hare. A moment of stunning energy, brilliant attack:

And my lord Yvain spurs impetuously after him, as hard as he can go. As a gyrfalcon, swooping from a distance, hotly pursues a crane and comes so close to it that it snatches at it but misses . . .

Chrétien de Troyes, **Yvain** lines 880 ff

The beauty of the hawk (the great explorer Hakluyt describes a falcon 'of golde with a great Emerald in the breast thereof'), its speed, ease and agility of flight, lent it naturally to metaphor; but that is a commonplace of mediaeval literature. As Alanus de Insulis (Alain of Lille), 1125 – 1203, the Cistercian thinker, wrote:

omnis mundi creatura
quasi liber et pictura
nobis est in speculum.

('Every creature in creation presents as it were a book or picture to us, a mirror of inner nature.') The falcon became a favourite mediaeval metaphor of woman's pulchritude. In Gottfried von Strassburg's *Tristan*, lissom Isolde is said to carry herself with the elegance of a sparrowhawk; her combed hair sleek as a parakeet's well-preened feathers. Most fetching are her eyes. Bright, wide open and alert, they rove like a falcon's on a bough, inquisitive for prey, catching at any slightest movement.

In Chrétien's *Erec et Enide,* the hero wins a Competition of the Hawk. A fine sparrowhawk of five or six moultings is set on a silver perch. Whichever champion deems his lady unsurpassed in beauty, wit and purity of heart must send her to lift the bird down, or face any challenge from the other knights for his presumption.

When a sparrowhawk tramples on her perch in a fret of hunger, that gives Chrétien an exact picture of Erec and Enide's sexual longing. A lark cornered by a merlin describes a beaten knight cowering at Lancelot's feet.

From its mastery of God's heavenly realm, the hawk symbolised spiritual energy; from the voluptuous muscularity of its flight, earthly pleasure. The hawk which flies off into the blue, never to return, is lost love; the painful and lengthy moult is a girl's assumption of womanhood, or a man's loss of honour (there's male chauvinism for you). And so on. For a fascinating exposition of the whole subject I heartily recommend the reader to John Cummins' indispensable *The Hound and The Hawk*.

Finally, here is Isolde, stunned by love, depicted as a falcon caught in lime:

When Fair Isolde found herself beguiled, caught fast in the deep cloying lime spread by love, she struggled to escape. But, no matter how hard she fought, she could not get free, the lime dragged her back.

Gottfried von Strassburg, **Tristan** chapter 15

Love has struck like the sun out of the blue. In Welsh the word for hawk is *gwalch*. This is the root of Gawain's name in the *Mabinogion* – Gwalchmai, or 'hawk of May', symbol of the new summer sun. And on the third day when Gawain's host goes out

Two lovers go hawking in May (from a mediaeval calendar).

to hunt, the lady visits him once more, stunning in beauty as a hawk:

> In a ravishing robe that reached to the ground
> Trimmed with finest fur from pure pelts;
> Not coifed as to custom, but with costly jewels
> Strung in scores on her splendid hair caul.
> Her fine-featured face and fair throat were unveiled,
> Her breast was bare and her back as well . . .

While Gawain feints and weaves away from the seductive pursuit of the lady huntress, her lord and the open-air huntsmen out on the holt side have failed to run any real prize to earth. Cheated, they chase, instead, a snapping fox, symbol of unredeemed human nature . . . a creature 'perfect in all villainy' says Queen Reason in the fable . . . stinking, skulking, worthless thief . . . the Devil himself.

Nor Will We Spare To Hunt The Crafty Fox

. . . Lord and huntsmen return; their efforts wasted:

> . . . I have hunted all the day and have only taken
> This ill-favoured fox' skin, may the Fiend take it!

178

Inedible, unedifying, the fox provided no sport for the huntsmen; though, ironically, it and those other denizens of wood and stream never destined for the table – otter and badger – provide all the modern English huntsmen's game. 'The unspeakable in full pursuit of the uneatable', as Oscar Wilde put it. In Europe of the Middle Ages, the fox shared evil odour with the lynx and the wolf; this last animal, now virtually extinct, terrorised and wrought havoc on man and beast. Havoc, the same word as 'hawk', is Teutonic in origin, a shouted signal 'Havot!' for pillage and spoiling at the end of a battle. Gildas called the detested Scots and Irish Picts descending on the Britons 'wolves driven mad by gnawing hunger'. Never one to mince words, he likened them, also, in their coracles swarming over the sea to 'worms wriggling out of rocks warmed by the midday sun'. No better than vermin, in fact. Just like the fox who 'liveth of all vermin and of all carrions and other foul worms'. Cunning and shifty as he was, the fox provoked as much contempt as odium: a sneak thief, purloiner of hens, ducks, young geese; a mean-spirited creature, epitomised as such in Aesop's fables: sour grapes, low cunning, tendentious flattery.

Aptly, after Gawain's host catches the sly fox, Gawain tells a lie: he fails to own up to receiving from the lady 'the cincture of her gown / Which went round her waist under the wonderful mantle / A girdle of green silk . . .'. Wearing it, she promised him, 'he cannot be killed by any cunning on earth', and cunning is a vulpine trait. Gawain, due to lower his neck to the Green Knight's axe blade, all too humanly cannot resist the offer, so agreeably as it is perfumed with the sweet cooing of the lady who makes her gift, 'beseeching him for her sake to conceal it always / And hide it from her husband with all diligence'. So, foxily she persuades, and, outfoxed of a little honour Gawain accepts to elude the Green Knight's steel; and foxes her husband by

saying nothing; and takes himself off next day to the Green Knight's castle where . . . but you must read the story: there are wonders in it.

HERE BE MONSTERS . . .

In Gottfried von Strassburg's romance, Tristan rides out to fight a dragon. He sees it ahead belching flame-laced smoke like a Devil's brat, couches his lance, spurs his charger and hurtles precipitately into the beast. The lance drives deep into the dragon's throat, nearly as far as the heart. The shock of the impact kills Tristan's horse and he only just manages to scramble clear. The enraged dragon falls on the dead animal and eats it. Then, galled by the lance wound it makes for refuge up the mountain slope, bellowing hideously, uprooting trees, hosing thickets with sulphurous fire, with Tristan hot in pursuit. The dragon reaches shelter under the steep overhang of a cliff, and there Tristan attacks a second time. The dragon, like a self-contained army, launches at him smoke and steam, slashing teeth and claws, sharp as razors. But Tristan harries it as relentlessly as the buried lance yanking at its guts. The beast falls, writhing in agony. Quick as an arrow, Tristan darts forward and plunges the full blade of his sword into the dragon's heart.

> From its vile throat, the stricken monster roared so loud it seemed all heaven and earth were falling apart.
>
> chapter 12

With serpentine trunk and tail (Greek *dracon* means snake), eagle's feet and wings, lion's forelimbs and head, fish scales, antelope horns, the dragon lives, either below the mountain or at the bottom of lake or sea, but always coiled jealously about his vast treasure hoards. One such was the great fish of the deeps in Hebrew myth, Leviathan:

179

Who can open the doors of his face? his teeth are terrible round about. His scales are his pride, shut up together as with a close seal. One is so near to another, that no air can come between them . . . Out of his mouth go burning lamps and sparks of fire leap out.

Job 41 vv. 14–19

The Moslems called him Nun; every day he satisfies his hunger with a fish three miles in length. Leviathan is one of the eastern dragons, in Islamic myth those sons of heaven who control the watery element. Generally beneficent, he will, on occasion, eructate in displeasure and make the earth tremble or else gulp down the sun – as an eclipse. The western dragon, inhabitant of the oily dark cold waters of the Baltic and North seas, the grim lakes of the vast forestlands of northern Europe, the craggy mountain halls of frostbound ranges, is unexceptionably malign. He, as Wace records, also dims down the sun:

The Comet shone marvellously clear and cast a beam that was brighter than the sun. At the end of this beam was a dragon's head, and from the dragon's mighty jaws issued two rays. One stretched over France . . . the other ray went towards Ireland.

Le Roman de Brut (Everyman p. 31)

This dragon comet, which stirs Uther, Arthur's father, so deeply, may well be that comet mentioned in the Anglo-Saxon chronicle for the year A.D. 497. It portends the death of Uther's brother and his own kingship. So:

In remembrance of the dragon, and of the hardy knight who should be king and a father of kings,

which it betokened, Uther wrought two golden dragons, by the counsel of his barons. One of these dragons he caused to be borne before him when he went into battle. The other he sent to Winchester to be set up in the church of the bishop.

ibid.

Winchester is the old capital of England identified by some as Camelot. And though Uther's dragons were gold, the dragon we usually associate with Wales (old Britain) is red. The Saxon dragon was white; but to both Saxons and Britons the dragon stood for warlike invincibility. In fact, it is probable that the Saxons introduced the idea of dragons to the Britons in the first place. Michael and the angels fought against the red dragon 'called the Devil and Satan, which deceiveth the whole world' (Revelation 12 v. 9) and so, too, Arthur and his knights face monsters. However, their monsters are very Celtic in nature, mostly the human grotesques, ogres and giants of Celtic legend. Dragons were Scandinavian or Teutonic, like Fafnir, the dragon king of Hades who cannot bear the light and has robbed the earth of gold, slain and despoiled by Sigurd. Or else dragons came from the east, via Greece – the Lernaean Hydra and Ladon, guardian of the Garden of Hesperides vanquished by Hercules; or from Rome. The dragon of the north is the darkness of winter, kin to Surt, 'black smoke', with his flaming sword who rules over the Land of Brightness: robbing the earth of gold is another way of describing the cold, blank, sunless days of winter; and spring that moment when the hero slays the beast of night and scatters the sun's rays like a gold shower, again.

The Celts had their sun heroes (Gawain, for one), but their way with the alien dragon was a cunning sidestep. They turned his evil powers back on him, as if flattering the villainous beast with a gilded mirror that overblazed his eyes with a reflection of his own ugliness: they made Dragon their word for Chief. So, Uther Pendragon is *Uther* (Welsh *Uthr:* terrible) *pen*: son of, *Dragon*: Chief. In this capacity, the dragon came to symbolise power, wisdom and astuteness in heraldry. The Vikings had used him to scare the opposition, carving his head on the boats they called their 'dragon barques'. Arthur's own association with the dragon shows a link to the Ancient Greek belief that dead men turned into dragons once they descended below the earth: sow a dragon's teeth and armed men sprang out of the ground, as Jason discovered. But Arthur, the Chief, or Dragon, comes to life, too.

St George, whom the Crusaders brought back with them from Asia Minor and honoured with their own red cross on white tunic, had slain a dragon, just as Arthur, his coat emblazoned with the sign of the Virgin Mary, had crushed the white dragon of the Saxons and driven it back into the grey sea. But here was no secular victory: Arthur, George, the Crusaders all fought against dragons, as Christ had fought and overcome the powers of darkness:

Done is a batell on the dragon blak
Our campioun Chryst confountet has his forces.

Dunbar, *'On the Resurrection of Christ'*

The slaying of dragons – scaly monsters who crawl out of sea (the Kraken), or lake (the Loch Ness monster?) or well (the Lambton Worm) to devastate the countryside – has a root in practical myth-making. A lord wins land by force; he secures his power by the rule of the sword; he strengthens his stewardship by wise authority and good management. The local story grows (encouraged, doubtless, by him) that he brought prosperity where before there had been disorder and ruin, just

like the rampaging of dragons, against which the people, with no lord to protect them, had been powerless. So, whenever a new Prince Bishop was installed in Durham, the lord of Sockburn Manor was obliged to meet him at his first entry into the county and, standing over the river Tees on Croft Bridge, hand him the family falchion (sword):

My Lord Bishop, I here present you with the falchion wherewith the champion Conyers slew the worm, dragon or fiery flying serpent which destroyed man, woman and child; in memory whereof the king then reigning gave him the Manor of Sockburn [near Darlington] to hold by this tenure, that upon the first entrance of every Prince Bishop into the country this falchion should be presented.

Quoted in Jacqueline Simpson, ***British Dragons***
(p. 54)

The Prince Bishops of Durham exercised the power of feudal lords over the Palatine county, an autonomous principality within the greater kingdom. Everywhere else in England the king had first claim on a beached whale; in Durham that right was ceded to the Bishops.

Just as Arthur, the dragon of the Britons, bides his second coming from sleep under the hill, so not a few dragons lie below hills round Britain: the dents in Linton Hill, Roxburghshire, were impressed by the tight coiling of a dragon's tail, they say; and Dragon Hill, near Uffington in Oxfordshire, hides another slumbering, silver-scaled brute.

WONDERS WHICHE THAT BEEST THE ANTICHRIST SHALL SHEWE . . . (*The Pilgrimage of Perfection*, 1526)

St John talks of the beast called Antichrist in Revelation:

And I stood upon the sand of the sea, and saw a beast rise up out of the sea, having seven heads and ten horns, and upon his horns ten crowns, and upon his heads the name of blasphemy. And the beast which I saw was like unto a leopard and his feet were as the feet of a bear and his mouth as the mouth of a lion; and the dragon [Satan] gave him his power, and his seat, and his great authority.

13 vv. 1–2

The Middle Ages saw the emergence of a number of composite beasts – monsters with the characteristics of several creatures. The Ancient Greeks had the chimera (lion's head, goat's body, dragon's tail) but the Biblical sources, especially St John's apocalyptic vision, probably encouraged the idea most. Moorish influence again has play; thus the griffin, from India, thence to Arabia, had the legs, head and shoulders of an eagle, king of birds; the rest of him a lion, king of animals.

His becke was marvaylously greate, his eyes as great as a basyn and more redder than the mouthe of a fornays and his talantys so great and so longe that fearful it was to beholde hym.

Huon of Bordeaux

The fascination with monsters was not new. Latin *monstrum* simply means 'wonder, marvel', translating the Greek *deinos*, 'strange' and therefore 'terrible', which gives us *dinosaur*; a lizard so unusual in appearance it scares you half to death just looking at it.

The classification of animals was a late science. Aristotle's work in the subject, rudimentary as it was, had not resurfaced; and, if Nature constantly astonished the mediaeval mind she unremittingly intimidated, too. Curious beasts emerged from the sea, to be glimpsed sprawling on rocks; or else, a creature darting across a half-lit forest glade . . . The mediaeval eye tended to believe what it saw or even half saw. No less august a father of the Church than St Augustine himself encouraged belief at face value: facts were facts and not to be argued with. But from the slim testimony of the eyes came the eloquent description of the tongue, given full rein by fancy and imagination. If the Devil walked abroad, could it be wondered that his monsters roamed alongside him especially if Satan's brood, the Saracens, described them in their books? A seal bewigged with seaweed became a mermaid; a straggle-armed squid became a fantastically drawn squamous prelate – the Bishop Fish. But every fruit of observation (or imagination) had to have a place; nothing could be left unexplained; and every living creature in earth or in air had its equivalent in the watery element. Only the fabled salamander could inhabit fire, the last of the four elements, inhospitable to all others.

We can actually monitor the birth of one such mediaeval curiosity: the Old Testament Antlion. In the Septuagint version of the Book of Job, the Syriac word for *lion* (Latin *leo*) in the original text seems to have been mistranslated into Greek as *ant* (*myrmex*). A later scholar spotted the error but, this being Holy Writ, concluded that if God had allowed ant *and* lion to mingle then he must have intended them to mingle, so he invented the *myrmicaleo*. Ants usefully encourage us to work hard ('go to the ant, thou sluggard; consider his ways and be wise'), but how does an ant couple with a lion? Here the Bible plainly suggests it *does*; and so it must be. The Antlion monster comes into existence, with carnivore father and vegetarian mother, doomed to early death since he cannot properly settle on a diet. This conveniently gets rid of the monster as soon as he arrives, in fact if not in fiction. In fiction the monster lives on.

And the florid creations of the Bible bestiary encouraged the fiction; the book of Revelation supplies many examples:

> And the shape of the locusts were like unto horses prepared unto battle; and on their heads were as it were crowns like gold, and their faces were as the faces of men.

Revelation 9 v. 7

In the Middle Ages, all animals were deemed to exist for man's use; except the monkey which appeared to have not a shred of usefulness in it. (Perhaps a sneaking, pre-Darwinian register of the physical resemblance between monkeys and man) It was an age when too much sniffing of basil would, doctors said, plant a scorpion in your head, and when a cock might find itself put on public trial for laying an egg. It happened in the courts at Basle. Unreliable fowl, the cock: symbol, at once, of the risen Christ ('Lo, the day star now arises!') and of the Devil whose egg it was the cock laid. Out of it would hatch the very quintessence of evil, the incarnation of poisonous nastiness: a cockatrice. Winged beast with the body of a cock and the tail of a snake. Deadliest monster ever born: no living creature, except a weasel, could look at, touch, smell or even hear the hissing brute and not drop stone dead on the instant. The venomous exhalations of its rotten throat blasted and shrivelled vegetation. An English soulmate of St Patrick, the famous snake-scorcher, cleared the mainland of cockatrices by festooning himself with mirrors from head to toe and walking the whole country up and down. Any cockatrice, or basilisk to give its other name, catching sight of its own hideosity reflected back keeled over: an evil eye for an evil eye. In Iceland they called the basilisk a skoffin, and the

The Cockatrice 'From powerful eyes close venim doth convay/Into the looker's hart and killeth farre away' (Spenser); but when Christ comes to glory 'the weaned child shall put his hand on the cockatrice' den' (Isaiah 11 v. 8).

only thing that would carry off a skoffin was a silver bullet scored with the sign of the Cross. Now you know where the Lone Ranger came from; him on his white palfrey.

THE QUESTING BEAST

There were many other such invented monsters, just as there are to this day in travelling fairs in southern France; but the strangest of all is, perhaps, the Questing Beast of Arthurian romance:

> And this meanwhile there came Sir Palomides, the good knight, following the Questing Beast that had in shape a head like a serpent's head, and a body like a leopard, buttocks like a lion,

and footed like an hart; and in his body there was such a noise as it had been the noise of thirty couple of hounds questing, and such a noise that beast made wheresomever he went; and this beast evermore Sir Palomides followed, for it was called his quest.

Malory Book IX chapter 12

This animal wonder sometimes goes by the name Glatisant, 'Yelping' Beast. It appears in the *Perlesvaus* as a female, 'bigger than a fox, slighter than a hare, of colour white as the driven snow; of gentle semblance, her eyes seemed as it were two emeralds'. She is constantly rent by a questing pack of twelve hounds in her belly. She approaches the sanctuary of a cross in the forest. The hounds, ugly faced and savage, leap fully alive out of her belly. She crouches, making as if to cry mercy; but they spring at her and 'tear her all to pieces with their teeth, but no power had they to devour her flesh'. The hounds run off. Perceval and the damsel who have observed this affecting scene, place the torn and bloody gobbets of the body in a golden dish, lay them reverently before the holy cross and make devotion. A sweet smell emanates – always the sign of divine presence as anything malodorous betrays the lurking Devil, redolent of sulphur.

Later, this curious episode is explained by the king hermit, Perceval's uncle: the Questing Beast is Christ; the twelve hounds the tribes of Israel, condemned to the wilderness, as a forty-year trial of their love for God, and God's Son. They abandon him. (Can you wonder?) The manna he has sent by miracle and grace, and which they have stored in subterranean caverns, He transforms to 'newts and adders and worms'. They see they have done evil and scatter to the four winds. (The Diaspora.) Then, rounding on their tormentor, supposed protector, they crucify Him in vengeance, thus tearing Him to pieces; but cannot destroy his divine flesh. He lives on. That neatly summarises the prevailing anti-Semitic propaganda of the thirteenth-century theologians.

Malory's Questing Beast seems to me to have its origin in John's Antichrist beast; though Malory, himself not sure of the origin, has planted a decent mystery, another bafflement to thicken the web. For this is as strange a monster as you will encounter anywhere in mediaeval literature, amongst the weird menagerie of inventions, of afanc, ecidemon, wyvern, calygreyhound, hippogriff and a host more. One clue to the Questing Beast's nature, which, along with the puzzle of the sword in the stone, has intrigued me greatly, may emerge from an episode later in Malory's story. Soon after Sir Bors and Sir Galahad have received 'all manner of meats and drinks' from the Sangrail (here a censer borne in the mouth of a white dove); and when they have 'kneeled down and made their devotions . . . there was such a savour as all the spicery in the world had been there'. But that perfumed hint of God's presence quickly turns sour. Sir Bors faces a marvellous adventure, as it were an animated nightmare sprouting from the pursuit of the Questing Beast. The doors and windows of his chamber are suddenly 'Shot of arrows and of quarrels, so thick that he marvelled, and many fell upon him and hurt him in the bare places'. Thereupon, he is attacked by a hideous lion whose head he smites off. A dragon instantly appears:

passing horrible, and there seemed letters of gold written in his forehead, and Sir Bors thought that the letters made signification of King Arthur. Right so there came an horrible leopard and an old, and there they fought long and did great battle together. And at the last the dragon spit out of its mouth as it had been an hundred dragons and lightly all the small dragons slew the old dragon and tare him all to pieces.

Malory Book IX chapter 197

Dragon spits out his own teeth . . . leopard and lion . . . all marks of the Antichrist. Surely that *is* our Questing Beast? And now there swims into view St Carantoc's floating stone altar which, God has promised him, will come to shore one day and show him where to found his church. The Saint meets King Arthur, who has come to the region to search out and kill a serpent which has laid the fields waste. The Saint asks Arthur if he has seen the floating altar; the King says he has and will tell the saint where if the Saint uses his divine power to remove the evil serpent. The bargain is struck; the Saint whistles up the serpent who comes, mild as a lamb, to his bidding; and the King indicates Carhampton where the altar has landed. This story might explain a number of things but, alas, it comes from a mediaeval Latin text printed by Wynkyn de Worde in 1516, far too late a mishmash to be of any but curiosity value.

I caution against drawing any firm conclusions about the Questing Beast and many other marvels: there is as much uncalculated detail in the romances about Arthur and his Round Table knights as calculated; as much conscious invention as unconscious contemporary allusion. Exotic and esoteric facts and fancies appealed for their own sake. In a time of visions – grotesque, fearsome, devilish, or glorious, ecstatic, rapturous – writers, whether in monastery or town, church house or hermitage, reached for bestiaries, cosmologies, astrologia and almanacs for the enriching of their tales. Illuminators in the monastic *scriptoria* (writing rooms) had been drawing fiendish reptilian creatures in the margins of manuscripts long before Hieronymus Bosch let rip with his own brand of anatomical distortion to scare the fifteenth-century audience away from the earthly fleshpots. To the mediaeval imagination, it was all colour, all the teeming product of God's extraordinary creation, and not always of exact classification.

Many and various prodigies of the mediaeval bestiary adorn illuminated manuscripts, the more loathsome in aspect of them put there to jolt the alarmed reader into more godly thoughts. One, the camelopard, actually a giraffe, was thought to be a cross between a camel and a leopard, hence the name. Yet, what better image than that of a frightful beast to paint on a shield to shake in the face of an enemy on the field of battle? The Roman legions had carried dragon banners into war for just that purpose. Heraldic blazon spawned a whole family of hybrid beasts, therefore: griffon, wyvern, yale, opinicus, double-headed eagle, and so on. However, early blazon was not a precisely ordered science. Indeed, it matched the riot of imaginative invention to be found in the illuminated manuscripts.

On a White Shield a Blood-Red Cross

Arthur and the Round Table knights gather in Noauz for a jousting competition. The principal combatants arm themselves in readiness and pace restively up and down the lines of gaily coloured pavilions. From the stands, Queen Guenever and her ladies watch; they know the champions by the shields they carry: Governal of Roberdic, golden band on red field (background); the son of the king of Aragon, eagle squaring up to dragon; Ignaures (how the ladies sigh after *him*!), green and azure halved field, on the green a leopard; Coguillant of Mautirec, two pheasants beak to beak;

Semiramis, on gold field a sable (black) lion;
King Yder, a stag issuing from a gate.

> Chrétien de Troyes, *Lancelot* lines 5726 ff

Here Chrétien tries an amateur hand at blazon; that is to say, 'the description, according to the rules of heraldry, of armorial bearings'. In fact when he wrote *Lancelot*, about 1180, *any* blazon would be, so to speak, amateur since a strict, legal codification did not arrive for another seventy years. We cannot, therefore, expect significance, beyond the vaguest, from Chrétien and his contemporaries; nor is there any evidence to suggest that the first of the Arthurian romancers wished to do more than enliven his writing with chivalric colour, to lend his description the sort of intensity and brilliance of the miniatures which adorn mediaeval texts. That he assuredly does. But if the identity of King Arthur is not so much secret as obscured by multiple candidacy, the blazon of the romances gives a very fragmentary idea of the heraldic picture, like scattered pieces of a jigsaw which has still to be fully assembled. For example: the arms of the King of Aragon. Raymon Berengar IV, king of a newly united Barcelona and Aragon from 1137, had no eagle or dragon on his shield, but carried the gold field with four vertical red bands still used by Catalonia today. On the other hand, this King Yder's shield rings a bell: the stag issuing from a gate is the old heraldic device of Ireland. The turreted gateway to the castle isn't right, though; that must be an urbanised version of a thicket, the stag breaking cover. Over the years the whole badge has changed and, finally, been stylised as maiden, thrust forward like a ship's figurehead, forming the bowed side of a gold harp with silver strings.

BLAZON

The Greek historian Anna Comnena, daughter of the Emperor Alexius Comnenus, recorded the shields of the first Crusaders as being plain; even if they had rough scarlet crosses of cloth stitched to their surcoats. Few of the shields on the Bayeux Tapestry, made about the same time, sport any device (heraldic emblem), either. One Norman, hacking at an English soldier with such vigour that he has come out of his saddle to sit astride his horse's neck, carries a shield adorned with what appears to be a white dragon. Perhaps the Norman embroiderer intended a nasty dig, there: the white dragon of the Saxons come back, in the shape of the Normans, to discomfort and overrun the inhabitants of Albion once more . . . the Saxon beast reawakened to devour its own people.

Within thirty years or so of the first Crusade, the Franks, and especially the Normans, were decorating their shields with what blazon calls the cognisance: an image or coloration or pattern which served as an identifying badge of the bearer. The *History of Fuke Fitz-Warine* (written between 1256 and 1264 and mentioned in connection with Dinas Brân) although much later gives a nice example:

> Merlin saith that in Britain the Great a Wolf shall come from the White Launde with twelve sharp teeth six above and six below. He shall have so fierce a look that he shall chase the leopard out of the White Launde . . . in the time of Arthur what is now called the White Town was known as the White Launde . . . King Arthur bore as shield indented as the heralds devised with 12 teeth argent [silver/white] on gules [red i.e. bloodstained] of the Wolf. By the leopard may be known and understood King John, for he bore in his shield the leopards of beaten gold.

This appears to refer to the detested King John who captured and then murdered, in 1203, his rival for the English throne, Richard I's designated heir, his nephew Arthur of Brittany. The disgruntled Shropshire romancer revives the dream of Arthur in the hapless prince beloved and favoured of his uncle, the great crusading Lionheart. The shield he carries bears his name and fierce aspect. In the ancient world, to look a wolf in the eyes killed you on the spot.

Eventually, the shield with painted device became standard and necessary for recognition when most knights wore closed-in helmets and thus hid their faces. To begin with, though, all Crusaders wore the open-face helmet shown on the Bayeux tapestry, or variants on the design. Facing the Saracen arrow clouds, however, proved a nasty experience: King Harold, remember (if indeed it *was* him), died, as the monologue puts it, of 'an eye full of arrow'. Visors were introduced, for them who could afford it; and, whilst offering excellent protection, the encasing helmet seriously reduced the range of vision and made identification on the battlefield, never easy in the confusion of mêlée and dustcloud, even more problematic. Not identification of the enemy, though: no Crusader, however fired up with bloodlust and alcohol, could mistake the swarthy, light-armed, flowing-robed Moors on their wheeling horses; but, in the feudal age, where lords and vassals had to stick together either side of ransom and booty, identifying friends was crucial. The introduction of banners, duplicating the colours and devices of the shields, expedited that. And one must be circumspect about the grand pageantry of battle. It may have been a brave palette of colour before the fighting, but once the battle was joined it was dust, confusion, sweat and unmitigated terror which blurs reason as well as focus. In the sandy war zones of the Holy Land, identification, even of brightly painted shields, must have been nigh impossible during the battle; only useful afterwards, for the picking through the scattered corpses and

wounded. A very unromantic mayhem.

Heraldic blazon must, I think, have grown out of a necessity, or requirement away from the battlefield. The Crusader armies were always a hotchpotch of small feudal regiments owing separate allegiance to their feudal lord, and each one intensely jealous of its own standing and achievement. Heraldic badges and colour schemes probably owed as much to Frankish swagger as to practical usefulness. Charles Martel's ice-wall of Franks needed no blazon to keep their ranks tight against the Moors outside Poitiers. I think the display mattered more than the military purpose. Lord Cardigan, who commanded the Light Brigade at Balaclava, made his regiment, the 11th Hussars, the best-dressed regiment in the British army, at his own expense. The Cherry Pickers they were called; and best-dressed, in his and others' view, meant best fighters. All pride and vanity. Blazon had a similar purpose *and* was yet another stealing from the Moors. *Their* love of florid colour and abstract design – pavilions decorated with checkers and lozenges, stripes and fringes – plus the fluttering banners of azure, emerald, white, scarlet and gold which they carried into war impressed the drably furnished Europeans, dun-coloured as the Roman soldiers had been, with their pomp and show. Most of the Crusaders being illiterate and unacquainted even with the outside of books it's not likely, but the Arab ostentation may have prompted connection with the pictorial glories of mediaeval religious art: notably the illuminated manuscripts. The Irish illustrators, in particular, beavering away through the Dark Ages at vellum parchment and wells of tinted ink, developed a brilliant decorative skill harking back to the great flourishing of Celtic art. The Celts loved abstract design as did the Moors, who, however, were banned from the representation of nature on religious grounds, its being considered disrespectful to God the Creator. The

Catholic Church, denouncing abstraction as the product of a diseased mind, a Devil-inspired fantasy, pronounced an exactly opposite ban. I don't think it is too wild a surmise, either, that the secular lords and knights saw heraldry as offering them a share in the brave chromes that had, for a long time, been monopolised by the Church.

There was, too, the matter of expense. Paints did not come cheap, being made of crushed gemstones and specially prepared metals. Arab wealth and culture far outstripped European, emergent from the Dark Ages. But, as the western kingdoms grew richer, they splashed out more lavishly from the coffers filled from the plundering of the east.

The Normans led the way, as haughty and vain a crowd as you could find this side of a Prussian duelling club. They, evidently, brought the idea of painted and decorated shields back from Palestine and a rudimentary style of heraldry was born. Pope Alexander II, the first bishop of Rome to offer indulgence to knights who fought the Saracen in Spain, bestowed on William the Conqueror a banner of red cross on white field, though where he had the design from we cannot know; nor whether it was given as reward or bribe. St Bernard roundly castigated the vanity of the new fad:

> You paint your spears, shields and saddles; your bridles and spurs are adorned on all sides with gold and silver and gems, and with all this pomp, with a shameful fury and a reckless insensibility you rush on to death. Are these military ensigns or are they not rather the garnishment of women?
>
> St Bernard, ***In Praise of the New Chivalry***
> sermon quoted in Brault, **Early Blazon**

The unspoken accusation is also there: all *Moorish* and infidel.

In Hoc Signo Vinces

In the 1130s Geoffrey of Monmouth, writing for his Norman masters, makes one of the first references in European literature to an identifiable heraldic device: before the battle of Bath, Arthur takes up a circular shield on which is painted a likeness of the Virgin Mary. This detail comes from the history of William of Malmesbury (1125) who wrote of Arthur: 'he put his faith in an icon of the Mother of our Lord, sewn onto his armour' (therefore a sort of badge threaded onto the mail coat). The source must be Nennius, ninth century: 'Arthur carried a statue of the ever-Virgin Mary on his shoulder', but the Latin chronicler has muddled the Welsh/British *ysgwyd* ('shoulder') and *ysgwydd* ('shield'). A statue (*imago* in Classical Latin; thence 'image, picture') would be an impossible encumbrance for a fighting man.

At any rate, before long, all the Crusader lords, following the Norman vogue, had painted their shields with individual colours and markings; as the Greek aristocrat citizen army had embellished their shields with painted animals, abstract design and so on, and the Roman professional army had shields adorned with stylised thunderbolts, symbol of Jupiter. And Uther's dragons, too, which began as totems on poles, much like the legionary Eagles, became eventually the dragon banner under which the men of Wessex mustered and fought. Wolfram von Eschenbach describes another royal banner, that of the Burgundian Orilus de Lalander:

> On his shield a life-like dragon; on his laced-on helmet another dragon, rearing; and numerous tiny golden dragons on his armour and surcoat, embellished with precious gemstones, the eyes set with rubies.

Dragons aplenty, then, at first, but all manner of animals, real and imaginary, made their way into

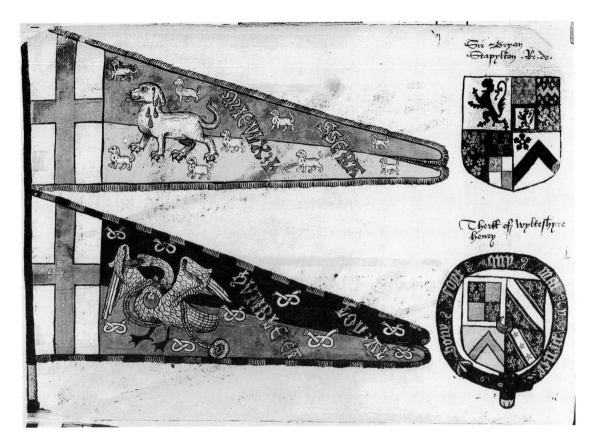

Heraldic blazon at its height. The faithful hound, though wounded, limps doggedly on: Mieulx Ssera: Better Late than Never.

the catalogue of blazon: the golden eagle of the emperor Lucius (Wace) and Gawain (*Perlesvaus*); Percival's white hart on sinople, that is green in heraldry, though originally a red earth pigment (*Perlesvaus*); Tristan's gold lions on scarlet and so on. This last has invited much speculation. The lion stands for courage; as Arthur, in the *Perlesvaus*, 'holdeth him at bay like a lion when the staghounds would attack him'. (Where else would Europeans see a lion encircled by hounds but in Syria or Palestine?)

The tomb of Geoffrey of Anjou, founder of the royal Plantagenet line, in Le Mans cathedral, bears the heraldic badge: gold lion rampant (that is rearing, paws raised for the attack) on an azure field. A shield of this design had been hung about his neck by Henry I when he married the English king's daughter Matilda in 1127. There can be no certainty what Geoffrey's son Henry II sported on *his* shield, but his grandson, Richard the Lionheart, I of England, bore what became the established Angevin device: three gold leopards (heraldic lions)

189

on a red field. The fact that the French king used blue may have influenced the contrary choice of red. Tristan's arms would seem, then, to hint at an Angevin cognisance; except that one translation of Gottfried's poem suggests that Tristan in fact had a boar for his device. Appropriate for a knight associated with Cornwall, as was King Arthur himself, and described in an English romance as the boar who comes out of Cornwall.

Now, red shields and red knights feature prominently in Arthurian romance; and red is the colour of the bloody war god Mars; the Apocalyptic horseman of war and strife is red; red is also a Celtic sun colour; and, in mediaeval chromatography, the symbolic colour of Justice and Wise Judgement, which fits ill with a pagan god noted for his demented battle fury. But let that pass. In fact, the red of the Angevin shield as of Tristan's shield and many others in romance and real life, probably denotes nothing more than a rich, a very regal (and costly) hue: a handsome shade, too, that suits well with gold, another sun and royal colour; that rare crimson dye squeezed out of the elusive shellfish the Mediterranean *murex*.

As Gerard Brault points out in his *Early Blazon*, little conclusive evidence emerges from a study of the romances to give credence to the idea that the numerous references to heraldic device have any significance at all. Scholars read far too much into what amounts, simply, to authorial sparkle – the strong embellishments of good storytellers. Agreed, black knights tend to be evil and white knights virtuous; and whole treatises could be written on symbolism of the favourite colour of both the visionary St Hildegard and the waxen-hearted Henry III, green, without even the sketchiest glance at Gawain's pentagram. Green was, too, one of the most expensive paints to manufacture being made from crushed malachite, a semi-precious stone of emerald or brilliant green colour.

For the most part the blazon of the romances, as in contemporary life, appears to have only one driving reason behind it: show; it looked well. Otherwise it is a haphazard affair, lacking form, regulation or effective record. However, round about 1250, blazon underwent the rigorous scrutiny of lawyers in a studious effort to bring it to order. This may have been a repercussion from noblemen's quarrelling over land and disputed property claims, fighting the dragon, if you like. Much more likely it stemmed from arguments as to who had the right to bear which coat of arms. A poem of 1300, 'The Siege of Caerlaverock', mentions just such a case. Litigation was in the air. The European warrior class, for 150 years cock of the walk as victor in the Holy Land, had lost its footing. Now that the Crusades were over, and with skirmishes against neighbours frowned on in the new state-conscious, religiously bound Europe, what function did the armed knight serve? Riding in the lists and foreign war; avoiding the disreputable tag of 'mercenary' if possible. So, just as the schoolmarmish Victorians invented Scottish tartans, three colourways per clan, blazon achieved official legal status. The heralds, hitherto a despised class of non-combatant busybodies lounging on the sidelines, scrambled to the fore to establish themselves as the precious experts in the niceties of heraldic achievement. *And* they took to themselves that old warcry of Charlemagne, name of the hill overlooking Jerusalem: Mountjoy became their official title.

My own feeling is that the tournament formed heraldry: scene of a brave display, a martial strutting of peacock knights.

Whatever historians say, early blazon had little use on the Crusades beyond the satisfying of vanity in the European camp, and rivalling of the pageant in the Moorish camp. Its idiosyncratic nature is well-mirrored in the chaotic muddle of heraldic jargon in the romances, and its codification in about

1250 ties in with trends elsewhere.

For, all at roughly the same time, heralds and theologians set up official shop to lay down the law and the writing of Arthurian romance dwindled. Blazon found itself turned over to legal eagles, busy at rules and regulations and their illustrators, who produced the heraldic rolls, exact records of coats-of-arms, as gorgeously illuminated with polychrome badge and escutcheon as Bibles and sacred texts in the monasteries.

The Catholic Holy War against the Infidel had, effectively, been lost, although the last Crusaders did not return till near the end of the century. But Papal attention had shifted to heresy on the much nearer at hand. The Angelic Doctor, Thomas Aquinas, defined orthodox theology in his massive tomes of *Summary*, and the law of truth was laid down; a fellow Dominican, Bernard Gui, would soon be pursuing those who deviated, with the full weight of the Inquisition behind him; and Clement V, shortly before he agreed to the destruction of the white-robed Templars, would preach a Crusade against the natural heirs of the Albigensian Cathars, the Italian Apostolici, as well as the few remaining Albigensian communities who eked out existence in Provence, after the bloody massacres at Béziers and Monségur. The Church succumbed to introspection and paranoia. One predicted millennium, A.D. 1000, had passed; but official opinion had long reckoned the real millennium to have commenced with the Donation of Constantine in A.D. 324. Time was running out for the world and her people of the true Faith. Arthur, Christian knight at war with the Moors, those spawn of Satan, now proved an irrelevance, if not an embarrassment; a bothersome relic, anyway, of the heady, yet better-forgotten days of the lost Crusades. Once upon a time, Arthur's knights (the Crusaders, red cross on white ground) had ridden forth from Camelot (any fortified hilltop citadel, any castle in Europe or the Holy Land) to do battle, in the words of Revelation 9 v. 17, wearing 'breastplates of fire and of jacinth and brimstone: and the heads of the [ir] horses . . . as the heads of lions; and out of their mouths issued fire and smoke and brimstone'. The army of the Apocalypse. Their adversary? Isaiah had described him, 'the piercing serpent, even leviathan that crooked serpent . . . the dragon that is in the sea'. And the fruit of victory would be 'that the great trumpet shall be blown, and they shall come which were ready to perish in the land of Assyria, and the outcasts in the land of Egypt, and shall worship the Lord in the holy mount at Jerusalem' (Isaiah, chapter 27). The romance had died. Now Pope and Church put on the breastplate of Dogma, laced up tight with codes and orthodox opinion. The quarrels would continue, as long as there were theologians to wrangle; but fact had established itself over romance; the sword of faith swung at the heads of heretics, clinging to their dangerous fictions, not at the Pagans, who were lost (and had won) anyway.

Gone the untrammelled days in brilliant Provence, home of romance, when Guilhem IX, protector of Albigensian Cathars, and grandfather of Eleanor of Aquitaine, ran off, or so the story went, with a certain minor nobleman's wife. Imprudently, since he still had wife of his own, Guilhem, so burning with love of his lady, had her portrait painted on his shield. The reason he broadcast, not caring who heard, was that he would bear her up in battle as she bore him up in bed. This 'strange device' the heralds of early blazon discreetly termed *jambes de s'amie,* 'his sweetheart's legs'.

That seems a good note on which to end a book about love and war in the Middle Ages and Arthur and his knights who fought for love of fair damsel.

POSTSCRIPT

I called this book *Arthur the King* first and foremost to provoke curiosity, in the hope of challenging a conventional, even trite, view of the legendary hero which blurs distinctions between the shadowy Arthur of Roman Britain and the singing king of a tinseltown Camelot. *Arthur the King* fixes itself as a study of a mediaeval phenomenon in mediaeval, rather than fake olde worlde, terms. For, though King Arthur is claimed, in one incarnation or another, by every successive age, I wanted to stress his original historical and social importance as *the* king, par excellence.

The period between Geoffrey's *Historia* (*c.* 1135) and the composition of the *Quest of the Holy Grail* (*c.* 1240) saw the emergence of great royal dynasties in Europe, the absolute monarchs who, after the protracted uncertainties of several hundred years, came to rule by the grace of God, the right of succession and less and less by the inevitable exercise of force. If the army was never far away, now theory and principle of royalty came to the fore. To power ('you *will* obey') was added authority ('you *must* obey'). This authority often relied on the connivance of the Church; and the popes in Rome modelled their own spiritual monarchy on that of the kings. So kings and popes, backed by God's word, headed the pyramid of established order which embraced all creation.

In so many respects, Arthur *the* king inspired these Christian leaders of this new and relatively stable order. He had fought for and won national freedom. At his feet emperors and paynim lords bowed the knee. To his court flocked men and women of high birth.

For the first time since the darkest miseries of pagan/barbarian invasion, Europe enjoyed a measure of regulated peace. Kings basked in glory; they acquired wealth and showed it off in magnificent style, in rich pageant. ('The boast of heraldry, the pomp of power/And all that beauty, all that wealth e'er gave', in Gray's words.) Arthur epitomised every royal splendour, of material and moral possession. He was the king, the quintessential monarch; Camelot, and his other courts, the cities whose streets were paved with gold and silver. The romances of Arthur and his favoured Round Table knights celebrated the high goals of heroism, chivalry, opulence and empire, magnanimity, liberality – everything idealised by the crusading Christian warrior. Above all, romance glorified the conflict between Christian good and Satanic evil; the virtuous (manly) white knight versus the impious black knight.

Moreover, reflecting on Arthur's immortality,

the noble chevalier of the twelfth and thirteenth centuries dreamed of his own survival beyond the grave, in the memory of his great deeds. Arthur inspired him to believe that his courage would endure, that fame would extend to him a glorious eternity. The Celtic afterlife of heroes becomes the life everlasting in God's mansions promised by Christ. The sword of the Crusader becomes the sword of faith; Excalibur the hard steel of God's universal omnipotence.

The extensive and long-lived popularity of early Arthurian romance proves that the audiences of men and women who listened to countless story-tellers in Norman England, France, the Holy Land and across Europe, heard exactly what they wanted to hear: that life might be glorious and opulent, marked by grand gesture as well as by intimate passion. Quick to emotion, to weep or be thrilled, they adored the Round Table legends, which offered, in more objective terms of course, an escape from cold reality. In the world of Arthur and his knights and ladies, they observed life as it might be if only . . . if only . . . The storytellers merely gave their version of the finished sentence, filling out the dream with imagination and drama, with exploit and tension.

Geoffrey called his book *Historia* for an obvious reason: he wanted to tap his audience's nostalgia while at the same time implying that the romance was true because it was historical. The new lords and ladies of Europe could then interpret their glory as *old* glory, glory with the added weight of tradition. However, their sense of antiquity was not as ours; they thought of Arthur only in contemporary terms, their memory being childlike in its short perspective.

After the romances peaked in popularity, they enjoyed a second life: new translations and editions but very few new versions. The nostalgic element came to the fore: as the ruling dynasties grew older, history began to expand to a more distant past.

All post-mediaeval Arthurian romances are, to an extent, direct heirs of the most nostalgic of all Arthurians, Malory. The first Arthurian romance had declared: 'The glory is now, *yours*'. In contrast Malory's theme was 'The glory is departed'. So, after the cataclysm of the First World War, for example, the Irish composer Bax and the English Rutland Boughton tried, as it were, to roll out the green sward of Camelot over the stinking, bloodstained mudfields of the modern, mechanistic world. And, in the first flush of a crusading war against communism, Americans called President Kennedy's White House Camelot.

Most recently, it is Arthur as penumbral Celtic freedom fighter who has inspired authors to pepper their pseudo-chronicles with authenticating, unpronounceable Welsh names. One Belgian mystic, supported by a British mythologian, even calls Arthur an Anglo-Roman. So much for historical verity.

Yet Arthur's appeal lives on, evergreen. Surely this is because the stories themselves are so powerful, most particularly in their first, mediaeval telling. If God no longer fascinates us twentieth-century hardheads, black-hearted Satan, in all his manifestations, does; the crusade against his evil minions and designs goes on.

Every version of Arthur's story is, however subliminally, rooted in its own age. The names may change but the age-old themes persist. Who is Luke Skywalker but young Arthur come again? Who are Batman, Superman, James Bond, Dick Tracy, even Popeye and My Brother Sylvest but the heirs of Gawain and Lancelot? We cannot, apparently, do without an Evil Empire; it needs no fixed name or topography. There will always be a hero sleeping under the hill, ready to surge out to save the world. The best we can hope is for him, or her, to be of the stature of Arthur.

CHRONOLOGICAL OUTLINE OF ARTHURIAN LITERATURE

PRINCIPAL SOURCES

Various early writings mention Arthur in passing. Most were recorded long after they were composed, in the eleventh and twelfth centuries, when the oral tradition was beginning to disintegrate.

*c.*540 Gildas *De Excidio Britanniae* (though Arthur not mentioned)

*c.*600 (or *c.*900) Welsh elegy *Gododdin*

*c.*800 Nennius *Mirabilia* (part of the *Historia Brittonum*)

*c.*ninth/tenth century *Verses on the Graves of the Heroes* Welsh poem

*c.*950 *Annales Cambriae*

late eleventh/early twelfth centuries Various Lives of Welsh Saints written in Latin. Arthur usually appears as a king, not a saint, but is converted by a miracle

pre-1100 Welsh poem about Geraint (Chrétien's *Erec*)

*c.*1100 *Culhwch and Olwen* (included in the later collection *Mabinogion*)

Welsh *Triads*, a gallimaufry of early Welsh poems

PSEUDO-HISTORY AND ROMANCES – ORIGINALS OF ARTHURIAN LEGEND

Chanson de Roland written about the end of the eleventh century)

1135/1150 Geoffrey of Monmouth *Historia Regum Britanniae*

Adaptations of and from Geoffrey:

*c.*1150 Gaimar *Estorie des Engles*

*c.*1155 Wace *Le Roman de Brut*

*c.*1190 Layamon *Brut* (in English)

*c.*1210 Robert de Boron *Merlin*

*c.*1155–85 Thomas *Tristan* (under patronage of Henry II?)

*c.*1160–70 Béroul *Tristan*

*c.*1160–70 anon. *Folie de Tristan*

*c.*1160–90 Marie de France *Lais*

*c.*1170–90 Chrétien de Troyes

*c.*1195–1225 Wolfram von Eschenbach *Parzival*

end twelfth century Hartmann von Aue *Erec*

*c.*1210 Gottfried von Strassburg *Tristan*

early thirteenth century *Vulgate Cycle*:

Lancelot du Lac

Quest of the Holy Grail

The Death of King Arthur

GRAIL AND HOLY GRAIL TEXTS

Arthurian knights visiting a Grail Castle located in Britain:

early twelfth century (?) Welsh *Peredur* (*Mabinogion*) from same Celtic tradition as that later used by Chrétien

*c.*1190 Chrétien de Troyes *Perceval*, written for Philippe of Alsace (and Flanders) who died on Third Crusade, June 1191

*c.*1191–1212 *Perlesvaus*

early thirteenth century Four long continuations of Chrétien's unfinished story: two anonymous; Manessier (*c.* 1206–44) for the grand-niece of Philippe of Alsace; Gerbert de Montreuil (probably 1226–30)

early thirteenth century Wolfram von Eschenbach *Parzival*

early 1200s Didot *Perceval*

early thirteenth century *Quest of the Holy Grail* (Malory's sourcebook)

History of the Grail from the time of Christ to the time of Merlin and its journey from the Holy Land to Britain:

early 1200s Robert de Boron *Joseph d'Arimathie*

1215–30 *Estoire del Saint Graal*

thirteenth century Various French romances based on Chrétien and others

*c.*1320 *Sir Tristrem* English

*c.*1350 *Le Morte Arthure* stanzaic poem in English

*c.*1350 *Gawain and the Green Knight* in English

*c.*1400 *Morte Arthure* alliterative poem in English

*c.*1450 *Merlin or the Early History of King Arthur* (English)

1460 Malory *Morte D'Arthur*

CHRONOLOGY OF THE CRUSADES

1096–99 Capture of Jerusalem

1115 Bernard Abbot of Clairvaux

1147–9 Second Crusade defeats in Ascalon and Damascus

1187 Saladin takes Jerusalem

1189–92 Third Crusade. Acre captured by Richard the Lionheart's army. Christian right of pilgrimage to Jerusalem ceded by Saladin

1202–4 Fourth Crusade. Sack of Constantinople

1212 Children's Crusade: thousands of boys and girls transported by corrupt merchants to Marseille and sold into slavery

1244 Jerusalem lost to Moslems for good

1244 Capture of Monségur in southern France. Massacre of Albigensians

1248–54 Sixth Crusade. King Louis IX defeated and entire army taken captive

1270 Seventh Crusade. Death of Louis

1291 Last Christian stronghold, Acre, conquered by Mameluke Turks

1304 Suppression of Templars

ROMANCES

Béroul *Romance of Tristan* and *The tale of Tristan's madness* (Classics) Penguin, 197?

Chrétien de Troyes *Arthurian romances* (Everyman) Dent, 1975.

Death of king Arthur (Classics) Penguin, 1971.

Lancelot of the lake (World's classics) Oxford U.P., 1989.

Mabinogion (Everyman) Dent; (Everyman Classic) Dent, new edn., pbk., 1983.

Malory, Sir Thomas *Le morte d'Arthur* Vols. 1–2 (Classics) Penguin, 1969.

Morte Arthure, alliterative, and Morte Arthur, stanzaic (Classics) Penguin, 1988.

Perlesvaus Brewer, 1978; J. Clarke, pbk., 1986.

Quest of the holy grail (Classics) Penguin, 1969.

Sir Gawain and the green knight (Classics) Penguin, 1982.

von Eschenbach, Wolfram *Parzival* (Classics) Penguin, 1980.

von Strassburg, Gottfried *Tristan* (Classics) Penguin, 1970.

HISTORY AND PSEUDOHISTORY MISCELLANEOUS

Celtic miscellany (Classics) Penguin 1971.

Earliest English poems (Classics) Penguin 1970.

Early Irish myths and sagas (Classics) Penguin, 1981.

Geoffrey of Monmouth *The history of the kings of Britain* Penguin, 1966. op.

Gildas *Ruin of Britain, and other works* (Arthurian period sources, 7), Phillimore, pbk., 1978.

Gregory of Tours *History of the Franks* (Classics) Penguin, 1974.

Mandeville, Sir John *Travels* (Classics) Penguin, 1983.

Marie de France *Breton lays* published as *Proud Knight, fair lady: lais of Marie de France* N. Lewis Hutchinson, 1988.

Mediaeval English verse (Classics) Penguin, 1970.

Rolle *The fire of love* (Classics) Penguin, 1972.

Wace and Layamon *Arthurian chronicles* (Everyman) Dent, 1962.

Woledge, B. ed. *Penguin Book of French verse. Vol. 1 To the fifteenth century* Penguin 1968. op.

COMMENTARY

Ashe, G. *The quest for Arthur's Britain* Paladin, 1971.

Baigent and Leigh *The Temple and the Lodge* Cape, 1989.

Baigent, Leigh, Lincoln *The holy blood and the holy grail* Cape, 1982.

Billings, M. *The cross and the crescent* BBC, 1987.

Blair, C. *European arms and armour* Trustees of the Wallace Collection, 1986.

Cummins, J. *The hound and the hawk: the art of mediaeval hunting* Weidenfeld, 1989.

Davis, R.H.C. *The mediaeval warhorse* Thames & Hudson, 1989.

Delaney, F. *The Celts* Grafton, new edn., pbk., 1989.

Gautier, L. *Chivalry*

Girouard, M. *Return to Camelot: chivalry and the English gentleman* Yale U.P., 1981; pbk. 1985.

Jones, T. *Chaucer's knight: portrait of a mediaeval mercenary* Methuen, 2nd edn., pbk., 1985.

Lewis, C.S. *Allegory of love* Oxford U.P., pbk., 1977.

Loomis, R.S. ed. *Arthurian literature in the middle ages* Oxford U.P., 1967. op.

Loomis, R.S. *Arthurian tradition and Chrétien de Troyes* Clarendon P., 1959. op.

Loomis, R.S. *The grail: from Celtic myth to Christian Symbol* Wales U.P., 1963. op.

Loomis, R.S. *Wales and the Arthurian legend* Wales U.P., 1956. op.

Morris, J. ed. *The age of Arthur* Vols. 1–3 Weidenfeld & Nicolson, 1973.

Nykyl, A.R. *Hispano-Arabic poetry* Clarendon, 1974.

Partner, P. *The murdered magicians: Templars and their myths* Crucible, pbk., 1987.

Piggott, S. *The Druids* (Ancient people and places) Thames & Hudson, pbk., 1985.

Runciman, S. *History of the Crusades* Vols. 1–3 Cambridge U.P., pbk., 1951–90.

Severin, T. *Crusader: by horse to Jerusalem* Hutchinson, 1989.

Sheard, J.A. *The words we use* Deutsch, 1954. op.

Simpson, J. *British dragons* Batsford, 1980. op.

Topsfield, *Troubadours and love* Cambridge U.P., 1978.

Weston, J. *From ritual to romance* Chivers, 1980.

Page numbers in italic denote illustrations

Picture Credits

Front cover, Bibliothèque Nationale, MS Fr. 343 Queste, f.3; page 10, British Library, MS Roy. 20 A II, f.4r (photo Bridgeman Art Library); 14, British Library, MS Roy. 20 A II, f.3r; 23, British Library, MS Add. 28681, f.9; 26, British Library, MS Roy. 20 D IV & 14 E III, f.89 (photo Bridgeman Art Library); 33, Bibliothèque Nationale, MS Arabe 5847, f.79; 35, British Library, MS Cotton Nero C IV, f.39r; 41, J. Allan Cash (Eric Lewis); 47, Barnaby's Picture Library (Mustograph); 52, Bibliothèque Nationale, MS Fr.5594, f.19; 61, British Library, MS Add. 42130, f.82; 70–71, La Ville de Bayeux (photo Giraudon); 75, Bibliothèque Nationale, MS Fr.782, f.160 (photo Giraudon); 81, British Library, MS Add. 38120, f.39v; 83, Kestner-Museum, Hannover; 87, Bibliothèque Inguibertine, MS 403, f.7v (photo Giraudon); 91, Universitäts Bibliothek Heidelberg, Cod. Pal. Germ. 848, f.178r; 95, Giraudon, MS Fr. 118, f.219r; page 97, British Library, MS Add. 10294, f.94 (photo Bridgeman Art Library); 98, British Library, MS Cotton Nero E II, f.172v; 99, Bibliothèque Nationale, MS Fr.9087, f.85v; 100–101, Bibliothèque Nationale, MS Fr.2692, f.67v–68; 102, British Library, MS Harl. 4425, f.12v; 103 (top), British Library, MS Cotton Nero D IV, f.93v; 103 (bottom), Bibliothèque Nationale, MS Fr.12577, f.18v; 104, Ashmolean Museum, Oxford; 107, Bayer. Staatsbibliothek München, MS Germ. 51, f.90r; 114, British Library, MS Egerton 745, f.78; 120, Bodleian Library, MS Laud. Misc. 720, f.225; 123, Trinity College, Dublin, Book of Kells, f.89r; 127, British Library, MS Roy. 2 B VII, f.180v; 137, Bildarchiv d. Öst. Nationalbibliothek, Cod. 609, f.4; 144, Bibliothèque Nationale, MS Fr. 112, f.15v (photo ET Archive); 152–3, Barnaby's Picture Library (West Air Photography); 168, A. F. Kersting; 173, British Library, MS Harl. 3244, f.38; 178, Victoria & Albert Museum, MS L475, f.5r (photo Conway Library, Courtauld Institute of Art); 183, British Library, MS Harl. 4751, f.59; 189, British Library, MS Add. 45132, f.63b.